SEABIRDS: A NATURAL HISTORY

SEABIRDS:
A NATURAL HISTORY

ANTHONY J. GASTON

Yale University Press
New Haven and London

Published 2004 by Christopher Helm, an imprint of A & C Black Publishers Ltd.,
37 Soho Square, London W1D 3QZ, and in the United States by Yale University Press

ISBN 0-300-10406-5
Library of Congress Control Number: 2004100690
Printed and bound in Italy by G. Canale

Typeset by J&L Composition, Filey, North Yorkshire

A catalogue record for this book is available from the British Library.

Paper produced with elemental chlorine-free pulp, harvested from managed sustainable forests.

The paper in this book meets the guidelines for permanence and durability of the Committee on Production
Guidelines for Book Longevity of the Council on Library Resources.

10 9 8 7 6 5 4 3 2 1

For Anne-Marie
Thank you for being yourself

Contents

List of Figures

List of Tables

Preface

Delightful, I think it be, in the bosom of an isle, on the peak of a rock,
That I might often see there the calm of the sea.

That I might see its clear strand of smooth headlands; no gloomy thing;
That I might hear the voice of the wondrous birds, a joyful tune.

That I might see its splendid flocks of birds over the full-watered ocean;
That I might see its mighty whales, greatest of wonders.

St Columba's Island Hermitage, Irish, 12th century,
author unknown (Jackson, 1951)

Every great group of land animals has made some attempt to re-invade salt water. Turtles, crocodiles, snakes, dugongs, seals and whales; all have terrestrial ancestors, all returned to the sea. Not so, flying animals. Bats are virtually confined to land, and even that most prolific winged order, the insects, are only marginally represented at sea. This leaves the birds to dominate the air above the oceans. Though most bird species are terrestrial, about 5% of them live their lives partly or wholly away from land, except while attending their nests. Most seabirds spend a great proportion of their lives quartering the broad face of the ocean; they are quintessentially peripatetic. This makes them a very conspicuous element of the seascape.

We all carry images of the ubiquitous 'seagulls', marking their presence with hoarse screams and leaving their chalky calling cards on rooftops, beacons and jetties. On the horizon, those with a keen gaze may discern ribbons of passing seaducks or the rhythmic rise and fall of wave-soaring shear-waters. In the harbours, loons paddle among the moored ships and cormorants spread their tattered wings like heraldic griffons. On some long, windswept, coastal dune, a cloud of terns rises with grating complaint as the walker passes; tourists toss chips and sandwiches to the retinue of assorted long-winged birds gliding in the wake of a ferry. Such sights and sounds are the common residue of seaside holidays and other coastal journeys.

Although seabirds are a rather obvious element of the marine environment, most people do not think of them as sea creatures in the same way that they think of whelks or whales. Because they are often seen in flight or perched on rocks and islands, and because they must return to land to breed, they do not qualify as genuine marine organisms in some peoples' minds. Nevertheless, because they derive their food from the sea, they are indisputably a part of the marine environment. The sea is their home as much as it is for crabs and corals.

In the days before jumbo jets, when people travelled abroad by ship, journeys overseas must have yielded other seabird images: petrels and albatrosses and other denizens of the open ocean. Those who spent their lives at sea, especially under sail, were very familiar with the diversity of birds that shared the waves with them. They gave them fanciful names: mollymawks and boobies, hagdowns and looms, Mother Carey's chicks, stormy-petrels, sea pigeons, sea parrots and the like. They provided companionship after weeks at sea, and the appearance of inshore species, such as auks, gulls and cormorants, gave warning of the nearness of shore: a welcoming beacon in fine weather, an evil omen in fog or gale.

For peoples of the sea: Inuit, Bretons, Polynesians, Aleuts, Vikings, Basques and Newfoundlanders, seabirds were central totems and important sources of food, clothing, fertilisers and information. For sailors and fishermen, the sound of their harsh cries was a harbinger of hope or a warning of impending disaster. For thousands of years, seabirds and people lived side by side, sharing, whether willingly or otherwise, the harvest of that great biological factory, the sea.

For seafarers, kittiwakes, gulls, fulmars, shearwaters and petrels are their constant company. Scarcely a net or fish trap is hauled, from the Barents Sea to the Bay of Bengal, without the close attention of an avian patrol. The flensing decks of whalers and the try-pots of sealers, in their day, were a magnet for seabirds. For a long time they have been our companions, fair weather and foul. Some have suffered at our hands, even to extinction, as others have fattened on the residues of our harvests.

Despite our long familiarity with seabirds, there is much about them that we know or understand little. As we insulate ourselves ever more securely from the wild, wet and windy, the uncomfortable and the insecure, so nature becomes something remote from us, and we from it. Seabirds today are a part of everyday life for few but the patient inshore fisherman or long-distance sailor. As scientists, we may record every last feather and every slightest movement in our computers. We may digitise nest sites and telemeter heart rate, track them with satellites, probe them with ultrasound and perform a thousand tests on their DNA. But, we too are becoming more distant from our subjects. The constant insistence on the quantification of knowledge can tend to separate us from that sense of communion with our study subjects that characterised the generation of naturalists who first made watching birds not only a recreation but also a science.

I would not want to glamourise seabirds too much, or exaggerate their role in the marine environment. Nor would I wish to inflate the benefits to human life and health that might accrue by knowing them better. There may not be many who would wish to brave the hardships of the North Sea shores in order to glimpse a midwinter Razorbill, as a wind from Siberia whistles off the waves. And, perhaps rightly, there are few who pine for the smell of decaying guano on some shadeless tropical reef, when the sun is so high that the observers, and the breeding boobies that they observe, cast no shadows.

But for those who would know more: who have been crossed by the shadow of a giant petrel floating above the liner's stern, who have been wakened in their tent on some forested islet by the gentle crooning of storm-petrels or the awful shrieking of shearwaters, who have lain in the short grass atop some crag to peer at ranks of murres and kittiwakes, or swum in an atoll lagoon where terns hovered overhead; and for those who have not, but might like to do so, this book is for you. An account of how these beautiful and engaging birds fit into the economy of nature.

Acknowledgements

I would like to thank everyone who has worked in the field with me over the years, from Prince Leopold Island, Nunavut, to South Island, New Zealand. I cannot mention anyone by name without having to list you all: that would make a much thicker book. It would be easy to ramble on about companionship and the spiritual bond of sharing harshness and solitude. It is all true. But for those of you who shared that spirit with me, I do not need to say it. You know who you are and you know that it has been amazing!

In addition, I would like to acknowledge that I have been very fortunate in my managers at the Canadian Wildlife Service, George Finney, Hugh Boyd, Graham Cooch, Richard Elliot and Peter Blancher, who gave me every support in pursuing my seabird interests. Chris Perrins and Linda Birch made me very welcome in the Edward Grey Institute Library, where I have done much of my reading over the years. David Lack, whose ideas make frequent appearances in the book, was my first supervisor at Oxford: I owe him a huge debt for accepting a rather dubious fossil-collector as a bird student in the first place and, through his writings, for providing me with much inspiration. Additional thanks for a variety of reasons go to Sandy Bartle, Christine Eberl, Grant Gilchrist, Mark Hipfner, John Piatt, Larry Spear, Bill Sydeman and Kerry Woo. Parts of the book were read and commented on by David Ainley, Hugh Boyd, Tony Diamond, Ricky Dunn, Tim Lash, Bob Ricklefs and Ron Ydenberg. I thank you all for your encouragement (no, really, you were encouraging!). To Tim Lash and to John Chardine, I owe enormous thanks for contributing many of their photographs.

My particular thanks go to the Polar Continental Shelf Project of Natural Resources Canada and to the pilots of the De Havilland Twin-Otters that have been an essential element in all my seabird research in the Canadian Arctic. It is difficult to describe the sensation when, standing under a cold, grey sky on some windswept beach or barren tundra, watching the fingers of a nearby fog bank creeping inexorably closer, listening to the crackle of the high-frequency radio and surrounded by the litter of boxes and bags that hours before was your camp, you first become aware of the throb of the twin-turboprops. Then, from the lowering cloud, the broad, square-tipped wings appear, dangling fat tyres made for a far larger aeroplane. The approach is absurdly steep, like a kamikaze pilot. If the wind is blowing across the landing strip, the aircraft comes on like a crab, edging sideways towards the tyre-marks that form the only guide for the pilot. Then the rear wheels touch, the nose dips and the engines roar in reverse thrust. Almost before you can blink, the plane is down and slewing round to bring the cargo door level with the pile of gear.

Up until that moment, perhaps for 2–3 months on end, you have been responsible for the lives of your students and assistants, working in an environment where dangers from Polar Bears, from climbing on fragile cliffs, or from travelling icy waters in small boats, were frequent and real. From the moment that they clamber into the aircraft, the members of your crew become the responsibility of the pilot. Then, and only then, you are free; as free as I am now from this book. I love the field work and I acquire great satisfaction from writing. But sometimes it is nice not to do either.

NOTE ON ENGLISH NAMES

I have used 'European' English names for the most part, but I have used the North American 'murre', rather than 'guillemot' for the genus *Uria*, confining guillemot to the genus *Cepphus*. In addition, I have confined the term 'skua' to the genus *Catharacta*, using the North American 'jaeger' for *Stercorarius* species. Also, I felt that using 'divers' for *Gavia* spp. might lead to confusion with 'birds that swim underwater', so I have preferred the North American 'loons' for that genus. I recommend these arrangements to the folks in Europe, they save some ambiguity and circumlocution. For groups, I have used 'auks' as equivalent to all members of the Alcidae, 'cormorants' for all Phalacrocoracidae, 'boobies' for all Sulidae, 'albatrosses' for all Diomedeidae, 'gadfly petrels' for all *Pterodroma, Lugensa* and *Bulweria* spp. and 'petrels' as including all members of the Procellariidae. To refer to the entire order Procellariiformes, I use the term 'tubenoses': ugly, but accurate.

CHAPTER ONE

Introduction

I arrived at Prince Leopold Island, in the Canadian high arctic, in May 1975, never having been farther north than Inverness, Scotland, and never having visited a major seabird colony. The single-engine Otter aircraft that flew me out there felt like very flimsy protection against the immense wilderness of ice and snow that unfolded below me. We had been delayed for two days in Resolute Bay by a blizzard. No land was visible but occasional rocky cliffs. Only a few small chinks were apparent in the armour of ice that sealed in the sea. Surely, I was arriving far too early—nothing would be happening for weeks.

But, after the informalities of a field camp arrival were over and I made the short walk to the cliff edge, it was clear that I had been mistaken. The land might be shrouded in snow and the sea gripped by ice, but the Northern Fulmars and Thick-billed Murres that thronged the cliff ledges seemed quite unmoved. Thousands of years of experience told them that this was the place and now was the time. The murres were still a month from laying but the business of establishing their right to a former site, or finding and winning another, was going forward apace.

I had come directly from a study of passerines in tropical forests and scrub, where most of my time was spent simply finding and identifying individual birds. Acquiring a sample of 100 birds had required substantial industry. Now, here I was looking at thousands of birds at a glance, each one firmly rooted to a particular site on the cliff, like rows of beach huts on the Bournemouth promenade. This was going to be really smooth!

And in a sense it was. My companions and I collected enough data on Thick-billed Murres in three years to write a thick book. But in another sense, things were a lot more challenging in the world of seabirds. To see where and what my forest birds were eating, I needed only to follow and watch, but this I could not do with the murres. The best I could manage was to follow them through a telescope until they disappeared from sight, or go out in a boat, shoot a few where they were feeding and look in their stomachs. It was another ten years before David Cairns designed activity recorders that allowed us to measure exactly how much time they spent swimming and flying, and almost another decade before Don Croll put the first time-depth recorders on Thick-billed Murres to give us a glimpse of their underwater lives.

In 1984, I began systematic ringing of Thick-billed Murres at Coats Island, in northern Hudson Bay. I wanted to know their survival rates, the age when they began to breed, and their reproductive success at different ages. I expected the programme to last eight years, but it has run for more than twice as long and is still going: there are many interesting things about Thick-billed Murres that I would still like to learn. We need the patience of decades, not months or years, to understand seabirds.

Birds get to be old, but they don't get to be wise. The wisdom of birds is largely in their genes; either they are born with it, or they lack it. But when you deal with long-lived birds, like murres, you see their individuality very clearly. Each year when you go ringing, it is the same birds that stand their ground and attack you, or ignore you altogether as you remove the chicks from under their breasts, the same birds that panic and struggle while being handled or that slip unresisting into the bag so that their weight can be recorded (fewer of the latter, I must admit). To me, they are like old friends, though I fear this feeling may not be entirely reciprocated.

I have always liked to know birds as individuals, rather than as statistics. Many years ago, I was greatly influenced by Jane Goodall and her wonderful sagas of the Gombe stream Chimpanzees Pan troglodytes. *This book on seabirds is mainly about big pictures and trends, not about individual birds, but every bird is different. No generalisation in ecology is ever 100% valid. Somewhere, sometime, there is or will be a guillemot that plunges like a gannet and a tern that swims underwater. In an age when the computer speaks with the voice of unerring certainty, I find the unpredictable character of birds rather reassuring. They were here before us, and they will surely outlive us. Their lives have a reality and immediacy that may escape us in our increasingly secure and synthetic world.*

WHY SEABIRDS?

Why should I write a book about seabirds? What things do these birds have in common that distinguish them from the rest of the world of birds, and how are these differences related to their marine existence? How does the study of seabirds rate in terms of distinctness from other areas of science, especially other areas of ornithology?

Marine ornithology has two components: one is taxonomic (it is about birds) the other environmental (it is about the sea). Seabirds have a taxonomic definition (Procellariiformes, Sphenisciformes, Pelecaniformes and selected Charadriiformes: phalaropes, gulls, terns, skimmers, skuas and auks, with sheathbills sometimes included as honorary members). These are the birds that Leverett Loomis (1918), William Backhouse Alexander (1928), Robert Cushman Murphy (1936), James Fisher and Ronald Lockley (1954), and Philip Ashmole (1971) wrote about in the books and papers that served to define the field. When Peter Harrison (1983) produced his path-breaking identification guide to seabirds he included loons (divers) and grebes. I shall include loons because some species are marine throughout the year (most Pacific and Red-throated Loons), and all species are almost entirely marine during the non-breeding season. On the other hand, no grebes are marine while breeding and some species are mainly freshwater year-round, so they get little mention.

Most seabirds are found away from the shore, many out of sight of land. Once we move more than 1 km offshore, and excepting migrants forced to cross the ocean between winter and summer quarters, we encounter few birds not included within the taxonomic definition of seabird: principally the eiders and a few other seaducks, and some loons (especially Pacific Loon). Hence, seabirds seem to be those families that may be found well away from the shore and we may characterise marine ornithology as 'the study of birds adapted to living at sea, well away from land (but not including sea ducks, because they are studied by waterfowl biologists)'. This is rather an ugly definition, but it seems to fit the customary usage of the term.

Seabirds have frequently been defined in taxonomic terms, but there is no neat phylogenetic classification that divides birds found at sea from others. Many ducks, shorebirds, rails, herons, and kingfishers, all thought of as predominantly freshwater birds, occur in saltwater environments. A few raptors, especially the sea eagles, feed in nearshore waters or specialize in feeding on marine birds (e.g. some falcons). Even some songbirds are partial to the seashore: the Rock Pipit of British shores haunts the tidewrack, while the dainty, if somewhat macabre, Blackish Cinclodes or Tussacbird of the Falkland Islands participates in the marine food chain by pecking scabs off elephant seals and drinking blood from the wound. However, the Northwestern Crow is probably the only passerine that actually goes to sea, foraging on floating kelp beds far from shore.

All species belonging to the petrel, albatross, storm-petrel, booby, frigatebird, tropicbird and auk families feed exclusively at sea (Table 1.1). In addition, many species of loons, cormorants, gulls, terns and skuas and some grebes, ducks and shorebirds, feed either entirely or mainly at sea. Here, I shall include mention of some birds not traditionally considered seabirds, because some populations, at certain times of year are predominantly found at sea. On the other hand, I shall not concern myself much with those members of typical seabird families that inhabit fresh water, such as certain terns, gulls, pelicans and cormorants, except to contrast them with their marine relatives.

Table 1.1   Species of marine birds and their families

Family	Genera	Wholly marine spp.	Partially marine spp.	Non-marine spp.
Penguins	6	17		
Divers/Loons	1		5	
Albatrosses	4	25		
Petrels	13	79		
Storm-petrels	7	20		
Tropicbirds	1	3		
Pelicans	1	1	1	6
Boobies/Gannets	3	9		
Cormorants	2	24	2	7
Frigatebirds	1	5		
Ducks/Geese				
Phalaropes	1		2	1
Skuas/Jaegers	2	5	3	
Gulls	7	29	18	3
Terns	10	28	12	3
Auks	11	23		
Totals	**65**	**222**	**72**	

Although the shore, with its characteristic biological communities dominated by kelps and sea-weeds and typically marine invertebrate groups, is undoubtedly a member of the marine environment in good standing, I am going to deal mainly with the waters of the sea. The intertidal zone is a complete avian realm in itself: one where birds are important players in the ecological cast. However, my subject involves birds and the ocean, how they use it and how they are adapted to it. The land will feature in my tale mainly through its role as a breeding site for seabirds.

Three types of animal inhabit the air above the continents: birds, bats and insects. Neither the bats nor the flying insects have been successful at colonising the sea, although the occasional bat operates close to shore. As the bats are practically all either flying insect or fruit-eaters, and as neither is available at sea, their absence from marine habitats is unsurprising. The near absence of insects, so ubiquitous and diverse on land and well represented in fresh waters, is more puzzling. Moreover, the sea is full of all kinds of arthropods, demonstrating that having a horny body and many-jointed legs is no handicap at sea. We can ask ourselves why no insects inhabit the sea, but we might just as well ask why not one of the thousands of crustacean species has taken to flying.

This type of deep historical question is hard to answer. Insects, like birds, have become addicted to breathing air. For crustacea, the tides and currents of the oceans can serve to disperse them just as well as the winds of the atmosphere. But these are merely statements of how things are. While we can examine how the whale or the penguin has adapted from land to sea by contrasting them with their terrestrial relatives, we cannot say exactly why there are no flying crabs. Flying crabs are surely not impossible, in some parallel universe not unlike our own, but until we find some, any explanations for the current situation must be entirely speculative. Likewise, among seabirds, none builds a floating nest upon the ocean. There are many good reasons why it might not work, but it is impossible to categorically state that such a thing is impossible. In *The Thousand and one Nights*, Sinbad the Sailor, on his third voyage, reported seeing a species that nested in a floating shell, so we cannot completely rule out the possibility. Consequently, I shall confine myself to considering why things are as they are, rather than why they are not some other way.

WHY MARINE ORNITHOLOGY?

There is something about seabirds that promotes their separation from other birds in the minds of their students. What is it about birds that live at sea which encourage marine ornithologists to form separate societies and produce their own specialist journals? First, consider breeding biology: practically all seabirds are colonial, compared to only a small percentage of landbirds. When we study the breeding behaviour of seabirds we are dealing with problems such as information centres, extra-pair copulations, parent/offspring recognition, prostitution, predator mobbing, cliff-nesting, nocturnal or fossorial breeding, which otherwise apply to only a small proportion of birds and to hardly any other vertebrates.

Likewise, consider habitat selection and community ecology. Habitat selection for landbirds is, for the large part, dependent on vegetational structures. The vegetation is, for most birds, the matrix in which they live. At sea, once we get away from shoreline features, there are few physical barriers. Instead, the variation in seabird habitat is created by variations in temperature and salinity that structure the marine food webs of which seabirds form a part. As far as community ecology is concerned, the type of niche differentiation that separates species of forest birds, based on nuances of foraging behaviour (twig-gleaners, versus sallying flycatchers, bark-probers versus drillers), is reduced to the single fundamental constraint of diving performance. In many communities of seabirds, the principal prey is common to most species, something normally seen on land only during vole plagues or caterpillar and locust outbreaks. This observation has led to the notion that competition among seabirds, if it occurs, must be of a rather transitory type.

Notice that both the fields that I have instanced (breeding biology and habitat selection) set seabirds apart from the otherwise marine birds of the intertidal and nearshore zones: the latter are not necessarily colonial and their habitat ecology is similar to that of landbirds in taking cues from structure (sandy versus rocky shores, kelp beds, mussel beds, etc.). Of course, there are always exceptions. The study of Marbled Murrelet breeding biology is clearly a part of terrestrial ecology. Similarly, studies of arctic-nesting jaegers have much in common with studies of other tundra-breeding raptors.

The emphasis on oceanographic correlations in seabird habitat studies creates a fundamental division between marine and terrestrial ornithology, but places it close to marine biology. However, it is only recently that marine ornithology has begun to be accepted as a branch of marine biology. I think the rather reluctant acceptance of marine ornithology within the larger field relates to a minor law of ecology: ecologists don't look up the food chain they only look down. This is especially evident in the marine environment. Those who study phytoplankton are concerned mainly about water chemistry and temperature; those who study zooplankton are concerned about water chemistry and phytoplankton dynamics; those studying fish are interested in plankton, while those studying marine mammals are interested in the whole food chain. Everyone is interested in what is below their chosen organism, because they believe that food is an important limiting factor. No one is very interested in the parts of the food chain above their chosen group, because no one thinks that predation has much effect. Seabirds, being at the top of most marine food chains, and having, by the standards of fish and invertebrates, minuscule standing stocks, are considered by marine biologists, if they consider them at all, to be relatively insignificant. Like spume cast up by storms at sea, they are symptoms of great forces at work, but not part of those forces.

So, seabirds never received much attention from marine biologists. As nature abhors a vacuum, it was left to ornithologists to extend their investigations to the marine environment. This must be why, in Canada, where I work, seabirds are the responsibility of the Canadian Wildlife Service, while every other marine organism is the preserve of the Department of Fisheries and Oceans.

Overwhelmingly, what sets seabirds apart from other birds is their participation in food chains not only separate from the vegetation associations that define the ecology of the land, but arranged in a manner that promotes entirely different strategies for finding and capturing food. It is not that food in the ocean is patchier than in terrestrial environments: actually, it is probably less patchy on certain scales (e.g. over hundreds of kilometres), but that patches are, by terrestrial standards, extremely ephemeral. If we accept certain near-shore zones of tidally induced upwellings (which fluctuate on a tidal cycle), then most concentrations of food for seabirds probably vary over timescales of minutes to weeks, rather than the predictable annual fluctuations that characterise most terrestrial associations. Thus, the study of seabirds becomes a study of opportunism and above all travel: each individual bird must cover large distances. The issue of territoriality, so important for many landbirds, hardly ever arises for seabirds once they leave their nests.

People living in Western industrial societies nowadays can hope to live for the biblical three score and ten years; many will exceed four score. This longevity places us among the longest-lived mammals. Like most long-lived mammals, we do not begin to reproduce for many years and when we do it is usually a single birth, with an inter-birth interval of more than one year. Hunter-gatherer societies, presumably leading a lifestyle that would have characterised most of our species until the Neolithic revolution some 10,000 years ago, begin to reproduce at a similar age, and have an inter-birth interval of 2–3 years. With life expectancies of 40–50 years, women bear children until near the end of their lives, giving a total potential lifetime reproduction of 10–15 children. These demographics, possibly typical of pre-agricultural humans, are very similar to those of Emperor Penguins, albatrosses and large petrels.

However, there is one big difference between the situation for humans and seabirds: in humans, child rearing proceeds up to at least puberty. In modern industrial society it may extend, in an attenuated form, into the twenties (student support), and at the death of the parent it is usual for a valuable legacy in the form of land, property and power (money) to be transferred to the offspring. In this respect humans resemble cooperative breeding birds, where the family territory is inherited through succession from one generation to the next. In seabirds, the dependency of the offspring does not exceed one year (about 280 days in Wandering Albatross and *c.*300 days in King Penguin) and there is no territorial property to inherit. The argument from humans and great apes, that in a saturated habitat it is the quality, rather than the quantity of offspring that counts, cannot be applied to seabirds. Although some aspects of the demographics of seabirds resemble those of large mammals, the differences suggest that the selection pressures moulding them may have been different.

THE 'SEABIRD SYNDROME'

Now we are coming to the core of what distinguishes the ecology and adaptations of marine birds from those of their terrestrial relatives. The essential elements are scale and mobility, but constrained by the need to return to land for breeding. This combination gives rise to coloniality, and this, in turn (if you are prepared to follow Philip Ashmole, 1963), has led to the many characteristic features of seabird demography and life history. If you must travel far from your breeding site to feed, the frequency with which you can return to provision your nestlings is severely constrained. Low provisioning rates lead to a reduction in clutch and brood size, lowering annual reproductive output and, hence, promoting adaptations towards longevity. This leads to deferred maturity and to multi-year pair-bonds, putting a premium on correct mate choice. To maintain a sufficient rate of feeding, both parents must share the duties of rearing. This restricts options for sexual selection, reducing the degree of sexual dimorphism, though not the evolution of elaborate nuptial plumage. Hence, ecology has a strong role in determining social behaviour and life-history strategy.

Low reproductive rates, long lives, deferred breeding, coloniality, and sexes that behave alike and look alike, form part of a strongly correlated suite of adaptations that characterise birds which feed far out at sea. The inter-dependence of these adaptations, and their common origin from selection inherent in the choice of a marine life, is the theme that I shall attempt to elaborate throughout the book—I am giving away the plot in advance. My intention is not simply to provide a natural history of seabirds, but to meditate on the power of feeding ecology to affect every aspect of birds' lives, from their clutch size to their plumage. This grand unifying idea is not mine; either implicitly (Lack, 1968) or explicitly (Ashmole, 1963, 1971) it has been familiar to seabird biologists for nearly half a century. However, it is not universally accepted and, in fact, parts are much disputed.

I have dubbed the combination of behavioural and ecological attributes that I have listed, 'the seabird syndrome'. It makes sense of many phenomena that otherwise seem arbitrary. Some people will not be convinced; others may find what I have to say self-evident. If we examine seabirds piecemeal, we may find many individual observations that conflict with the grand design. That is why I want to paint the broadest possible canvas, looking at seabirds on a global scale. At that scale, I believe the co-evolution and interdependence of the different traits that comprise the seabird syndrome are indisputable.

Members of seabird families that inhabit fresh waters generally exhibit the seabird syndrome to a lesser extent than their marine relatives. Their lives are shorter and their offspring more numerous: some are non-colonial or form only very small colonies. By confining myself, for the most part, to birds that live at sea I have avoided the necessity of constantly qualifying my generalisations to take account of the freshwater species and populations. However, I shall turn to freshwater gulls, terns and cormorants occasionally, solely to emphasise the distinction between marine and freshwater environments.

COMPARISONS WITH OTHER BIRDS AND VERTEBRATES

There are some attributes of seabirds that are fairly unusual within ornithology, but shared by many aquatic vertebrates. For instance, underwater foraging may take place at very low light intensities, may require exceptional abilities in diving (e.g. to hold the breath for long periods), and exceptional resistance to pressure. These problems are shared with ducks, some rails, and the dippers, as well as aquatic mammals, reptiles and amphibians, but do not affect non-diving seabirds. Hence, although they form important elements of marine ornithology, these specialisations do not constitute problems specific to seabirds.

Can we find parallels for the salient features of seabird biology among other organisms? Of course, many organisms are colonial, from termites to prairie dogs, and their coloniality may derive from a variety of causes. Among birds, many that forage socially, and many that feed in freshwater habitats, are colonial. The ecological factors correlating with coloniality in birds were extensively reviewed by Lack (1968).

Coloniality can evolve only in the absence of multi-purpose (breeding and feeding) territories. The defence of feeding areas mainly occurs where resources are relatively stable and predictable and sufficiently dense for defence to be feasible and worthwhile, in terms of energy invested versus resources protected. Stable and recognisable boundaries may also be useful facilitators of territoriality. None of these features is characteristic of marine environments.

Likewise, many larger vertebrates have a low reproductive output and are long-lived. Among animals, especially birds and mammals, there are strong associations between high survival, deferred maturity and low reproductive rate. If a bird develops a life-history strategy that involves a small clutch size, it is likely to do so only if it has, or is capable of achieving, a high adult survival rate, which is a prerequisite for the evolution of deferred maturity. For obvious reasons, deferred breeding will not evolve in populations where individuals have a low chance of surviving to the following breeding season. Consequently, these three features of seabird biology cannot be regarded as independent responses to life at sea, but form part of a group of frequently co-adapted traits.

Parental care by both parents is commonplace among birds that feed their nestlings, which includes most terrestrial birds, as well as practically all seabirds. Lack of plumage differences between the sexes is less common and occurs especially among colonial breeders or those that live permanently in social groups of more than two birds, such as those that nest cooperatively. As birds in which the sexes look alike include species varying widely in ecology, it seems that the common factor preventing the evolution of sex differences is not directly related to habitat or feeding ecology, but is a consequence of the social behaviour adopted.

Hence, all of the elements of the 'seabird syndrome' can be found elsewhere in the world of birds: it is their combination in a single habitat grouping that distinguishes the ecology of seabirds. Where else can we find this particular array of traits?

Among birds, certain birds of prey, especially vultures, share many of the characteristics of seabirds: they are colonial breeders, they do not hold feeding territories, they are long-lived and they rear few young. Pairs share incubation and chick rearing and there is little or no sexual dimorphism.

Aggregations are usually on a much smaller scale than those of seabirds, with colonies of tens to hundreds of pairs being typical, and some rear two young per year. However, they appear to represent the closest approach to the seabird syndrome among terrestrial birds. Like seabirds, they forage over large areas looking for concentrated, but ephemeral, sources of food. This similarity points to food and foraging strategy as the main causes of their convergent adaptations.

If we look beyond the class Aves, it is clear that the pinnipeds (seals, sea lions and Walrus *Odobenus rosmarus*) confront many of the same problems as seabirds and have reached some of the same answers. Some are colonial while breeding and some, albeit fewer, are constrained by having to commute to and from distant feeding areas at that time (in science-speak, they are 'central-place foragers'). Some range over large areas of ocean looking for concentrated food. They do so more slowly than seabirds, but they can afford to do so because their energy reserves are much larger and their energy consumption per unit body mass much lower. But, because they are mammals, and therefore bear live young that are fed for a time on their mothers' milk, they have developed other strategies to cope with coloniality and its consequent local depletion of food. Moreover, few pinnipeds are truly oceanic, except those associated with sea-ice (a kind of land substitute): most remain close to shore throughout their lives, like loons, seaducks and other inshore seabirds.

In life-history adaptations, the seals are less extreme than seabirds: they do not live as long and (mostly) they start to breed at a younger age. In all these characteristics they resemble penguins, but not flying seabirds. Penguins rest somewhat uneasily among their fellow seabirds and for many topics that we shall touch on they provide a special case. In lineage, they are birds, but in terms of their ecology, they more closely resemble seals.

Cetaceans are even less like seabirds in their life-history adaptations than seals. Being able to give birth at sea frees the whales from the tyranny of colonies and central-place foraging and the huge size of some whales means that feeding can be highly discontinuous over time. Like seabirds, they are faced with the need to locate small, ephemeral food patches spread over vast areas. It could be that, if we make allowance for the difference in timescales, the foraging behaviour of whales and seabirds is very similar. The deployment of satellite telemetry, certain to be a huge growth area for seabird and cetacean biologists over the next decade, should allow us to make that comparison very soon. However, the huge difference in reproductive strategies between whales and seabirds makes them very different in other aspects of their biology. Overall, those that study whales have little in common with seabird scientists.

There is one other group of mammals that is worth setting alongside seabirds, and that is bats. Having dismissed them for their inability to invade the sea, I should now point to their striking demographic similarities to seabirds. Relative to their size, they are very long-lived and have a slow reproductive rate, most rearing only 1–2 young annually. In addition, many roost and breed communally in enormous numbers, taking advantage of sites that confer protection from diurnal avian predators. Many bats make long journeys from daytime roosts to feed at night on intermittently available fruit, though this food may be seasonally predictable. The causes of the demographic convergence between bats and seabirds are unclear, but foraging range may be a common factor.

ELEMENTS OF MARINE ORNITHOLOGY

Before we discuss the seabirds' adaptive syndrome, we must consider the essential elements that form the matrix within which seabirds have evolved and hence the constraining variables that seabird scientists must understand. The list is a little daunting and illustrates the breadth of disciplines that marine ornithologists must master in order to understand the objects of their study.

Marine ornithologists must be concerned about oceanography and its effects in structuring marine communities, as well as fisheries and their impacts on both the fishes being harvested, on other fishes caught incidentally, and on their predators, competitors and prey. They need to address foraging theory in the context of highly ephemeral resources, spread over areas unthinkable in most studies of terrestrial birds and over timescales from minutes to centuries. They must consider demographic theory in a context where reproduction is highly variable and long deferred, generations are hugely overlapping and senility is an important phenomenon. They must consider social behaviour in the context of the largest and densest reproductive aggregations found for any bird or mammal. We should not say that terrestrial ornithologists necessarily view their ecology on a smaller scale, although most do. The essential thing is that the marine ornithologist has no choice but to consider whole oceans, because the events affecting seabirds are typically large-scale phenomena.

Is there a science of marine ornithology? I can imagine those people who go to sea in ships and count birds in different ocean currents and water types nodding their heads. Yes, this is marine ornithology and we are the ones doing it. Surely all that seasickness should get some kind of accolade? Well, maybe. The trouble is that the field pioneered by Roger Bailey (1966), Warren King (1967, 1970, 1974), Dick Brown (1975, 1980), Richard Pocklington (1979) and company is really good, solid marine biology, applied to birds. The paradigms and methods are identical to those of any marine zoogeographer: go forth and sample as many things as possible for as many bits of ocean as possible and look for correlations and concordances.

There is nothing wrong with such an approach—in fact I am very much in favour of it. However, there is nothing intrinsically unique to construct a field of science from it. Only when distributions at sea are mapped onto the constraints of coloniality, when densities of birds can be adjusted by their travel times and calibrated against the rate of change in their prey patches, do we begin to create something that is unique to seabirds, and hence begin to create a separate marine ornithology.

Likewise, a demographic study of albatrosses that informs us that the age of first breeding is adjusted in relation to expected lifetime reproductive success (Weimerskirch, 1992) is a lovely piece of science, but a straightforward application of population ecology. When the age of first breeding can be scaled to foraging radius and to prey density (e.g. Weimerskirch, 2002), then we begin to approach a uniquely seabird science. Proving that Crested Auklets prefer mates with long plumes (Jones & Hunter, 1993) provides useful support for one theory of sexual selection, but is just another cog in the big machine that is behavioural ecology. If it can be linked to the enormous scale of coloniality among auklets then it begins to fall within the separate ambit of marine ornithology.

There is no special virtue in developing a unique science. We could argue that answering questions unique to seabirds is a waste of time, because by definition the results can only be applied to seabirds. However, this could be said about studying any special adaptation. One of the positive things concerning the mixture of traits that I have identified as being at the core of marine ornithology is that they require integration of information and ideas from a broad range of scientific disciplines. If we view marine ornithology in a positive way, we can state that it is an interdisciplinary science looking at biological problems on a very large scale. And scale itself is a positive virtue, because, all too often, ecologists tend to study things at a scale that is far smaller than that on which natural populations and natural events really occur. Seabirds, through their vast foraging ranges and migrations, force us to work and think on a large scale. This can be annoying and frustrating, but also it can be enlightening. I have tried throughout this book to emphasise large patterns and those constraints and compromises in behaviour and ecology that are unique to marine birds. This is my excuse for the somewhat uneven treatment of seabird biology that I present.

OCEANOGRAPHY FOR ORNITHOLOGISTS

Many people view the ocean as a flat, featureless plain. But this is an erroneous perception. In truth, it is a place of great complexity and diversity, filled with excitement and hidden drama. The extraordinary things that occur within its vast spaces and corridors must in most part be deduced, for the sea is not a great communicator but the strong and silent type—a mute and patient, though sometimes wildly destructive, companion.

Roger Payne, *Among Whales*, 1995

The world's oceans cover two-thirds of the Earth's surface. If the planet's crust was completely flat, but for the gentle curvature of the globe, it would be covered by a layer of water more than 2 km deep. In its deep troughs, the ocean floor descends further below sea level than Mount Everest rises above it.

PHYSICAL FACTORS

The world's oceans are a huge field of study, drawing on physics, chemistry and biology. The understanding of large-scale current patterns and interactions with climate requires knowledge of thermodynamics and planetary motion. This great mass of saltwater is constantly in motion. Cooling at the poles, especially in the vicinity of the Antarctic and heating at the equator, create currents that transfer heat from low to high latitudes. Winds deflect the movement of water, driving it east or west, depending on latitude. Surface currents of warm water are replaced by currents that return cold water towards the equator at great depth. Imposed on this is the twice-daily rhythm of the tides. In addition, the input of major river systems can contribute variations in salinity and temperature far from their estuaries, and such input may fluctuate enormously over seasons and years. All these movements of water form part of a huge and somewhat unstable mechanism, changing almost by the hour, that transports huge quantities of water and heat from the equator towards the poles and in so doing is an important part of the Earth's climate generation.

FOOD CHAINS

Currents and depth layering have strong effects on water chemistry, especially in coastal areas, causing variations in dissolved salts that have a big impact on the distribution and abundance of micro-organisms, such as planktonic marine algae (diatoms and flagellates). These tiny plants form the basis for most food chains in the sea, with several layers of animals balanced above them, beginning with tiny herbivores such as copepods, moving through the larger crustacea, such as amphipods, euphausiids, mysids and other shrimp-like creatures, arrow-worms, comb-jellies, jellyfish, pteropod molluscs and small fish. Above these are the predatory larger fish and squid, as well as the huge baleen whales, some seals and seabirds. Right at the top of the chain come really big predators, such as sharks, tuna-like fish, the toothed whales, sea lions, some seals, Polar Bears *Ursus maritimus* and the largest seabirds.

Then there are the food chains based on corals, seaweeds, kelps and sea grasses, that are confined to the waters of continental margins or tiny patches around oceanic islands and seamounts, and which are mainly grazed by animals larger than those typically taken by seabirds: dugongs, sea-turtles and large molluscs. However, the annual breakdown of kelp and sea grass, which occurs at the termination of the growing season, casts large quantities of biological material into the ocean, providing copious food for filter-feeding animals, such as clams, mussels, scallops and tube worms. These, in turn, provide food sources for inshore seabirds, especially seaducks.

Simple food chains, such as those described above, cannot possibly do justice to the complexity of marine food webs. Large fish may move up several rungs of the food chain in the course of their growth. Some large fishes may be important predators on their own younger stages. Birds such as puffins and murres, as well as many seals and whales, may feed on organisms as low down the chain as copepods, or two stages higher, at the level of fishes. Leavings and faeces from all levels of the higher food chain provide nourishment for a myriad of benthic scavengers, such as crabs, amphipods and polychaete worms, which also provide prey for bottom-feeding birds. At the greatest extent, a food chain might pass carbon fixed by phytoplankton, through copepod, amphipod, small fish, larger fish and seal, to reside eventually in a Polar Bear. Conversely, much carbon fixed by algae passes to sedentary filter feeders and returns via decomposition to loops far back in the food chain.

BIOLOGICAL PRODUCTION

In terms of productivity, it is usual to distinguish shallow waters of the continental shelves from deeper, oceanic waters. Between these two, there is the continental slope, a zone of variable width where the sea floor shallows abruptly from the ocean depths. The continental shelf zone is generally one of high productivity, with a constant exchange of biomass between the faunas of the seabed (benthos) and the overlying waters. Beyond the continental slope, the opportunities for any biological exchange between air-breathing animals and the denizens of the depths are very limited. Moreover, bottom topography has little effect on the surface waters, except where seamounts rise close to the surface; hence there is little renewal of the mineral nutrients necessary for phytoplankton growth. Continental shelf waters provide more than 90% of fishery takes worldwide, although they occupy only 5% of the area of sea. The ratio of the density of seabird biomass in shelf, versus oceanic, waters is probably similar.

Although the broad expanse of the oceans, beyond the continental margins, is generally a zone of low biological production, exceptions occur where the major current systems meet. This is especially true of the subantarctic polar boundary, which encircles the southern hemisphere at about 50°S, but to a lesser extent it is also true wherever major currents interface. Moreover, the tiny coral atolls that are scattered across tropical latitudes far offshore in the Indian and Pacific oceans create, in their lagoons, tiny oases of biological production.

MARINE REGIONS

The ocean can be divided into several major water types, defined by their surface temperature characteristics: tropical, subtropical, subpolar and polar. The terms low and high arctic are sometimes substituted for subpolar and polar in the northern hemisphere, but the latter seem to be more symmetrical with the tropical terminology. In the northern hemisphere, subpolar is frequently replaced by 'boreal'. However, although the southern counterpart of boreal should be austral, that word is not usually applied in an oceanographic context. Boreal is a lovely word, recalling old maps showing explorers in funny hats menaced by unicorns, and large blank places beckoning the adventurous, but regretfully we prefer subpolar in this context.

Only tropical and polar waters can be unambiguously defined, the other categories being varying mixtures of these. Moreover, surface water temperatures, especially at continental margins, are much affected by large-scale upwellings of cold subsurface waters, which create seas with temperate characteristics even at the equator. Roughly speaking, temperatures at sea are arranged in decreasing order from equator to pole, but exceptions abound: the waters off Newfoundland, at 45°N are colder year-round than those that lap the shores of the Barents Sea at 70°N, while those off the coast of Chile are 10°C cooler than those at the same latitude in the central Pacific. Unsurprisingly, temperature is a far more important factor in seabird distributions than latitude.

TRENDS AND FLUCTUATIONS

On an oceanic scale, seabird populations vary closely with the production generated by marine ecosystems (Brown, 1980; Hunt & Schneider, 1987; Hunt, 1990). On smaller scales, they are frequently affected by physical mechanisms operating on the availability of prey, rather than the rate of production (e.g. Brown, 1980; Cairns & Schneider, 1990; Gaston *et al.*, 1993). Because of the dynamic nature of many marine ecosystems, and because of the perturbations that have been brought about by human impacts on seabird populations, either through direct harvesting or by alien predators, most seabird populations have fluctuated strongly during the period for which records are available (the last few decades for most species). Consequently, there are few places where we might reasonably assume that seabird populations are in natural equilibrium.

Change is a constant element of the marine environment and it occurs on timescales ranging from seconds to millennia over areas of a few metres up to oceans of millions of square kilometres. The lives of seabirds may be affected by the capricious vagaries of storms and hurricanes, by the predictable daily and monthly rhythms of the tides, by annual changes in productivity created by the progression of the seasons, and by changes taking place over several years, such as those associated with the El Niño Southern Oscillation events that transform the surface waters of the Pacific, and to a lesser extent the other oceans, every 4–6 years. Even longer-term cycles are recognisable, operating over decades and centuries, and each level of variation contains within it every other. The only constant element in the seabird's world is change. On top of this, there are directional changes taking place in the Earth's climate and oceanography that may be the result of human activities that have altered the composition of the atmosphere. What the outcome of these changes may be for seabirds is a matter for conjecture, but, like the rest of the biosphere, seabirds seem destined for even more turbulent times in the future than their chosen habitat customarily inflicts on them.

SEABIRD REALMS

I have already used the terms inshore and offshore fairly liberally. They will be used even more frequently hereafter, because the distance from shore that birds habitually feed has many fundamental implications for their ecology and reproduction. Foraging range is probably the most important single factor determining variation in those characteristics that distinguish the seabird syndrome.

Although I am going to use these terms extensively, I do not want to attempt a rigorous definition and as far as possible I follow the terminology of Ashmole (1971). Most people would consider sea within 8 km of the coast to be 'inshore', but where land slopes steeply to deep waters, we may find birds, such as albatrosses, typically found far out at sea, regularly approaching to within a few kilometres of shore. Conversely, where shallow waters extend far from shore, even normally coast-bound species, such as guillemots and scoters, may occur far from land. There is no firm definition of inshore and offshore within waters of the continental shelf (these are known as 'neritic' by oceanographers). Nor is there necessarily a close connection between inshore/offshore feeding and foraging range. During breeding, some inshore-feeding species may travel long distances to feed (e.g. Marbled and Kittlitz's Murrelets). However, on the whole, offshore feeders do travel further to find food during breeding than inshore feeders.

Two other words that require definition are 'pelagic' and 'oceanic'. Pelagic is a clearly defined technical term used by oceanographers to denote the waters away from continental shelves. In this context, I use it interchangeably with 'oceanic' to describe species that forage predominantly beyond the continental shelf. These are necessarily species that are independent of land outside the breeding season. Likewise, oceanic islands are those that rise from the ocean floor away from the continental shelf.

A confounding factor that affects these categories is the presence of seasonal sea-ice cover at high latitudes in both hemispheres. Sea-ice provides a platform on which seabirds can perch and develops a characteristic food web associated with its underside. It enables otherwise inshore birds, such as Black Guillemots, to occur far offshore in winter. A distinctive seabird community is associated with sea-ice at both poles.

MY SOURCES

In a fully scientific treatise, every assertion and every factual statement would have to be given solid backing from the relevant peer-reviewed literature. However, I have not written this book as a scientific text, but as a natural history book. To reduce the number of references, I have omitted them for statements that I feel are generally accepted by marine ornithologists. However, I have included them where I am describing an unusual or unique observation, an idea that may be unfamiliar to readers, one for which there may be only one or two sources, or one that is especially associated with a particular researcher. I plead forgiveness of those who would have wished for more references (as well as those who would have wished for fewer).

In my comparisons among seabird families, of which there are more than a few, I am greatly indebted to several recent compilations. I mention them here and will not refer to them again, except in the context of some particular idea, but they form the basis for many of my generalisations concerning particular groups: for penguins, Williams (1995), for albatrosses, Tickell (2000), for other tubenoses, Warham (1990, 1996), for cormorants, Johnsgard (1993), for skuas and jaegers, Furness (1987a), for all these groups the accounts in del Hoyo *et al.* (1992), for gulls and terns the contributions of Joanna Burger and Michael Gochfeld to del Hoyo *et al.* (1996), and for auks my own book with Ian Jones (Gaston & Jones, 1998).

I distinguish natural history from science on the basis of numerical content. Much of what I discuss is supported by hard numbers in scientific publications and I have included numbers ('data' as they are often known) where they seem necessary. However, I have tried to avoid probabilities and I make shameless use of the 'telling anecdote'. I am not attempting to prove anything, but simply to provide an overview of seabird ecology, based on ideas that seem, if not proven, at least reasonable. I include some graphs to illustrate trends. Although I present no statistics, all trends shown are significant at the normal level of acceptance: $P < 0.05$, for what that is worth (it is wise not to place too much faith in probability tests). I have relied rather heavily on my own observations, though I am familiar with only a small proportion of the world's seabirds. I have tried to make it clear where I am presenting my own ideas, as opposed to those that are widely accepted, by shifting to the first person. In places, I speculate, I hope within reason. I take heart from a comment of the Nobel Laureate, François Jacob, on the nature of science:

> *Whether mythic or scientific, the view of the world that man builds is always largely a product of his imagination.*
>
> François Jacob, *The Possible and the Actual*, 1982: 11

Northern Fulmar gliding just above the sea: note the downward dihedral of the wings, with one tip skimming the surface. (Tony Gaston)

CHAPTER TWO

Types of seabirds

One evening, not long ago, I was watching the television in my health club, while I patiently strode to nowhere on the exercise machine. At the club, there are ten televisions in a row. My habit is to watch a comedy channel while keeping my headphones tuned to the news channel. While thus engaged, out of the corner of my eye I caught sight of a familiar shape on the rock video channel. Among a welter of abstruse bodies and movements was the merest glimpse of a bird. Even as I switched my attention it was gone. I was left only with the impression of long, stiff wings and a high leisurely arc, above a green, heaving sea. I had no doubt that it was a gadfly petrel, though I could not recognise the species.

Information psychologists estimate that the human consciousness can process a maximum of c.50 bits of information per second. That means the equivalent of 25 individual letters of the alphabet, or hitting five keys on the piano. Yet, in not even a fraction of a second, my brain had formed a detailed image of a bird, its shape, proportions, colour and movement, as well as some background. Clearly, I could not have consciously 'seen' all this. Instead, a few salient points of information in the video had triggered the explicit picture that my mind presented. What pieces of information produced such an unexpected image?

Birders in England have a word for it, 'jizz': the indefinable quality that attaches to a particular type of bird. Normally the jizz does not have anything to do with colour: too many birds are coloured the same, at least to our eyes, and colour changes with light. Jizz is about proportions and movements. For seabirds, among the world's least colourful birds, jizz is always an important clue to identification.

Being keen to discover what rock band had used an image of a gadfly petrel in its video, I attempted to switch audio channels. Alas, in my haste, I confused the channel selector with the treadmill speed regulator. My hasty attempt to change channels resulted in the treadmill giving a sudden spurt. I was precipitated onto the floor, where young women on adjacent machines stared pityingly at me. Probably, the image of the petrel had passed across their vision without producing a conscious ripple. But for me, the image of that bird, so far in time and place and environment from the sunless basement in which I trod the machines, was the most significant event of the day.

Much more than landbirds, every type of seabird has its own peculiar shape and movement. To me, each characteristic jizz comes with an accompanying image of seascapes and islands where I may have first encountered it. And these characteristics not only trigger memories, they carry clues to the whole lifestyle of the birds. Meditating on southern oceans, great waves and trade winds; on unimaginable journeys on wheeling wings; on time and wide spaces and the unbearable lightness of being a petrel, I went to take a shower.

HISTORY

Life originated in the sea and all the major phyla of animals began there. Many groups of organisms that evolved on land subsequently returned to the sea: reptiles, flowering plants, mammals and birds. The last, like their warm-blooded cousins, the mammals, became most abundant after the demise of the dinosaurs at the close of the Cretaceous, but well before that there was a diversity of seabirds. Some of the earliest fossil birds inhabited the marine environment and there is even a theory that flight itself evolved at sea and that the origin of seabirds preceded the development of flight. Today, the largest bird other than ratites (Emperor Penguin) and the one with the longest wings (Wandering Albatross) both live at sea.

Different groups of birds invaded the marine environment at different times. By the Cretaceous period, *c*.100 million years ago, there was a wide variety of marine birds inhabiting the shallow, continental seas of the period, including the flightless, loon-like Hesperornithiformes, which had virtually no wings, and the tern-like Icthyornithiformes. Both groups had reptile-like teeth in both jaws. Both died out, along with the dinosaurs, at the end of the Cretaceous and were replaced with modern bird types. Both the penguins and the tubenoses are recognisable from the Eocene period (60 million years ago), as well as ancestors of today's gull/shorebird assemblage. All modern seabird families were present by the Miocene, approximately 20 million years ago.

Depending on the classification that you espouse, modern birds appear to contain several lineages in which marine life has developed independently: penguins (Sphenisciformes), petrels and albatrosses (Procellariiformes), loons (Gaviiformes), pelicans, cormorants and relatives (Pelecaniformes), ducks and geese (Anseriformes), where it may have happened frequently, and the gull/shorebird assemblage (Charadriiformes), where it appears to have occurred at least twice (phalaropes and the gull/tern/auk/skua lineage). Many more marine bird lineages are extinct, so it is clear that the boundary between land and sea is not one that birds have had much compunction about crossing.

CLASSIFICATION

Biologists have been arranging the world's organisms according to their natural affinities since well before Darwin, but the idea of evolution created a rationale that had previously been missing.

Classifications since Darwin have sought to combine species of common ancestry into a hierarchy of genera, families and orders that reflect their descent. For seabirds, the identity of discrete units at the level above genus (variously Families, Infra-orders, Sub-orders) has been relatively stable. However, the arrangement of these blocks within the class of birds as a whole has been rather variable, reflecting the difficulty of identifying the course of events that took place in the early part of the Tertiary period.

Following the great impetus to classification given by the publication of Darwin's *Origin of Species* and a period of intensive comparative anatomical investigations, the late 19th century witnessed a plethora of competing classifications, from which a consensus developed that persisted for much of the 20th century. Gadow's (1892) classification (Table 2.1) is characteristic of such arrangements. From the point of view of seabirds, the important feature is the separation between Charadriiform seabirds (auks, gulls, terns), which he placed with the shorebirds, and the Steganopodes (pelicans, etc.; more recently known as Pelecaniformes), which were classed with storks, herons and flamingos. The chief uniting feature of the pelicans and allies was the 'totipalmate' foot, in which a web connects all four toes. All other web-footed birds have webbing connecting only the three forward-pointing toes.

Fürbringer (1902) created an alternative arrangement in which the division between the Charadriiformes and the rest of the seabirds was deepened to the level of sub-classes, with the sub-class Charadriornithes containing not only Charadriiformes, as outlined by Gadow, but also the cranes and rails (Gruiformes). All other seabirds were included in the sub-class Pelargornithes, which included an order for the loons/divers and grebes (Podicipediformes) and another very large order, Ciconiiformes, which embraced the flamingos, herons, storks and birds of prey, as well as the Pelecaniformes. Significantly, Fürbringer also classified penguins and petrels, both given their own order by Gadow, as 'probably' Ciconiiformes.

Table 2.1   Typical arrangement of seabird families based on comparative anatomy (Gadow, 1892); not all non-seabird orders and families are shown

Subclass	Order	Suborder	Family	Contains
Neornithes	Colymbiformes	Colymbi		Loons/divers
		Podicipedes		Grebes
	Sphenisciformes	Sphenisci	Spheniscidae	Penguins
	Procellariiformes	Tubinares		Tubenoses
	Ardeiformes	Steganopodes	Phaethontidae	Tropicbirds
			Phalacrocoracidae	Cormorants
			Pelecanidae	Pelicans
			Fregatidae	Frigatebirds
		Herodii	Ardeidae	Herons
		Pelargi	Ciconiidae	Storks
			Phoenicopteridae	Flamingos
	Falconiformes			Birds of prey
	Anseriformes			Waterfowl
	Gruiformes			Bustards, cranes and rails
	Charadriiformes	Limicola	Chionididae	Sheathbills
			Charadriidae	Plovers
			Glareolidae	Coursers, pratincoles
			Thinocoridae	Seedsnipes
			Oedicnemidae	Stone-curlews
		Gaviae	Alcidae	Auks
			Laridae	Gulls, terns, skuas and jaegers

Subsequent classifications tended to prefer something akin to Gadow's arrangement until the very comprehensive classification of Sibley & Ahlquist (1990) reconstituted a grouping (Ciconii; a suborder) that included flamingos, herons, storks, birds of prey and most Pelecaniformes, as well as loons, grebes, penguins and tubenoses. Another suborder, Charadrii, is equivalent to Gadow's Charadriiformes (Table 2.2). In this classification, the previous Pelecaniformes (Steganopodes) is split among three groupings. The tropicbirds have their own group (parvorder Phaethontida), as do the boobies and cormorants (Sulida), while both pelicans and frigatebirds are part of a grouping (Ciconiida) that includes herons, ibises, storks and New World vultures, as well as tubenoses, penguins and loons, the latter all combined with frigatebirds in a single superfamily (Procellarioidea). Under this classification, as few as three groups could have become marine independently, though it is equally possible that several of the superfamilies of the Ciconii could either have moved to saltwater independently or originated from a common ancestor that was already marine.

Unfortunately, these varied arrangements tend to confuse the issue of how often birds have adopted a marine way of life. Whether tubenoses and penguins are considered separate orders, or simply sister families among the same superfamily, does not inform us whether their common ancestor was or was not a marine bird; only the fossil record can do that and thus far it has not revealed the answer. However, that both groups, including all fossil species, as far as we know, are or were, exclusively marine, strongly suggests that their common ancestor may already have been a seabird. Similarly, the close association in all classifications between auks and gulls, and the fact that all genera of both families include marine representatives, makes the probability that their common ancestor was a seabird rather high.

Sibley & Ahlquist (1990) discuss the break-up of the former Pelecaniformes, pointing out that either the totipalmate webbed foot evolved several times, or it was lost in certain groups. The latter idea seems highly unlikely and there appears to be no reason to consider a multiple origin any less likely for four webbed toes than for three, a circumstance that is implied by all plausible classifications (in ducks, gulls and tubenoses/penguins at a minimum).

Whether the aquatic habits of ducks and geese evolved in marine or fresh water is unknown, but all have webbed feet and can excrete salt. However, the uniting characteristics of the group seem to relate to the use of vegetable matter for food, a habit that is most likely to have developed in fresh water (most seaducks are carnivorous, Brent Goose being the principal marine vegetarian). Hence, the several incursions of ducks into the marine environment (eiders and scoters, scaups, mergansers) have probably been secondary adaptations. Many species are equally at home on salt and fresh water and this ability may have been characteristic of the ducks and geese right from their origin.

Overall, the classifications of recent birds prior to that of Sibley & Ahlquist (1990) suggested three major incursions into the marine environment: the penguins and tubenoses, the Pelecaniform and the Charadriiform seabirds. The fossil record suggests that the first two groups are oldest, both being present by the Eocene, and that gulls and auks differentiated from the rest of the Charadriiform group some time during the first half of the Tertiary, with auks being clearly recognisable by the Miocene (15 million years ago). If we accept the Sibley & Ahlquist classification and ignore the possibility that the entire Ciconiida had a marine origin, we again find a minimum of three entries into the marine realm: the Charadriiform seabirds, the tropicbirds, boobies and cormorants, and the frigatebirds, tubenoses and penguins.

Whichever arrangement we accept, the evidence for return movement from marine to terrestrial habitats is small. The Charadriiformes contain many birds that exploit the coastline, both of the sea and of fresh waters; this applies to shorebirds, plovers and gulls. Within this grouping, only the auks are purely marine. Among marine families, only the jaegers, while breeding, and some gulls, have adopted terrestrial foraging. If we accept Pelecaniformes as originally a marine group, cormorants and

Table 2.2 Classification of seabird families according to DNA hybridisation data (after Sibley & Ahlquist, 1990)

Parvclass	Superorder	Order	Suborder	Infraorder	Parvorder	Superfamily	Family	Contains
Galloanserae	Anserimorphae	Anseriformes		Anserides			Anatidae	ducks, geese
Passerae	Passerimorphae	Gruiformes						cranes, rails
		Ciconiformes	Charadrii	Charadriides	Scolopacida	Scolopacoidea	Scolopacidae	shorebirds, phalaropes
			–		Charadriida	Chionidoidea	Chionidae	sheathbills
							Burhinidae	thick-knees
						Charadrioidea	Charadriidae	plovers
							Glareolidae	coursers
						Laroidea	Laridae	gulls, terns, auks; birds of prey
					Podicipedida		Podicipedidae	grebes
					Phaethontida	–	Phaethontidae	tropicbirds
					Sulida	Suloidea	Sulidae	boobies
							Anhingidae	snakebirds
						Phalacrocoracoidea	Phalacrocoracidae	cormorants
				Falconides	Ciconiida	Ardeoidea	Ardeidae	herons
			Ciconii	Ciconiides		Scopoidea	Scopidae	hammerheads
						Phoenicopteroidea	Phoenicopteridae	flamingos
						Threskiornithoidea	Threskiornithidae	ibises
						Pelecanoidea	Pelecanidae	pelicans
						Ciconioidea	Ciconiidae	storks; New World vultures
						Procellarioidea	Fregatidae	frigatebirds
							Spheniscidae	penguins
							Gaviidae	divers/loons
							Procellariidae	tubenoses

anhingas have reverted to fresh water, but not to terrestrial foraging. All classifications make it likely that using fresh water is a secondary adaptation in these groups. If divers/loons are part of a marine assemblage, which fact is supported by their wintering habitats, then breeding on freshwater lakes also may be secondary. Overall, it seems that adaptation to the marine environment is a development that is rarely reversed.

A BRIEF INTRODUCTION TO MODERN SEABIRDS

Penguins (Spheniscidae)

Stout flightless birds with torpedo-shaped bodies, very robust legs, webbed feet, and tiny, flipper-like wings. Their feathers are stiff, short and relatively undifferentiated, compared with those of flying birds, forming a dense matt over the entire body. A layer of fat below the skin also helps retain heat in the frigid waters in which the majority live. They stand and walk upright and employ 'porpoising' while travelling at sea. Most lay two eggs, either on the surface or in burrows. Confined to the southern hemisphere, though extending north to the Galápagos Islands.

Tubenoses (order Procellariiformes)

A large family of mainly gliding birds, globally distributed, but most species breeding in the southern hemisphere, united by their possession of raised tubular nostrils on top of the upper mandible, the mandible being strongly hooked. Tubenoses mostly have long, narrow wings and rather weak legs (except albatrosses), All breed in colonies, laying a single egg. They produce stomach oil, which is regurgitated to the nestling, causing it to become very obese partway through the growth period. Most, perhaps all, have a keen sense of smell, being attracted to fish oil from far downwind. All but storm-petrels and albatrosses will swim underwater, using their wings as paddles, though the frequency of this behaviour varies from being the exclusive feeding method among diving-petrels, to being only occasional among gadfly petrels. **Albatrosses** (Diomedeidae) are the largest, with stout bodies, short tails and extremely long, narrow, rather blunt, wings; they nest on the surface on remote islands. **Storm-petrels** (Hydrobatidae) are the smallest, and the smallest of all marine birds, having a very low weight to wing area ratio and long, feeble legs that they dangle as they flutter just above the sea surface. They nest in burrows or crevices. The remainder of the tubenoses are placed in the family Procellariidae: **prions** (*Pachyptila* spp.) are somewhat like large storm-petrels, with an erratic, flickering flight, but their broad-based bills possess fringing lamellae on the palette. **Gadfly petrels** (*Lugensa*, *Pterodroma* and *Bulweria*) are even larger, but have narrower bills, longer wings and a low weight/wing area for their size; they often soar in great arcs, like albatrosses. **Shearwaters** (*Puffinus* and *Calonectris*) are similar in size to gadfly petrels, with stiff, narrow, pointed wings and, having relatively heavy bodies, flap frequently in flight; most nest in burrows or crevices. They feed at the surface and underwater, swimming strongly with their wings and feet. The *Procellaria* petrels are like heavy-bodied shearwaters, but fly more like fulmars: all are predominantly black or grey. **Diving-petrels** (*Pelecanoides*) are like small, short-winged shearwaters, which feed almost entirely underwater. The **fulmarine petrels** (*Fulmarus*, *Daption*, *Thalassoica* and *Pagodroma*) are generally heavier bodied with broader wings and have especially long nasal tubes; among them, giant petrels (*Macronectes*) have the longest nasal tubes, giving them an especially ugly look that seems to befit their predatory way of life.

LOONS (*GAVIIDAE*)

A small and rather uniform family of dagger-billed, web-footed, foot-propelled, underwater swimmers with small, narrow wings; poor fliers that require a long run to take off from water and cannot take off at all from land. Solitary open nesters beside lakes and ponds, laying two eggs. Found only in subpolar and polar regions of the northern hemisphere.

FRIGATEBIRDS (*FREGATIDAE*)

A small, uniform, pan-tropical family; buoyant and delicate fliers with long, slender, hooked bills, huge, rather broad wings, long, deeply forked tails and very small legs and feet. They build stick nests in trees and bushes or on the ground, and lay a single egg. Females are larger than males. Feed by piratical attacks on other seabirds, or by snatching food from the sea surface. According to my Brooke Bond Tea card (*c*.1955), "dare not alight on the water because it would never be able to rise again" (true). Among seabirds, the most likely to be observed soaring on thermals over the ocean.

TROPICBIRDS (*PHAETHONTIDAE*)

Small, isolated pan-tropical family with mainly white plumage; adults have long central tail streamers; bills somewhat downcurved, not hooked; legs weak and set far back. They feed by snatching from the sea surface or, more frequently, plunge-diving, often to substantial depths. Nest on the ground among rocks or in crevices in cliffs, laying a single egg.

PELICANS (*PELECANIDAE*)

Legendary for their enormous beaks, equipped with an extensible membrane in the floor of the lower mandible, which forms a balloon-like scoop while feeding. Huge birds with long, broad wings, designed for soaring. Mostly found on large freshwater lakes in warm-temperate and subtropical areas of the northern hemisphere, where they feed by dipping their bills from the surface, but the one marine species feeds by shallow plunge-diving as well as surface-dipping. Build stick nests on the ground, laying 2–3 eggs.

CORMORANTS (*PHALACROCORACIDAE*)

A large, uniform and widespread family with short, broad wings, rather slender bodies, long tails (compared to other seabirds) and long necks. The bill is long and narrow with a pronounced hook at the tip. Most are all black, some black above and white below. Most feed predominantly on fish, caught while swimming underwater, foot-propelled. They breed in the open, mainly in trees, sometimes on barren islets, laying up to six eggs. Feed in coastal waters, lakes and rivers; absent from most oceanic islands.

PHALAROPES (*PHALAROPINAE*)

Small, rather delicate shorebirds with lobed toes that assist them in surface swimming. Breed on arctic tundra in the northern hemisphere and winter at sea in tropical or subtropical latitudes. Feed by picking small animals from the water surface, sometimes spinning around to create a vortex that brings prey within reach. Nest solitarily beside boggy pools on sedge meadows, laying 3–4 eggs.

SKUAS/JAEGERS (*STERCORARIIDAE*)

A small family comprising only two genera, breeding only in polar latitudes, though some winter in tropical waters. Medium-sized, they have long wings, pointed in the jaegers *Stercorarius*, blunter in the larger skuas *Catharacta*. The central tail feathers are elongated in the smaller genus, which has rather small feet and weak legs. Nest in the open, solitarily or sometimes in loose aggregations, laying two eggs.

GULLS (*LARIDAE*)

All-purpose seabirds with long wings, somewhat broader and noticeably more flexible than those of petrels. In flight, they make greater use of flapping than petrels and the wings are less rigid, permitting improved manoeuverability at low speeds. The bill ranges from slender and straight in the smallest species to deep and sharply hooked in the largest. The legs are robust, fairly long, and placed under the centre of the body, so that they can run easily on land, like shorebirds. Solitary or more usually colonial nesters in the open, on the ground or occasionally in trees; nest usually of grass or moss. Most lay three eggs.

AUKS (*ALCIDAE*)

Very diverse family of wing-propelled pursuit-divers found only in cool waters of the northern hemisphere. Mostly black above and white below; wings short and pointed, flying with rapid wing-beats. Bills vary from narrow and dagger-like, to deep and laterally compressed, or stout and parrot-like. Legs are stout, and placed well back on the body in most genera, though not so far in puffins (*Fratercula*) and auklets (*Aethia*), which run actively on land. Most nest in crevices or burrows, some on open cliff ledges and two of the three *Brachyramphus* species, on tree branches; lay 1–2 eggs.

ON DIVERSITY

The diversity of living things is one of the great miracles of life. How can so many designs for catching fish all be equally viable? To look at it another way, how can the apparently trivial differences between a Common Tern and a Forster's Tern, or between a Sooty Shearwater and a Pink-footed Shearwater, determine that one is very abundant and widespread, while the other is rather uncommon and has only a limited range? This is one of the core problems of ecology.

According to current theories of evolution, all of the diversity that we see is founded on direction-less and arrhythmic mutations that create the variation permitting natural selection to work. And selection comprises all those factors that influence an individual's chances of replicating itself in the next generation: the physical environment, with its waves and winds, rocks, icebergs, reefs and mud-flats; the predators, ever watchful for the slow, the unwary or the indiscreet; the prey, always straining to outrun or outwit; and the competition, never far off in the race to get to the prey first.

When we consider the many ways that birds can adapt themselves to this multiplicity of forces, always changing, over centuries, years, seasons and from day to day, the diversity becomes less amazing, though no less fascinating. The process by which we seek to explain much of this variation is known as reverse engineering. When an engineer wants to produce a practical device, he or she considers what it needs to do, and the capabilities of the materials to hand, and designs the mechanism necessary to achieve the objective at the least cost and lowest hazard. When we see a bird in flight we see a biological device that is extremely well suited to its function, which is to nourish itself and reproduce. The trick in reverse engineering is to determine how the size, shape and movement of the various organs interact to produce the required function. Stephen Pinker (1997) likened this process to finding an unusual object in an antique shop and gradually working out from deduction that the object is a device for removing the pits from olives.

For seabirds, we do not need to consider why they have wings and feathers, why they have bills and not teeth, why they have four, not five toes, why they have two eyes, or why they lay eggs. These are all characteristics of all birds. These attributes pose fascinating questions about evolution, but these are not the questions that I shall deal with. Instead, I shall concentrate on how they are adapted to the ocean environment and how their diversity fits them for the varied ways of life that they pursue. This is the theme of the next chapter.

A Red-tailed Tropicbird. Note the short legs and the elongated and very slender central tail feathers. (Tony Gaston)

CHAPTER THREE

Adaptation

The Pelecanoides *[diving-petrel] . . . offers an excellent example of a bird evidently belonging to one well-marked family, yet in its habits and structure allied to a very distinct tribe. The form of its beak and nostrils, length of foot and colour of plumage show that this bird is a petrel: on the other hand its short wings and consequent little power of flight, its form of body and shape of tail, the absence of a hind toe to its foot . . . make it at first doubtful whether its relationship is not equally close with the auks.*

Charles Darwin, *Journal of Researches*, 1845.

Cook Strait, separating the North and South Islands of New Zealand, can be a really rough stretch of water. In addition to the incessant, nagging wind of the southern forties, strong currents surge through the Strait, raising standing waves where there are shallows and reefs. Just off North Brother Island, where I stayed several weeks in an abandoned lighthouse keeper's cottage, in 1990, big standing waves were a permanent feature of the surrounding seas, except at slack tide.

My companion, Paul Scofield, and I spent most of the daylight period seawatching, either from the front porch of the house or from a vantage point at the top of the island. On some days, usually when it was windy, a steady stream of seabirds passed through our field of view: ponderous Wandering Albatrosses, dainty prions, rakish shearwaters, gadfly petrels, gulls, jaegers, even once a flock of introduced Canada Geese—a little reminder of home. When the wind dropped, watching the horizon for passers-by became less profitable and on these occasions we often resorted to observing the local birds, pre-eminent among them being the Common Diving-petrels.

When I planned my New Zealand trip, I was especially keen to study diving-petrels. They had been a major reason for the choice of North Brother as a study site, as the island supports a breeding colony of about 600 pairs. The reason for my interest was the striking convergence, first remarked on by Charles Darwin (above) between these atypical tubenoses and certain of the smaller auks. In size, shape and proportions, and in their bumblebee like flight, they are strongly reminiscent of auklets. In plumage, they most closely resemble Cassin's Auklet, even down to the pale blue feet and legs. Their breeding strategy also seems to converge with the auks, having shorter incubation and chick-rearing periods than other petrels of similar size.

Fortunately, North Brother proved to be not only a good place to study their breeding, but also an excellent site to see them foraging. The standing waves off the island provided attractive feeding conditions, with diving-petrels concentrating particularly in the waters between North and South Brother islands. The largest standing waves occupied a fairly small area, no more than 10 ha, where we estimated the current speed, except at slack tide, at more than six knots. Consequently, birds feeding in the waves were carried fairly rapidly downstream and had to constantly take off and fly back to the top of the main current area. One of their most striking habits was that they did not care to fly over the waves, but instead flew straight through them, disappearing with a splash to emerge on the far side of the crest a second or two later. Their strong affinity with turbulence created by the bottom topography was reminiscent of the feeding habits of auklets, especially the Whiskered Auklet, among the strong tidal currents spilling through the narrow passes of the Aleutian Islands. The auklets and diving-petrels provide a 'textbook' case of convergent evolution, where two organisms of different ancestry come to look and behave alike in order to exploit similar ecological niches.

When organisms change under the influence of natural selection they are said to have adapted. Features of their structure and behaviour that have obvious applications for their particular ecology or way of life (heavy insulation in cold climates, strong bills in woodpeckers) are referred to as adaptations. Hence, in this chapter I shall be discussing the more obvious ways in which seabirds are structured for life in the marine environment. Strictly speaking, if we believe that natural selection is the main force in evolution, then everything about an organism is in one way or another an adaptation. However, it is customary under this heading to deal with physical traits, like wings, bills and feet, as well as the senses. These are areas where we can most readily perform the reverse engineering that I referred to earlier, to infer the reasons for the variation that we observe.

SIZE

HOW BIG ARE THEY?

The smallest seabird is the Least Storm-petrel, weighing a mere 20 g and the largest, the Emperor Penguin, at 30 kg, the heaviest bird outside the ostrich family (Struthionidae). The distribution of size shows that *c.*80% of species weigh 80–2560 g: this is far larger than the size distribution of landbirds, which cluster at 5–300 g (Figure 3.1). In addition, flightless seabirds (range 1–30 kg) tend to be larger than those that fly (range 0.2–9 kg). However, when we compare flightless seabirds with flightless landbirds, seabirds are generally smaller (Figure 3.2). This is true even if we take into account extinct species, because extinct flightless landbirds (moas *Dinornis* spp. and elephantbirds

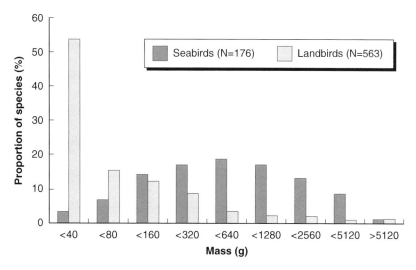

Figure 3.1   Size distribution of seabird species, compared to European landbirds.

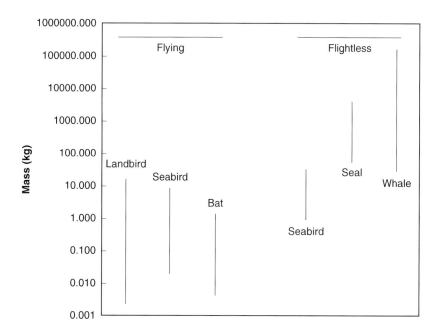

Figure 3.2   Size distribution of flying and flightless birds, mammals, etc.

Aepyornis sp.) were much larger than their surviving relatives and much larger than the largest extinct penguins, the latter estimated at *c*.130 kg body mass (Simpson, 1976). As marine mammals (whales) and marine reptiles (turtles) are generally larger than their terrestrial counterparts, this is somewhat surprising.

The absence of small flightless landbirds from continental landmasses is presumably the result of competition with, or predation by, small mammals. Even in the relatively large, mammal-free area of New Zealand, few birds less than 1 kg in weight were flightless, perhaps because of predation by the diverse and often rather large reptiles. Small flightless reptiles succeed in coexisting with small mammals, but unlike birds, they do not have to maintain a constant high body temperature, so they spend much less time foraging, an activity that makes both birds and reptiles especially vulnerable to predation. And, of course, some reptiles have a highly poisonous bite.

The lack of small flightless seabirds can be accounted for by the way wing size scales with body size in underwater swimming. In the auks, the relative size of the wings decreases sharply with body mass, thus the largest species capable of flight (murres) have very small wings compared to their mass. At the other end of the scale, the smallest auklets have wing areas comparable with those of the smaller gulls and petrels (see below). There may be no advantage for the smaller wing-propelled diving birds in reducing their wing area below the size necessary for flight. This also may account for why the smallest shearwaters appear to be the most accomplished underwater swimmers (Brown *et al.*, 1978), a trend that culminates in the auk-like diving-petrels, which are smaller than any shearwater.

WHY AREN'T THEY BIGGER?

The lack of whale-size seabirds can be accounted for by their inability to deliver live young. Laying air-breathing eggs forces seabirds to return to land for breeding. The size of legs required to support a penguin the size of even a small whale on land would be enormous and these huge appendages would need to be dragged around throughout the year with little function outside the breeding season. Significantly, Martin (1980) noted that the rather large (up to 1.5 m long) and extinct toothed seabirds, the Hesperornithidae, which were flightless and propelled themselves underwater with their feet, were anatomically incapable of bringing their legs forward below their body. Hence, to come ashore, they would have had to push themselves on their belly, like seals. The articulation of their tarsal joint showed that the toes were turned sideways on the return stroke, as is seen in modern grebes, but not in other seabirds.

The penguins are not the only group of birds to have given up flight. At least two other families of flightless seabirds are known from fossils: the Plotopteridae, which lived from the Oligocene to the mid-Miocene and seem to have been related to the boobies, and the Mancallinae, a subfamily of auks, which existed a little later. The Mancallines were about the size of the smaller penguins, while the Plotopterids grew up to 2 m long. Both groups disappeared at about the time that seals and whales started to become common and it has been suggested that there could have been a connection between the rise of the seals and the decline of flightless seabirds (Olson, 1985). It is rather striking that the largest modern penguins are about the same size as the smallest seals. The inefficiency of a design that makes little use of a large part of its anatomy (the legs and feet) for substantial periods of time may have been one of the reasons that penguins were out-competed by marine mammals and large fish once they evolved beyond a certain size.

WHY AREN'T THEY SMALLER?

This leaves us with the lack of really small seabirds (<30 g) as the most outstanding unexplained difference between landbirds and seabirds. On land, tiny birds of 5–30 g inhabit practically every habitat, from the canopy of the rain forest, to the sand dunes of the desert. Many of these little birds, like warblers and flycatchers, are highly migratory and some, like the swiftlets and swallows, spend their entire lives in flight. So, we cannot argue that the lack of small seabirds is a result of the heavy demand for flight in the marine environment. Many small landbirds are insectivorous, but equally we cannot argue that their absence at sea is due to a lack of insects, because there are plenty of similar-sized arthropods, such as copepods, in the ocean.

I have a few suggestions as to the absence of really small seabirds, but all are very speculative. One possibility is the danger of predation by larger seabirds; another is that very small birds simply cannot cope with the storms that periodically sweep the face of the ocean, an explanation offered by Tennekes (1996). A similar, but more general explanation along the same lines would be that the demographic characteristics of seabirds couldn't be reconciled with very small size. Among animals in general there is a trend for larger ones to live longer, presumably because the larger you are, the fewer are the chance environmental hazards that could wipe you out. It is possible that a bird weighing less than 20 g simply cannot insure itself sufficiently against the exigencies of the environment to be assured of a high enough survival to cope with the low reproductive rate imposed by the seabird syndrome.

This plausible argument notwithstanding, it seems most likely that the true cause of the lack of very small seabirds relates in some way to the aquatic medium itself. The smallest duck, the Cotton Teal, weighs over 200 g, the smallest rail that habitually swims is of a similar size and the smallest grebe is *c*.100 g. The dippers, that remarkable group of thrush-like birds that specialise in walking underwater, range from 50–100 g. Even kingfishers, which do not immerse themselves in water for very long, if at all, are never really small. The smallest, the African Dwarf Kingfisher, may weigh as little as 9 g, but the majority of species weigh above 25 g. In other words, swimming birds or birds plunging into water, do not occur in sizes below *c*.20 g, whereas about 50% of non-aquatic birds are smaller than that.

There are several possibilities to explain why aquatic birds do not acquire the small proportions of so many that inhabit bushes and trees. The first is thermodynamic: small birds lose heat faster than large birds and loss of heat is always a problem in water, which conducts heat much faster than air. Then, energy expended in surface swimming increases rapidly above an optimum speed that is determined by waterline length (Woakes & Butler, 1983). This is because the waves created by surface swimming are related to the length of the body (or hull, in the case of a boat). The energy involved in travel increases steeply if the bird or boat attempts to travel faster than the speed of its bow wave. However, wave speed is related to waterline length, so the larger the object the faster it can go before it meets the speed of its wave. A foot-long murre reaches this point at *c*.2.3 km/h (Vogel, 1998). A waterbird the size of a hummingbird would either have to swim very slowly, or expend an enormous amount of energy to go faster. Young Ancient Murrelets, only about 27 g and 8 cm long when they first go to sea, overcome the bow wave effect by 'hydroplaning', literally running across the surface of the water, something that their huge feet and legs and tiny body enable them to do.

Circumventing the constraint of the bow wave is presumably the reason why penguins 'porpoise' (swim in a series of shallow dives interspersed by leaping out of the water) when travelling long distances). There are no accounts of Great Auks travelling in such fashion. If they did not do so, their travel would have been extremely slow. The bow wave constraint may be one reason why most seabirds have retained the ability to fly.

Plunge-diving is probably constrained by terminal velocity, which is lower in a small bird than in a large one (a larger proportion of a small bird comprises feathers, giving it a lower density than a larger bird), as well as by the strength of the skull to withstand the force of hitting the water. All of these factors may contribute to discouraging small seabirds. None seems likely to explain all cases and the argument from demography may contribute as well. Probably the absence of very small seabirds derives from many convergent causes.

SEX DIMORPHISM

In most seabirds, there is little difference in size between the sexes. Males tend to be slightly larger, but for most groups the difference in body weight is less than 10% (most tubenoses, auks, terns, skimmers, cormorants, pelicans and the smaller gulls). Males are substantially larger in loons, large gulls (those >1 kg) and in giant petrels, while females are larger than males among skuas and jaegers, phalaropes, boobies (except the Northern Gannet) and frigatebirds.

Among landbirds, males are slightly larger in the majority of species. In this group, as the contribution of males to chick rearing decreases, their relative size increases. Males are largest in those species where they undertake little or no parental care; this includes many polygynous species. Seabirds are nearly all socially monogamous (that is to say, like people, they behave as though monogamous, though there may be some hanky-panky on the side) and males nearly always make a substantial contribution to chick rearing. Hence, the fact that in the majority of seabirds males are similar to females, or slightly larger, conforms to the pattern for landbirds. However, among seaducks, which have precocial young, like other waterfowl, and where the male plays little role in rearing the offspring, males are substantially larger than females.

That females are larger than males in the predatory and piratical skuas, jaegers and frigatebirds accords with the differences found among landbirds, where females are larger among birds of prey. The actively predatory hawks and falcons, especially those feeding on birds taken in flight, have females considerably larger than males, whereas among the scavenging vultures there is little difference. Current theory holds that female hawks are larger than males because they need to protect their eggs and young while the male hunts, his smaller size conferring greater aerial agility. Similar behaviour is witnessed in jaegers, where the female undertakes more brooding than the male, while the male performs more hunting for the nestlings (Andersson, 1971, 1973). However, males and females of most seabird species, including frigatebirds and boobies, devote almost equal amounts of effort to brood rearing (although in the Magnificent Frigatebird the male deserts the young part-way through the nestling period; Diamond, 1972). Moreover, among the large *Larus* gulls, which tend to be the most predatory, males are much larger than females, by as much as 30% in body weight. The common feature of both bird-eating raptors, skuas, jaegers and frigatebirds is extreme aerial agility, so this feature would seem to be implicated in the evolution of reduced male : female size ratio. Beyond that, the selection pressures leading to larger females are unclear.

DRINKING

What does it take to invade the marine environment? The only really essential characteristic of seabirds is that they can drink saltwater. Being able to land on water is useful but not essential: frigatebirds and some terns and jaegers seldom do so. Seabirds manage without fresh water by excreting excess salt through specialised glands situated on top of the skull, either inside the orbits (Pelecaniformes) or in front of them (all the rest, including ducks). Because of their high body temperatures and metabolic rates, birds must respire rapidly; a major source of water loss. Compared to mammals, which need to excrete water in order to eliminate urea, they reduce water loss by excreting more or less solid uric acid, but notwithstanding this physiological trait they need to drink frequently. Without the ability to excrete salt, birds would be tied to within a few hours' flying range of a freshwater source.

Some terrestrial birds are also capable of excreting salt, so this is a physiological ability that birds are capable of developing fairly readily. Among seabirds, oceanic species and species feeding on crustacea tend to excrete more concentrated salt than others, but individuals may be capable of modifying the excretory ability in response to increased salt in the diet (Peaker & Linzell, 1975). Most seabirds choose to drink fresh water if they have the chance. Marine reptiles also practise salt excretion, but if we assume that birds evolved from terrestrial reptiles, birds must have developed this ability independently.

STAYING WARM

Feathers are a bird's main way of keeping warm and it seems very likely that it was for this purpose, rather than for flight, that feathers evolved in the first place. The density of seabird feathers has already been referred to. In addition to being dense, contour and down feathers are rather evenly distributed over the body, especially in underwater swimmers. For the latter, there is an inevitable compromise between the need for a deep layer of feathers to provide insulation and the need to reduce cross-sectional area to improve underwater swimming performance: contrast the long breast feathers of an eider duck, which does not need to pursue active prey, with the shorter feathers of a Razorbill, which does.

All birds store energy in the form of fat. In many small birds this is deposited in discrete depots, especially at the base of the neck and within the abdominal cavity. These stores alter seasonally in response to changes in temperature, day length and the demands of reproduction and migration. Seabirds must maintain substantial stores of fat throughout the year, because adverse weather, arriving without warning, may prevent them from feeding for days at a time. In diving birds, this fat tends to be rather evenly deposited below the skin and serves as an additional insulating layer. This is especially well developed in penguins. In murres, the thickest layer tends to be on the neck and upper breast and around the lower abdomen, again avoiding an increase in the maximum girth.

Loss of heat from the legs and the bare area around the eye is reduced by heat-exchange systems in which arterial blood flows through small blood vessels interspersed with returning venous blood so that, for a gull in water close to freezing, the temperature of blood reaching the tip of the foot may be only a few degrees above zero (Phillips *et al.*, 1985). To further reduce heat loss a standing gull may rest on one leg, keeping the other tucked in the feathers of the flank. Likewise, a swimming duck may paddle gently with only one foot when not going anywhere. It is worth noting that even the act of standing requires some muscular control and hence expends energy. A bird roosting on the water saves this cost.

In contrast, when it gets hot, the blood vessels in the legs dilate so that blood flow to the feet increases and the webs act as radiators to assist in cooling, which is otherwise dependent on panting and, in boobies and pelicans, fluttering of the throat pouch. When you first catch a Thick-billed Murre on a cold day its feet feel icy. However, as the bird struggles to get free (they are very feisty birds) it rapidly begins to overheat and the feet soon become warm to the touch.

BODY DESIGN: O, FOR THE WINGS OF A GULL!

To render the true science of movement of birds in the air, it is necessary to establish first of all the science of winds which will explain the movement of water and fluids. And this science will serve as the stepping stone for reaching an understanding of things flying in the air.

Leonardo da Vinci (in Sertilanges, 1992)

There are a small number of fundamental designs assumed by seabirds, and each group of birds, as they adapted to the marine environment, has evolved towards one or other of these. They can be characterised as either underwater or surface feeders and these categories can be further subdivided (Figure 3.3):

A. Surface divers: birds that catch their prey by swimming underwater, initiating their dive from the surface and actively swimming through the water (e.g. penguins, loons, cormorants, seaducks, diving petrels, auks);

B. Plunge-divers: birds that catch prey underwater by plunging from the air, using their momentum to carry them below the sea surface (e.g. gannets and boobies, tropicbirds, some terns, Brown Pelican). This category was divided by Ashmole into those that swim actively after plunging and those that do not: those that swim after plunging are known as pursuit-plungers; gannets sometimes do this and shearwaters nearly always.

C. Flying surface gleaners: birds that do not go below the sea surface, but confine themselves to prey that they can snatch in flight (e.g. storm-petrels, jaegers, some terns);

D. Floating surface gleaners: birds that take their food while sitting on the sea surface (e.g. albatrosses, petrels, most gulls).

These divisions are not clear-cut, because birds like petrels and kittiwakes may snatch food in flight or land on the water, making them general-purpose gleaners. Some terns may glean from the surface as well as plunge-diving, while many gulls occasionally and many petrels regularly indulge in shallow plunge-diving. Shearwaters swim well underwater, either from a shallow plunge or from the surface; they also feed at the surface and occasionally glean while in flight, or hydroplane over the water,

Figure 3.3   Examples of some seabird types: A: surface diver (cormorant) B: plunge diver (booby) C: flying surface gleaner/kleptoparasite (skua) D: general surface gleaner (kittiwake).

mandibles apart, trawling the surface, a method much better developed in the skimmers, where it is their chief technique.

Surface divers can be further divided into those that fly and those that do not (currently just the penguins and the Galápagos Cormorant), and into those that are foot-propelled swimmers underwater (cormorants, loons and some seaducks) and those that are wing-propelled (penguins, auks, shearwaters [also use their feet], diving-petrels, gannets and most seaducks). All surface gleaners are capable of flying, as are, of necessity, plunge-divers. All flightless seabirds are surface divers: clearly flightlessness would be a disadvantage for a gleaner, which must cover large areas to take advantage of scattered and ephemeral patches of food.

WING PROPULSION OR FOOT PROPULSION?

Somewhat puzzling is that penguins, as well as many deep-diving seabirds that also fly, use wing propulsion rather than foot paddling; this was also true of most fossil species. This habit contrasts with marine mammals that mostly use the modified hind limbs for propulsion, though sea lions use both sets of limbs and Polar Bears *Ursus maritimus* exclusively use the front paws.

I consider the reason why most flying seabirds swim with their wings is as follows. Flying birds must possess very large muscles to power them in flight. Although they require legs on land, if they use their legs as well for swimming they inevitably must uselessly transport the larger wing muscles most of the time. In addition, using the legs for swimming means that they have to be fairly muscular, as pushing a body through the dense medium of water is hard work. Hefty leg muscles require big flight muscles to ensure that the bird can get airborne, leading to further waste when the wings are not in use.

This vicious circle can be broken if the wings are used for swimming as well as flying, because then the two most power-demanding exercises are performed using the same set of muscles. The legs can be allowed to degenerate as much as the demands of walking and a little surface paddling will allow. Wing-propelled underwater swimmers, such as auks and diving-petrels, are often described as 'weak fliers', but this gives a false impression. These birds are strong fliers (compared with rails or wrens): they just have rather small wings, so they must do a lot of flapping (Figure 3.4). However, they do tend to be weak walkers.

The above theory suggests that, at some time long ago, the penguins had ancestors that flew, which is an idea not universally accepted, but one supported on the basis of fossil and anatomical evidence by Simpson (1976) and Olson (1985). Otherwise, as most dinosaurs, which are considered to have been ancestral to birds, had very large hind legs, we would expect the feet to be the main propulsion in water as well. By that logic, cretaceous seabirds, such as *Hesperornis*, that had large paddling feet and virtually no wings, may have evolved directly from flightless reptilian ancestors, as suggested on anatomical grounds by Martin (1980). It also explains why loons and grebes are such poor fliers (relying on foot-propulsion for swimming, they need to keep their wing muscles as small as possible) and why foot-propelled diving ducks (e.g. *Aythya*) are generally poor at taking off compared to dabbling ducks (e.g. *Anas*).

There are a few other associated effects of the split between wing-propelled and foot-propelled swimmers. Cormorants are very accomplished divers, which may reach depths of more than 100 m (Croxall *et al.*, 1991). As a result, they have very strong legs and large feet, set far back on the body, which tends to shift their centre of gravity rearwards. It is noticeable that this family is characterised by long necks, mostly stretched forward in flight (less so in the Double-crested Cormorant): this contrasts with the wing-propelled auks, which have rather short necks. Cormorants also have long, rather broad tails compared to most other underwater swimmers. The long neck may help to balance the

Figure 3.4 Murre using wings for swimming and flying.

weight of the legs and feet, while the tail, kept somewhat spread in flight, helps to generate lift for the rear end. All these characteristics are even more exaggerated in the snakebirds (Anhingidae), another group of foot-propelled surface divers that has very long, slender necks, reminiscent of herons.

A more trivial difference between wing- and foot-propelled divers can be seen in their means of submergence. As Rory Wilson *et al.* (1992) pointed out, foot-propelled divers bring their propulsive apparatus (the feet) out of the water as they upend. Consequently, they often need to preface their dives with an upward leap that carries them far enough vertically down to submerge their feet so that they can start kicking. Wing-propelled divers, which are not constrained in this way, kick with their feet to upend, then flick their wings to start swimming.

SHAPE

Compared to the average landbird, seabirds tend to have long necks and short tails. There are exceptions: auks and petrels tend to have rather short necks, while frigatebirds, tropicbirds and many terns have long tail streamers. Loons have the shortest tails in relation to wing length (<20%), followed by auks and diving-petrels (Figure 3.5). Only storm-petrels (45–50%), cormorants and terns (both >50%) have tails approaching those of landbirds, with the terns being very similar in proportions to swallows and swifts. Birds of prey, thrushes and larks all have longer tails, on average, than any seabird family.

Wing lengths range from very long in the far-travelling gulls and tubenoses, to very short in the auks and loons. Body shape tends to be somewhat elongated in underwater swimmers, such as cormorants and loons and very elongated in penguins. This is because water resistance is related to the cross-sectional area of the body: by elongating, the underwater swimmers can reduce their cross sectional area for a given body weight. The elongation is very evident when we look at the skeleton, as surface-gleaning seabirds tend to have short, deep breastbones, similar to

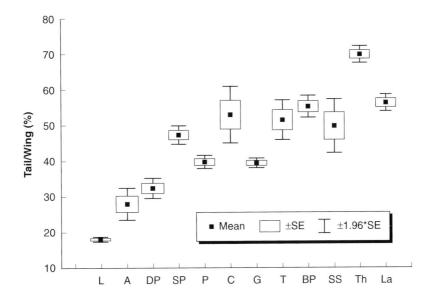

Figure 3.5   Tail length in relation to wing length for selected seabird and landbird families: L = loons, A = auks, DP = diving-petrels, SP = storm-petrels, P = petrels, C = cormorants, G = gulls, T = terns, BP = birds of prey (excluding vultures), SS = swifts and swallows, Th = thrushes (Turdidae), La = larks (Alaudidae).

those of birds of prey, whereas underwater swimmers have much longer breastbones, without as deep a keel.

WING SHAPE

At first sight, the most salient characteristic of seabird wings is their length. The Wandering Albatross has the largest wingspan of all living birds and even small gulls seem to have huge wings. However, when we examine wing length in relation to mass, we find that, for a given weight, the wings of seabirds are not dramatically different from those of other birds, especially swallows, swifts and birds of prey (Figure 3.6). The wings of seabirds appear particularly long for two reasons: the tail is usually rather short (compared with a songbird or a bee-eater *Merops* spp.) and the wings tend to be narrow. The latter characteristic is enlarged on below.

Although there is great diversity in size among seabirds, variation in wing design is more limited. Basically, aerodynamic designs can be divided into three classes: long-winged, high-endurance designs (petrels and albatrosses, tropicbirds, frigatebirds, gulls, terns and jaegers), with low weight/wing area ratios (wing-loading); short, broad-winged designs, with high wing loadings (cormorants) and short, narrow-winged, low-endurance designs (divers/loons, diving-petrels and auks) with even heavier wing-loadings (Figure 3.7). These variations correspond to a division between surface gleaners (the long-winged types) and surface divers (short-winged). Shearwaters (excluding certain tropical species) are somewhat intermediate between the two types, having longer wings than typical surface divers, but heavier wing-loadings than typical gleaners (Figure 3.8). Diving-petrels resemble auks in this characteristic. The cormorants, having short, broad wings that permit a lower wing loading compared to other underwater swimmers, are well-designed to make repeated short flights but are less efficient in prolonged flight. This seems to accord with their rather sedentary style,

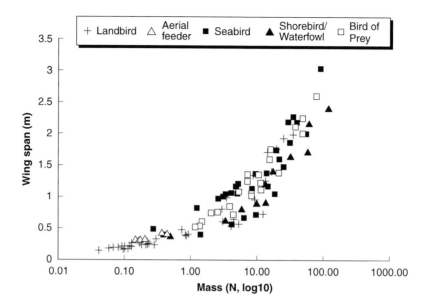

Figure 3.6   Wingspan in relation to body mass for selected landbirds (songbirds, owls and woodpeckers), aerial feeders (swallows, swifts), seabirds, shorebirds and waterfowl, and birds of prey (data from Tennekes, 1996).

Figure 3.7   Flight sketches of a murre, cormorant, loon, storm-petrel, albatross and shearwater.

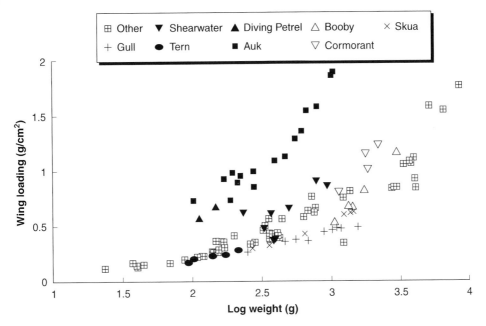

Figure 3.8   Wing-loading in relation to body mass among seabirds (data from Warham, 1977; Spear & Ainley, 1997). Other = tubenose other than shearwater or diving-petrel.

usually foraging within a short distance of their roost or nest. Few species migrate long distances. Their broad wings make them better at manoeuvring than auks, enabling them to nest in trees. Their wing shape would be poor for swimming with the wings, because it would be difficult to provide rigidity to the broad primaries.

The aspect ratio (wingspan/mean width) provides a measure of how elongated the wings are. Warham (1977, 1996) pointed out that, among the tubenoses, wing shape changes with size, with the small storm-petrels having relatively broad wings and the great albatrosses having extremely narrow ones (Figure 3.9). Aerodynamic theory predicts that the efficiency with which lift is generated from a given wing area increases with aspect ratio. The ratio of lift/drag (the glide ratio, or finesse) is used as a measure of this efficiency and varies from 4 for a House Sparrow to 20 for a Wandering Albatross (Tennekes, 1996). As wing-loading increases with size (as is evident from Figure 3.8), the need for greater aerodynamic efficiency also increases in larger birds, presumably creating the trend identified by Warham.

To see how wing-loading and aspect ratio interact, we need to correct both of these ratios for the effects of body mass. When we remove the effect of body mass by considering only the extent to which the wing-loading and aspect ratio of each species departs from the regression of these ratios on body mass for all seabirds (Figure 3.10), we find that two groups fall far from the rest: the auks, which have a much heavier wing-loading and the cormorants which have much lower aspect ratios.

It would be naïve to think that wing-loading is independent of aspect ratio. As wing-loading increases, there is an inevitable necessity to increase efficiency. Spear & Ainley (1997) suggested that, among tubenoses, aspect ratio increases with wing-loading, while in gulls it decreases. However, they did not consider the effect of body mass. When we correct for mass (Figure 3.11), there is a tendency among both tubenoses and gulls for aspect ratio to increase with wing-loading, but the effect is very weak for tubenoses. Terns, boobies and tropicbirds appear to share the same relationship between these ratios as tubenoses, but gulls and jaegers tend to have both lower wing-loadings and lower

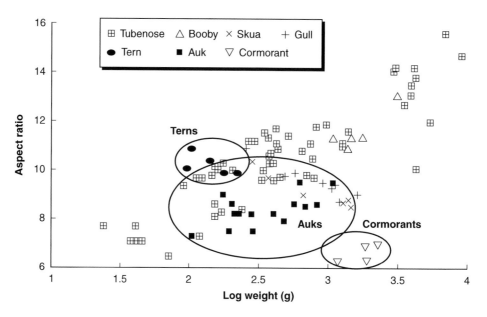

Figure 3.9   Aspect ratio in relation to body mass for the same species as Fig 3.8.

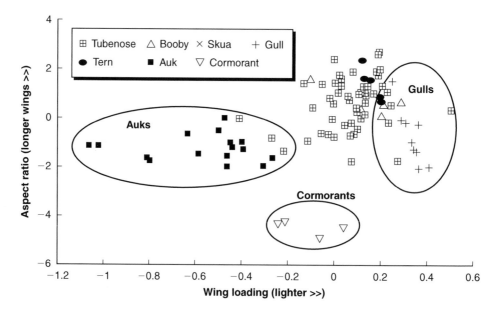

Figure 3.10   Aspect ratio in relation to wing-loading for the same species as Fig 3.8.

aspect ratios than tubenoses. In other words, gulls are a little lighter on the wing, for their size, but have rather less efficient wings for gliding. Skuas have the lowest aspect ratios relative to their size among any surface-gleaning seabirds, whilst frigatebirds have the lowest wing-loading, which makes sense for a bird that carries almost nothing in the way of undercarriage.

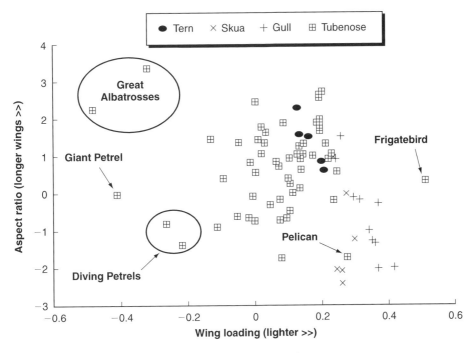

Figure 3.11   Aspect ratio in relation to wing-loading, excluding auks and cormorants.

Initially, the large gulls appear somewhat convergent with the medium-sized tubenoses (fulmars, gadfly petrels and shearwaters). However, the way that the two groups use their wings is very different. No one can mistake the flight of a shearwater for that of a gull. Despite the difference in relative wing length, shearwaters look much more like auks than like gulls, in flight. This is because they hold their wings very stiffly while flapping and gliding. Some albatrosses, large petrels and shearwaters have a very broad patagium (skin membrane) between the humerus and ulna, supported at the trailing edge by a tendon that is held away from the 'elbow joint' by a small bone. The patagium thus formed is an important part of the gliding surface (Warham, 1996), making these large tubenoses somewhat convergent with Pterosaur dinosaurs (pterodactyls: having no feathers they depended entirely on the patagium, like modern bats). In addition, the tubenoses have a system by which the elbow joint locks in place, reducing the muscular tension required to keep the wing extended, but reducing its flexibility (Yudin, 1957).

For underwater swimming, the primary feathers need to be very stiff, a condition that is reinforced by extended and rather dense covert feathers, but this means that in aerial flight the wingtips bend relatively little. In addition, the pressure on the articulation of the wing during underwater flight puts great strain on the joint, requiring it to be strengthened in ways that reduce its range of movement. Consequently, shearwaters are rather limited in the manner they can flap their wings, compared to gulls or even fulmars. A gull can arrest itself in forward flight, stalling and even hovering when it unexpectedly encounters potential food, whereas a shearwater has to keep going and instead must make a circuit and come back to investigate.

Watching Northern Fulmars and Black-legged Kittiwakes swooping and soaring around the cliffs of Prince Leopold Island makes this point rather well. Although fulmars weigh twice as much as kittiwakes, the two species have almost the same wing length, measured from the bend of the wing to the tip. However, the fulmar has a longer humerus, supporting more numerous secondary feathers, so that the wing area is 16% larger (Tennekes, 1996). In addition, the primaries of the fulmar are much stiffer than in the kittiwake, with a very stout rachis, built like a T beam, for rigidity. Both species glide, hover and soar on updrafts, but only the kittiwakes can turn on a penny, do somersaults and reverse in to their nest sites. Gulls may be less efficient than petrels at long-distance flight, but they are much more versatile and manoeuvrable at slow speeds (p 66).

Later, I shall discuss convergences between seabirds and large raptors, especially vultures, but in the matter of wing shape there is no similarity at all (p 66). For a given wing-loading, birds of prey have aspect ratios approximately half those of seabirds (Figure 3.12). Most vultures have broad, square-tipped wings, the primaries separating in flight to provide slots. This design is less effective for gliding than the long-winged design of most seabirds, but is more effective for creating lift in powered flight, hence making them better at taking off from flat ground. The broad-winged design is also better for gliding at low speeds, permitting large raptors to make use of rising thermals over land to soar for long periods with little expenditure of energy. Pelicans have long, broad wings that are good for soaring on thermals over land—this is one reason why I think of them as mainly a freshwater-adapted group.

An albatross, with a longer, narrower wing, also is capable of soaring in thermals (in theory—they never actually do so), but it would travel much further while doing so, because its wing is designed to generate lift through forward motion. Mostly, vultures are 'hanging out' waiting for some suitable victim to appear, so the additional travel distance might be a handicap; also, such long wings would be hopeless for taking off from land. Interestingly, the exclusively montane Lammergeier has narrower and more pointed wings than other vultures, perhaps because it depends more on up-currents along mountain ridges than on thermals (p 66). This type of 'slope soaring' is similar to the technique used by many seabirds, especially albatrosses. In addition, in most places where Lammergeiers land, they have some slope to assist them in taking off.

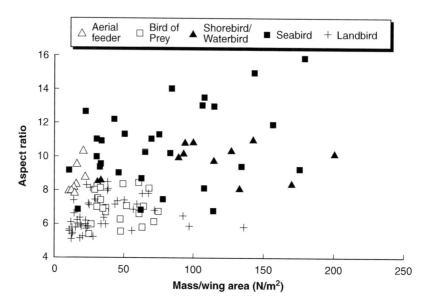

Figure 3.12   Aspect ratio in relation to wing-loading for selected landbirds (songbirds, owls and woodpeckers), aerial feeders (swallows, swifts), seabirds, shorebirds and waterfowl, and birds of prey (data from Tennekes, 1996). Seabirds have much higher aspect ratios for a given wing-loading than landbirds and birds of prey, but are similar to swallows and swifts.

Another feature that distinguishes the gliding of albatrosses and other large tubenoses from that of large raptors, is the angle at which the wings are held from the horizontal (the dihedral). When I used to build model aeroplanes, I found that giving the wings a positive dihedral (wings slightly angled upwards) created much greater stability in gliding than wings held strictly horizontal: an important factor in getting the plane to strike the intended victim. A slight positive dihedral occurs generally in raptors, though it is often only the tips that curve up. It is especially marked in Turkey Vultures and harriers (*Circus* spp.). In contrast, albatrosses have a negative dihedral, the tips of the wing drooping slightly. This configuration is even less stable than wings held horizontal, but minimises air spilling from under the gliding surface. Apparently, albatrosses cope adequately with stability by other means.

Taking off

Having long narrow wings is good for gliding, but can be a problem for taking off. In level flight, birds develop lift from the aerodynamic shape of their wings, but from rest, they must raise themselves entirely by muscular effort. In this process, wing-loading is an important constraint, so small seabirds are at an advantage over large ones.

When a teal or pigeon takes off, it raises its wings vertically, so that the wingtips almost touch, allowing it to generate lift before the wings hit the ground or water. However, the stiff wings of large petrels and shearwaters cannot be raised high above the back, giving them limited ability to generate lift. On land, they either launch themselves from a cliff or tree, or run into the wind to enhance the lift generated by their wings. The effect of wing-loading can be seen in the contrast between Streaked Shearwaters and storm-petrels, both of which breed on forested islands off Japan. The shearwaters must laboriously climb into the forest canopy, making use of slanting tree-trunks, in order to take off, while the storm-petrels take off easily from the ground, swerving and fluttering among the branches as they leave. This gives storm-petrels a much greater choice of nest sites in areas where islands are predominantly forested.

Murres and loons are especially handicapped in taking off, because of their very high wing-loading. Like swans and coots, they taxi along the surface, beating their wings in the air and running with their feet, when taking off from water. Because of their heavy wing-loading they gain altitude very slowly, even after clearing the water surface. After swans, the large loons seem to be the most constrained by their rate of climb. On the small lake in Quebec where I spend my summer weekends a Common Loon visits us regularly. When departing from the lake, the bird must rise to about 15 m altitude to clear the trees at the lake's outflow. To achieve this, on a windless day, the bird circles the lake twice: a distance of *c*.800 m, giving it an angle of climb of less than 1:50. The long taxi required by Pacific Loons to become airborne probably accounts for their restriction to larger lakes than their smaller relative, the Red-throated Loon.

Murres use a different technique for getting airborne if there is no wind. Initially, they practice a rather unique style of propulsion in which they beat along the surface with their wings (page 77). During this phase, they keep their heads down and body horizontal, striking the water as if they were rowing. Once they reach a certain speed, the head is raised, the body tilted upwards and the wings begin to beat the air. Puffins and Rhinoceros Auklets also use this technique, but not the smaller Ancient and Marbled Murrelets, which become airborne with little effort. However, even murres, in a strong wind, are able to launch themselves from the top of a wave.

LANDING

Compared to taking off, landing appears simple enough: just stop flying when you get where you are going. However, things are not that easy. A large bird possesses a great deal of momentum. In addition, birds with a heavy wing-loading have a relatively high stalling speed, making them incapable of slowing down much. Colin Pennycuick (1987) provides an excellent explanation of how the minimum and maximum speeds of petrel-like birds converge as size increases, so the largest albatrosses really only have a single gear. Either they fly fast or they do not fly at all. Large auks are in a similar situation. In both cases putting on the brakes by swinging back the wings (increasing the angle of attack) and spreading the feet, produces a very steep downward trajectory, potentially leading to a heavy impact with the ground.

Ground speed can be mitigated by flying into the wind and landing uphill, so that gravity assists the braking process. In the case of murres, their habit of breeding on cliffs allows them to use a ballistic technique, where they approach from well below their site, gliding up steeply so that they stall just as they reach their ledge. Those Common Murres that breed on flat rocks cannot use this strategy and often land very heavily. Where possible, they land on the sea and walk ashore. Loons and grebes are at an even greater disadvantage and will not normally come down on land at all. Instead, they land on the water and approach their nests by slithering from the water's edge.

Landing on water is easier, because it is a lot softer than land. Storm-petrels, prions, gulls and other highly manoeuvrable seabirds can alight from a hover. Species with heavier wing-loadings usually approach at a low angle and use the water as a brake. Waterfowl, pelicans and some cormorants brace their feet in front when touching down, but most true seabirds touch down first with the breast, like seaplanes, leaving the feet trailing, probably because the legs are set far back on the body. A few, like murrelets and diving-petrels, seem unconcerned about the need to brake at all and may fly into the water head first, a manoeuvre sometimes adopted by larger auks when pursued by other birds.

FLIGHT ALTITUDE

Though birds are capable of flying to great altitudes, most stay all their lives within a few metres of the ground or its vegetation. Probably, most landbirds keep close to vegetation to have somewhere to escape if attacked by a bird of prey. Exceptions occur during migration, when most birds fly more than 1,000 m above the ground. Other species, such as ducks and shorebirds, may make regular feeding or roosting flights at substantial altitudes, usually in flocks. Also, swifts and to a lesser extent swallows may feed hundreds of metres above ground, while birds of prey, crows, ravens and a variety of other large birds soar hundreds of metres up searching for sources of food.

At sea, most seabirds remain less than 100 m above the sea surface in flight. While seawatching, it is usually safe to keep the telescope sighted at or below the horizon, because few birds will pass higher up. Species such as albatrosses and large petrels, which make use of up-currents or differential wind speeds above the waves for soaring, clearly need to remain in the zone affected by the interaction of wind and sea. This mechanism is so well explained by Lance Tickell (2000) in his book on albatrosses that I will not repeat it here (see also Wilson, 1975).

Species that progress mainly by flapping may take advantage of the lower wind speed close to the sea surface when travelling against the wind. Downwind, the advantage of remaining close to the sea is less obvious and seabirds do tend to fly somewhat higher above the surface. Perhaps migrant terns and jaegers stay close to the sea on the off-chance of spotting feeding opportunities.

The only seabirds to regularly indulge in high soaring over the sea are frigatebirds, boobies and Sooty Terns. Frigatebirds take advantage of thermals at the base of tropical cumulus clouds in the trade-wind zone to travel long distances at altitudes of hundreds, perhaps thousands of metres (Pennycuick, 1983). Their low wing-loading and very high aspect ratio makes low-speed flapping flight very efficient, a characteristic they share with terns, especially noddies. It also makes them convergent with swifts: all these species feed largely on the wing. Like swifts, the frigatebirds' long wings cause them difficulty when taking off from flat ground: this is presumably the reason why most nest in trees or bushes (Nelson, 1975).

WINGS FOR SWIMMING

The wings of the Great Auk were very small compared to those of their flying relatives. Despite this, the skeletal modifications of the Great Auk were fairly trivial, compared to the changes in the length of the flight feathers. The wingspan, from tip to tip, was less than half that of their flying cousin, the Razorbill. The wings of modern penguins are even smaller. Small wingspan is related to the density of water, which makes flapping much more difficult than in air. It is notable that in all wing-propelled diving birds the wings are used to create forward thrust through the flexibility of the feathers as the wing is raised and lowered, as in flight. This contrasts with the 'rowing' motion exhibited by turtles, where the forelimbs are brought forward horizontally and then drawn back. This provides another clue that penguins probably had flying ancestors.

Luckily for birds the demands of flight have forced them to keep the main muscles very close to their centre of gravity, to reduce the leverage required to accelerate the wings up and down. The forearm and manus are very lightly muscled and consist mainly of tendons that deliver the force developed by contractions of the main pectoral muscles to the articulation of the skeleton. This accounts for why there is so little meat on a chicken's wing. For a swimming bird, this means that the forelimb is very slender in cross-section, cutting through the water easily, while the power unit is kept in the nice, hydro-dynamically efficient, torpedo-shaped, body. All the same streamlining that creates efficiency in air also helps to reduce drag underwater. The similarities between moving in air and moving in water that Leonardo da Vinci observed may be part of the reason why shifts to aquatic life have been relatively frequent among birds.

LEGS AND FEET

Among underwater swimmers, the feet are generally placed far back on the body, which has the advantage of minimising the drag set up by the body during swimming. Because of this, many seabirds either stand rather erect, in order to keep their bodies from falling forward (penguins, cormorants and murres) or lie prone on the belly when not moving (loons, fulmars, gadfly petrels, shearwaters, storm-petrels, tropicbirds and murrelets).

For birds that spend most of their time in flight, carrying a large pair of legs is an unwanted burden. Terns, frigatebirds and tropicbirds have very short legs for their size, reducing the weight that they have to carry in the form of undercarriage at the expense of being constrained to walk with very small strides (or hardly walk at all, in the case of tropicbirds and frigatebirds). Only the gulls, albatrosses, giant petrels and some auks (puffins, auklets) can run about fairly easily on land. Compared with other gulls, the pelagic kittiwakes have especially short legs, presumably because they spend little time on land.

Compared to other seabirds, petrels and storm-petrels have rather long slender legs and relatively large webs. Being set well back on the body, the legs appear to be designed for swimming rather than walking and certainly these birds have difficulty standing with legs straight. The tarsus being long relative to the humerus, they act more like oars than paddles.

Webbed feet, very useful in aquatic propulsion, are present in all seabirds except phalaropes. However, the marine habits of many grebes, which have palmate, lobed feet, demonstrate that webs are not essential to make a successful entry into the marine environment. The innovation of webbed feet must have occurred either three or four times in the evolution of birds, depending on which classification you choose to believe. It is noteworthy that this character is present in rather few aquatic birds of fresh water (ducks, pelicans and those members of seabird families found in fresh water, i.e. loons, gulls, terns and cormorants, but not among grebes, rails, finfoots, flamingos, herons or shorebirds). In most seabirds, the hind toe is very small and has no function in grasping, though it persists in the pelicans, cormorants, boobies, tropicbirds and frigatebirds, where the webs encompass all four toes (Figure 3.13).

The advantage of webbed feet for propulsion while swimming is obvious and is presumably the main cause of selection for this trait. Diving ducks have larger webs than dabbling ducks, presumably because swimming fast is more important to the divers (Raikow, 1985). Moreover, the webs frequently are used as rudders in flight, especially among species like auks where the tail is greatly reduced. The use of the webs in heat dissipation (many species) and in incubation (boobies and *Aptenodytes* penguins) is presumably secondary. Those seabirds that have retained the hind toe appear to be better at perching than those with only three functioning toes; many cormorants and frigatebirds and some boobies nest in trees, and perch on electricity wires, whereas few gulls or terns do so and only one auk (the Marbled Murrelet), which perches only on very large branches. Tubenoses do not nest in trees, although they may climb them in order to get airborne, where they breed within forest canopy (Streaked Shearwater and Westland Black Petrel).

All seabirds move on land principally by walking, rather than hopping (though many species hop occasionally), but the foot-propelled swimmers (loons, grebes, pelicans, cormorants and diving ducks) prefer to use their feet together, rather than alternately, while swimming underwater. In swim-

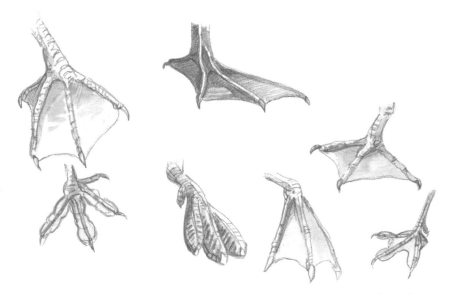

Figure 3.13   Some feet of swimmers. Clockwise from the top left: cormorant, gannet, murre, phalarope, loon, coot and grebe.

ming on the surface, ducks and auks may use their feet alternately or together, but at high speed they revert exclusively to paddling with both feet together. However, at take-off, loons, ducks, coots, shearwaters and albatrosses all run along the surface of the water with alternating strides.

These observations do not seem wholly consistent. The use of alternate strides at take-off, where the feet may function to raise the body off the water more than to create forward thrust, probably maintains greater continuity of thrust between wing-strokes than would be possible with feet together. However, the preference for using feet together underwater, rather than alternating, is harder to explain. It is consistent with the practice in frogs and marine mammals, but contrasts with the most efficient form of swimming in our own species (crawl beats breaststroke) and the technique preferred by Polar Bears.

Using the feet simultaneously, rather than alternately, makes forward propulsion more episodic and less continuous; this parallels the motion of wing-propelled swimmers. It also reduces any tendency to yaw from side to side. In fact, while hunting, both foot- and wing-propelled aquatic birds alternate brief bursts of propulsion with longer phases of gliding. I would like to make a wild guess that the glide phase is important for prey detection and that using the feet together permits birds to increase the proportion of time spent gliding.

As the legs do not need to support the body while swimming, the musculature of the leg is somewhat different from that of non-swimmers, with the gastrocnemius greatly enlarged. In addition, the stroke and retraction tends to be at the sides of the body, rather than below it, presumably because this keeps the body travelling in a straight line. The web is folded as it is brought forward, to reduce water resistance, then spread as it makes the power stroke. Birds have not adopted the up and down, tail stroke used by marine mammals, perhaps because the rigid design of the body skeleton, in which the majority of vertebrae are fused, prevents them from developing the sinuous body motion evident in seals and dolphins, and perhaps because even the most marine birds need legs that are somewhat functional on land.

In most seabirds, the lack of hind toe makes it impossible to grasp food with the foot, thus the bill becomes the sole organ for catching and manipulating food. In addition, food cannot be transported in the feet. This disadvantage appears to be exacerbated by the possession of webbed feet, further reducing the grasping power of the toes. Giant petrels and gulls will stand on a carcass in order to tear at it, but the inefficiency of a gull dismembering a carcass on land, compared to a hawk dealing with a similar repast, is striking. Even more odd is that skuas feeding on lemmings never attempt to catch them with their feet, as a hawk or owl will do. The skuas attack only with the beak. It takes two Long-tailed Skuas, one at each end, to efficiently dismember a lemming (Andersson, 1971). However, it is worth noting that pinning down the prey with the foot would be little use at sea, where there is nothing to pin it against.

BILLS AND MOUTHS

The design of the beak, generally a rather variable organ among birds, is limited in variety among seabirds, though there are a few really fancy types (Figure 3.13). Large gulls, shearwaters, storm-petrels, petrels, albatrosses, jaegers, frigatebirds, pelicans and cormorants all have hook-tipped upper mandibles, while most smaller gulls, penguins, terns and boobies do not, or have only small hooks. The hook is clearly useful for tearing open prey in gulls and albatrosses. Why fish-eating shearwaters and cormorants have hooked beaks, while boobies and terns do not, is hard to fathom. The most unique design among seabird beaks is that of the skimmers, where the lower mandible is greatly elongated and used to cut the water surface while feeding.

Auks are by far the most variable group in terms of bill design: part of the variation in summer is due to the bill serving a role in social communication (e.g. the coloured plates on the beak of

Figure 3.14   Variation in bill morphology among seabirds: a) Great Black-backed Gull, b) Audouin's Gull, c) King Penguin, d) Magellanic Penguin, e) Black-throated Loon, f) Caspian Tern, g) Little Tern, h) Great Cormorant, i) Magnificent Frigatebird, j) Wandering Albatross, k) Northern Fulmar, l) Short-tailed Shearwater, m) Common Murre, n) Parakeet Auklet, o) Marbled Murrelet, p) Horned Puffin, q) Great White Pelican, r) Great Skua, s) Red-tailed Tropicbird.

breeding puffins). However, the auklets possess some really unusual bills, culminating in the strange, upturned shovel of the Parakeet Auklet, one of the few seabirds that regularly eat jellyfish. By analogy with the horn of a rhinoceros, the horn of the Rhinoceros Auklet, a rather hard, fleshy protuberance from the upper mandible, looks as though it should have some social function. However, the horn is present in both sexes, appears in the nestling and persists throughout life, without any obvious seasonal changes. It is tempting to think that it might act like the 'rod' on an angler-fish, to attract prey, but this seems rather unlikely in view of the Rhinoceros Auklet's very active feeding style.

The tubenoses have an additional feature of the bill that is lacking in virtually all other birds: a raised bony canal running forward on top of the upper mandible and enclosing the nostrils. This is longest in the fulmarine petrels, especially the giant petrels. Because tubenoses are one of the few groups of birds to exhibit a strong sense of smell (see below), it seems probable that the tubular nostrils are in some way concerned with improving the ability to detect a given scent, but no one has convincingly demonstrated this.

Skeleton

The bones of birds frequently, though not always, contain air-filled cavities (they are 'pneumatized'). This is especially true of the skull bones. These cavities connect to the respiratory system via the air sacs that form an extension of the lungs. For the most part, seabirds are no different from other birds in this respect. However, they have a tendency to be less pneumatized than landbirds: penguins, loons, cormorants and auks have very little, but boobies show a good deal (McClelland, 1989). It may be that diving birds reduce the amount of pneumatization to decrease buoyancy, but this is not certain. Generally, pneumatization increases with size, because there is more room for a cavity in a larger bone: the wing bones of albatrosses are highly pneumatized. This characteristic was also found in the long bones of pterodactyls (Bellairs & Jenkin, 1960).

Underwater swimmers exhibit very distinctive skeletal adaptations relating to locomotion. In the case of foot-propelled divers, the pelvis is narrow with pronounced posterior elongation, which is most extreme in the loons. In these birds, the tarsus is generally laterally compressed, to improve streamlining. In all underwater swimmers, the breastbone is elongated to reduce the cross-sectional area while maintaining, or increasing, the muscle mass. In wing-propelled swimmers, the humerus is stouter than in other flying birds and stoutest in penguins. In the Great Auk, this bone was intermediate in shape between those of murres and penguins: a legacy of its fairly recent transition to flightlessness.

THE SENSES

Sight

Birds are renowned for their keen sight, which derives mainly from the fact that they have larger eyes, relative to their size, than other vertebrates. The eyes of the best-seeing birds appear to cram as many light-sensitive sensors per unit area as is theoretically possible. Hence, light sensitivity is mainly a function of the area of the retina. Large owls have larger eyes than we do and ostriches *Struthio* have the largest eyes of any land animal. Small passerines have small eyes simply because they have small heads, and as a result do not see well in the dark and few are nocturnal. As most seabirds are relatively large, they have good eyesight and this would seem to pre-adapt them to crepuscular or nocturnal activity (Martin, 1985). The relationship between head size and eye size means that seabirds need to be large to be deep divers, not only because large body size increases dive duration but because, as light levels decrease with depth, deep diving requires greater visual acuity. This can only be achieved through enlargement of the absolute size of the pupil, thus requiring a bigger eye.

Although seabirds share their acute eyesight with other birds, there are several ways in which they are specialised compared to landbirds. Because of the difference in refractivity between water and air, the eye lenses of aquatic birds must be able to accommodate over a far larger range than those of landbirds. There appear to be a number of mechanisms by which this is accomplished, including the deformation of the lens by squeezing it through the opening of the iris. Though diving birds are able to accommodate their eyes over a very large range of refractive conditions, those of penguins appear to be mainly adapted for focusing underwater. They have a relatively flat cornea compared to other vertebrates, reducing the amount of light focused by the cornea and making them mildly short-sighted in air.

King Penguins, which dive as deep as 300 m, have specially adapted pupils which are capable of expanding and contracting to a much greater extent than those of other birds, or indeed, ourselves. Martin (1999) has suggested that this great range of pupil size allows penguins to maintain visual acuity when they are switching from normal daylight to the equivalent of starlight in the course of a single dive lasting only a few minutes.

All birds are believed to be able to discriminate colours, but on the basis of pigments and oil droplets present in the retina, it is thought that the Humboldt Penguin, and presumably other penguins, can see much better in the blue-green part of the visible spectrum than the red part, and may detect ultraviolet light invisible to us. However, from my own experience, seabirds cannot detect infra-red light, so they exceed our own visual spectrum only at one end. Long-wavelength light at the red end of the spectrum is absorbed much more strongly by water than shorter wavelength blue light. Consequently, deep water is dominated by blue light, an obvious reason why deep-diving birds should adapt to improve vision at the blue end of the spectrum. Fish adopt similar tactics (Bowmaker & Martin, 1985).

HEARING

Vocal communication is an important element in the behaviour of most seabirds, as it is for most landbirds. Unlike dogs and bats, most birds seem to hear over approximately the same range of frequencies that we do and this may be one reason why we tend to find many of their calls and songs attractive. For the most part, seabird calls appear to be designed for rather close range communication, principally at the breeding site. This may be because conditions for communicating over long distances at sea are frequently disrupted by the ever-changing background of wind and wave noises. It may be, also, that there is much less to communicate about when the birds are at sea.

Using calls to communicate implies a certain minimum level of hearing ability. There is no evidence that any particular seabird has specialised hearing. Those that can identify mates and offspring from other birds on the basis of their calls may discriminate better than others, but do not necessarily have greater acuity. No seabird is known to emit calls, or any other form of acoustic communication, underwater. However, that does not mean they are not listening while swimming: some of their prey might be audible. At present we have no evidence for or against this idea. Though some seabirds are known to forage at night, none seems to specialise in hunting by sound. This is not a sense that has become specialized for marine life, but nor is it one that has been dispensed with.

Plate 1. Chinstrap Penguins on Penguin Island, South Shetlands, Antarctica (John Chardine)

Plate 2. A group of Adelie Penguins at Arctowski Station (Polish), King George Island, South Shetland Islands, show why they would have to flap their wings very fast indeed if they wanted to get airborne. (John Chardine)

Plate 3.   A group of Gentoo Penguins coming ashore at Petermann Island, Antarctic Peninsula. Synchronised arrival may help to reduce the danger of attacks by predatory marine mammals. (John Chardine)

Plate 4.   A Black-browed Albatross, ship following in Drake Passage, Tierra del Fuego. (John Chardine)

Plate 5. A Salvin's Albatross taking a good run to get airborne in calm conditions off South Island New Zealand, 1990. The wings are not raised as high as they appear, actually about 45 degrees from horizontal (Tony Gaston).

Plate 6. Immature Wandering Albatross in Drake Passage, Tierra del Fuego (John Chardine)

Plate xx.   A Light-Mantled Sooty Albatross with chick on South Georgia. This species has one of the longest chick-rearing periods known – about 5 months. The entire breeding cycle takes more than 7 months and successful breeders do not attempt to breed the following year (John Chardine).

Plate 7. *Adult Southern Giant Petrel – note the extremely large feet and broad wings, compared to albatrosses of similar size. (John Chardine)*

Plate 8. *White morph of the Southern Giant Petrel, in Drake Passage, Tierra del Fuego. This morph makes up about 10% of the population. (John Chardine)*

Plate 9.   Cape Petrel (Cape Pigeon), a typical fulmarine with a rather gull-like wing shape, but stiff, petrel-type primary feathers. (John Chardine)

Plate 10. *An intermediate morph Northern Fulmar on its nest at Prince Leopold Island, Nunavut, Canada: notice the hooked beak and prominent nasal tubes. (Tim Lash)*

Plate 11. *Prions (probably Broad-billed) demonstrating why their plumage may act as defensive camouflage – taken between South Georgia Island and Ushuaia, Argentina (John Chardine)*

Plate 12.   Nestling Imperial Shags with parent at Petermann Island, off the Antarctic Peninsula. Like most seabirds, shags reserve their gaudy colours for their bare parts (John Chardine).

Plate 13.   Masked Booby with chick: note the excellent binocular vision focused down the bill – Cayo Alcarraza, Culebra National Wildlife Refuge, Puerto Rico (John Chardine)

Plate xx.   Although chromatic colouration of the plumage is rare in seabirds, brightly coloured feet, bills and faces are common. This Red-footed Booby on Kauai, Hawaiian Islands, is a good example, with subtle variation of tones on the bill and face (Tony Gaston)

Plate 14.   Two Northern Gannets at Cape St. Mary's, Newfoundland. Like some other large, long-lived seabirds, gannets pass through several plumage states between the all-dark juvenile and the mainly white adult. The bird in the foreground, with dark feathers in the tail and coverts, is probably a third-year. (Tim Lash)

Plate 15.   South Polar Skua showing the hooked beak characteristic of the genus and very similar to that of the fulmars. (John Chardine)

Plate xx.   A Dolphin Gull foraging at a small sewage outflow in Tierra del Fuego. Gulls are the best walkers among seabirds, with stout legs set well under the center of gravity: skuas have smaller legs (see above), while those of jaegers are smaller again (John Chardine).

Plate xx. A small group of Ivory Gulls breeding on the summit of the Brodeur Peninsular, Baffin Island, about 400 m above sea level. Nowhere on Earth is more desolate: terrain like this, on nearby Devon Island, is being used by NASA as a stand-in for the surface of Mars (Tony Gaston).

Plate 16. Brown Noddy in flight: note the very high aspect ratio wings – Cayo Molinos, Culebra National Wildlife Refuge, Puerto Rico (John Chardine)

Plate 17.   An aerial view of Funk Island, Newfoundland and Labrador taken from 1300 m altitude. The circular green patch left of centre is turf-covered soil in which Atlantic Puffins burrow; up and left from there a whitish patch is Northern Gannets, while the dark areas surrounding and below the gannets, and stretching to right along the central part of the island are over 400,000 pairs of Common Murres. (John Chardine).

Plate xx.   The Atlantic Puffin, this one on Staffe Island, Scotland, is among the most colourful of seabirds during the breeding season, when the bill acquires exaggerated size and colour by the addition of horny plates (Anne-Marie Gaston).

Plates

Plate 18.   A flock of Thick-billed Murres crossing an ice pan in dense fog, close to the colony at Coats Island. The arrangement in an irregular 'V' and the height above the sea are typical. (Tony Gaston)

Plate 21.   Thick-billed Murre making a sharp turn close to the colony cliffs at Coats Island. The almost 90 deg. bend in the very stiff primaries of the Murre demonstrates the considerable force induced by this maneuver. (Tim Lash)

Plate 19.   A pair of Thick-billed Murres with a 15 day old chick: this is approximately the size at which the chick will leave the colony (Tim Lash)

Plate 20.   Thick-billed Murres wheeling along the colony cliffs at Coats Island in a storm (Tim Lash)

Plate 23.   (The horn of the Rhinoceros Auklet is a rather unique organ, among seabirds. Both sexes develop one, it persists throughout the year and even the nestling has an incipient horn. No one has yet suggested a plausible function for such a bizarre decoration. (Tim Lash)

Plate 24.   Tufted Puffin in flight at Triangle Island, British Columbia. This is the largest puffin species, with an exceptionally large bill. Note the legs spread, broadening the body surface to increase the glide area and positioning the feet to act as tailplanes. (Tim Lash)

Plate 22.   A group of Thick-billed Murres perched on snow-covered breeding ledges at Prince Leopold Island, Nunavut, Canada during the pre-breeding period. For some, their sites will be clear by the time they lay: for others, the egg will have to be deposited on the snow. Thick-billed Murres may not be the wisest birds in the world but they could definitely win prizes for pluck and determination (Tim Lash).

SMELL

'Do seabirds smell?' is a more ambiguous question than 'do seabirds see?'. In one sense, they certainly do: the musky odour of storm-petrels and shearwaters lingers on the bags in which they are held prior to banding, and even on the mist-nets in which they have been caught. After several years, I can still tell which nets were used to catch 'stormies'. A colony of Crested Auklets is detectable with the human nose for many kilometres downwind by its strange, tangerine-like odour, a characteristic shared with Whiskered Auklets (Jones, 1993). If an animal is deliberately manufacturing a substance that is chemically unique, volatile and persistent and spreading it in the environment, it is a fair bet that the substance is being used to either store or transfer information, and this implies that the animal 'smells' in the other sense: it can detect chemical substances in the atmosphere. It is surely no coincidence that the seabird families in which sense of smell is best developed (storm-petrels and petrels) are also those where most members produce a scent that is easily detectable by humans.

Actually, all birds must have the capacity to detect odours, as they all possess the sensory and neural apparatus to do so: they have a membrane within the nasal cavity that has sensory cells with nerves that connect directly to the olfactory lobe of the brain—the part that is known to be concerned with the detection and analysis of smells in vertebrates. However, the size of these elements and their apparent importance in the birds' behaviour appears to vary widely. It appears that the sense of smell is hardly used among most songbirds, in which the olfactory lobe may be as little as 3% of the size of the cerebellum, whereas in kiwis *Apteryx* spp. and the Snow Petrel the lobe is relatively ten times as large (Bang & Cobb, 1968).

Among orders of birds (other than kiwis, which being nocturnal are rather odd), the average ratio of olfactory lobe to cerebellum is highest among the tubenoses (29%). There is plenty of observational and experimental evidence to demonstrate that odours are important to tubenoses for finding food and their burrows. Within this group, the storm-petrels appear to be most reliant on a sense of smell for finding food, whereas diving petrels make little use of this sense, and have a correspondingly small olfactory lobe (18% of cerebellum). It may be significant that diving-petrels do not smell of much, as far as I am concerned.

As Lequette *et al.* (1989) noted, no seabirds that pursue prey underwater have been shown to use scent in detecting prey. This may be because the nostrils of all aquatic birds contain a special valve that shuts off the scent-detecting apparatus (olfactory membrane) from incoming water (Bang & Wenzel, 1985). As this device is found in all species that put their heads underwater, including ducks and kingfishers, as well as all seabirds, we can assume that (a) this type of valve has evolved independently several times and (b) it is really important to keep the olfactory membrane out of the water. Why that should be so may have more to do with the need to prevent water from entering the respiratory tract than with the care and maintenance of the olfactory membrane.

The fact that even 'olfactorarily-challenged' organisms such as ourselves can detect storm-petrel and Crested Auklet colonies at distances of kilometres raises the possibility that the sense of smell might be important to birds in finding their home colony, rather like salmon homing in on their native stream. This is a hard hypothesis to test and there is no evidence at present. Observations of incoming flight directions on clear and foggy days could give a clue, though radar or telemetry might be required to make the necessary observations.

CONCLUSIONS

The things that are most characteristic of seabirds, compared with other birds, are their well-developed salt glands, webbed feet and the rearward position of the legs. All of these characters are shared with ducks. Short tails and high aspect-ratio wings are very common, but not universal. Seabirds tend to be large and to have dagger-shaped bills and the use of a sense of smell is common, although apparently largely confined to the petrel/albatross lineage. Some seabirds have become very successful at foraging in terrestrial habitats: gulls on garbage dumps and ploughed fields and jaegers hunting for lemmings are obvious examples. This indicates that specialisations for marine life do not necessarily preclude a return to land. On the other hand, landbirds are totally excluded from moving out to sea by the wetability of their plumage. It is the development of methods for staying warm and dry at sea which constitute the essential element in colonising the sea.

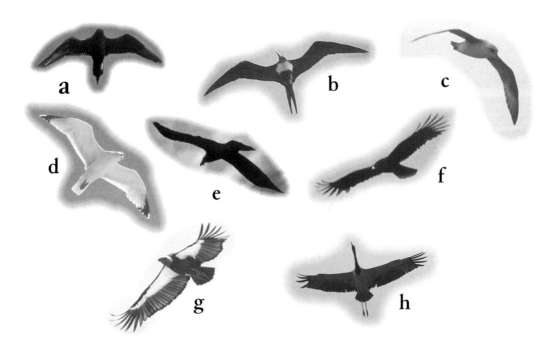

Flight silhouettes of seabirds and large land birds: a, Parasitic Jaeger; b, female Great Frigatebird; c, Northern Fulmar; d, Herring Gull; e, Lammergeier; f, Black Eagle; g, White-rumped Vulture; h, Demoiselle Crane. (Tony Gaston, Timothy J.F. Lash)

CHAPTER FOUR

Plumage

Prince Leopold Island is a great cliff-girt pancake of limestone, set in the icy seas of the Northwest Passage, at the junction of Lancaster Sound, Barrow Strait and Prince Regent Inlet. These are waters that are covered by unbroken ice for eight months of the year. The island's rock is uniform, horizontally bedded limestone, rising in tiers to a plateau nearly one thousand feet above the sea. The circumference of the island is about 25 km and Northern Fulmars breed over more than 75% of that perimeter, on rocky ledges and scree slopes and tucked beneath overhangs. They are strange birds, by turns stoic, irascible and comical.

When I returned to the island in the summer of 2000, one of my tasks was to census fulmars. From a distance, the cliffs are speckled with their white heads. Why bother to stand and count them in the bitter arctic wind? Much better to take a photograph, enlarge it and count the fulmars at leisure amid the comforts of the south. Indeed, this is the practice used for fulmar colonies elsewhere in the Atlantic. Sadly, at Prince Leopold Island, this technique is useless because the fulmars of northern Canada are very variable in their plumage and more than half the population is not white headed. The darker birds blend perfectly with the grey of the rocks. To make an adequate census of the Prince Leopold Island fulmars there was no option but to count them one by one, binoculars in one hand, tally-counter in the other, while the wind sang and our fingers froze.

Fulmars on Prince Leopold Island range from those that are sooty slate, perhaps tinged brown, over the whole body and upper wing (this extreme is known as dark-dark, or D²) to those that are the purest, gleaming white on the head and body, with dove-grey wings and a white wing-patch formed by the bases of the inner primaries (light-light, L². Every gradation in between occurs. Strangely, the birds take absolutely no cognisance of this variation: mating appears to be entirely at random. Nor is the variation in any way linked to age or sex.

The range of plumage colours seen in the fulmars of Prince Leopold Island covers almost the entire range observed among tubenoses. It makes them very confusing birds to identify at sea, especially when you are not expecting them. Depending on the type, they may be mistaken for Mew Gulls or Sooty Shearwaters.

At Prince Leopold, fulmars share the cliffs with Black-legged Kittiwakes: the two species also appear to feed in similar places and take similar prey. Both are masters of the air, wheeling and swooping around the cliffs and stacks of their home in all but the strongest winds. Despite their close association, an inspection of their feathers reveals that they are very differently adapted for flight. The wing length (as measured from the carpal to the wingtip) is almost the same in the two species, despite the fulmars weighing twice as much. The fulmars compensate in having a much longer inner wing and a larger number of secondary flight feathers. In addition, the primaries of the fulmars are much stouter in the shaft, and much more rigid, than those of the kittiwakes. Fulmars hold the articulation at the joint of the outer long bones and the 'hand' more or less rigid, thus the wing works as a single unit, whereas kittiwakes flex this joint liberally, with the primaries rowing like paddles at times, and the inner wing functioning merely as a glide surface. This makes them appear quite different in flight, with the kittiwakes blowing like snowflakes while the fulmars cleave the air like fighter planes. Lest we feel that feathers are just feathers, these species, ecologically very similar, remind us that there are different feathers for different fowls.

KEEPING WATER OUT

As I remarked at the end of Chapter 3, to be a seabird, it helps to have waterproof plumage. This is partially achieved through the structure of the feathers and partly through oiling the feathers from the preen gland, situated at the base of the tail (Rijke, 1971). Their ability to keep water away from their skin, where it would cause them to lose heat very rapidly, partly depends on the water-repellent capacity of the feathers, and partly on the resistance to penetration between the feathers.

Actually, most birds have waterproof feathers. The mechanical structure of the barbules on the feathers, when locked in place, is such that, rather like the 'micro-screen' fabrics that constitute modern rainproof clothing, water cannot penetrate them because of surface tension. The preen oil makes it easier for the feathers to retain their proper shape, as well as increasing their water-repellence, like spraying waterproofing on your nylon tent. A sparrow or thrush with well-preened feathers avoids getting waterlogged in rain due to the water-repellence of its contour feathers: the rain bounces or runs off, just like on a tiled roof. The tiling arrangement of the feathers, overlapping one another in rows, helps to shed water. However, when a passerine is caught and hanging upside down in a mist-net, the system breaks down, birds get wet rapidly and death by hypothermia quickly ensues. That is why we don't use mist-nets in the rain.

For diving birds, the problem is more complicated because once underwater, the water can work in between the feathers. This applies to the breast and belly feathers of a bird on the surface, but as they dive deeper the pressure of the water increases. Seabird feathers are not much better at repelling water than those of landbirds (Rijke, 1971). However, they are much better at preventing water penetrating them and they do this by being much more tightly packed, especially on vulnerable areas such as the belly. People accustomed to looking for a brood patch on a passerine get a surprise when they try gently blowing the belly feathers of a murrelet or a shearwater. Where the feathers of a thrush waft aside at the smallest breath, to reveal the naked belly, the feathers on a puffin are packed like pile on a Persian carpet. Only a very active raking with the fingers will reveal the naked brood patch.

Moreover, beneath the stiff contour feathers, interspersed among their roots, there is a dense layer of down feathers. When landbirds and seabirds are compared, the seabirds have vastly more feathers.

Cormorants differ from other seabirds in having feathers that permit water to penetrate them (Mahoney, 1984). They share this characteristic with the snakebirds. Allowing water to penetrate among their plumage reduces the buoyancy of cormorants and hence the energy they require to submerge and to remain underwater. However, it means that they have to work harder in ascent than birds that retain greater buoyancy. It also accounts for why, compared to loons, grebes and auks, cormorants look very low in the water when they are swimming, especially after they have been diving for some time. A darter becomes neutrally buoyant (i.e. the same density as water) at a depth of only 2–4 m and a Long-tailed Cormorant at 5–6 m (Hustler, 1992). In contrast, a murre, which traps air in its feathers, becomes neutrally buoyant only at *c*.40 m.

The negative aspect of having feathers that allow water to penetrate is that insulation is much reduced and weight after swimming is greatly increased, making flight more difficult and requiring more energy. That is why snakebirds and cormorants, especially those in the tropics, spend a great deal of their time sitting with wings spread, drying their feathers (Figure 4.1). However, the typical feather-drying pose is less often adopted by Double-crested and Pelagic Cormorants in the northern Pacific, suggesting that their plumage permits less water penetration than that of tropical cormorants. In addition, exposing the lightly feathered flanks and underwing to the air (lightly feathered flanks because the wing has to fit tight against the body for streamlining) is a really good way to lose heat, which is highly inadvisable in a cold climate. The poor insulating properties of cormorant plumage may be a factor in reducing the abundance and diversity of cormorants in polar regions, though several species occur in sub-polar waters throughout the year (Chapter 3).

Figure 4.1   Decorated bills and faces: Rhinoceros Auklet, Tufted Puffin, Rockhopper Penguin, Whiskered Auklet, Razorbill, male Magnificent Frigatebird, Double-crested Cormorant.

COLOUR: ANYTHING YOU LIKE, AS LONG AS IT'S BLACK OR WHITE

Plumage coloration among seabirds is far less variable than in landbirds; most are some combination of black, white and grey. In particular, there is a dearth of chromatic colours in the feathers of seabirds, though a few species develop a pink hue during breeding (Ross's Gull and Roseate Tern), Emperor and King Penguins develop a rich orange and some cormorants show subtle purple, blue or green iridescences. In this character, seabirds accord with many large non-passerine birds, especially storks, herons, ibises and spoonbills (all in Sibley & Ahlquist's Ciconii), where colours other than yellow are usually confined to bare areas. However, Red-tailed Tropicbirds have really red central tail feathers and Tufted Puffins and Rockhopper Penguins have really yellow plumes, so seabirds can sport colours if they want to.

BILLS, LEGS AND ORNAMENTS

Only the bill and legs of seabirds are regularly coloured: the bills, especially, can be quite ornate (e.g. in penguins, puffins and auklets; Figure 4.2). Among boobies, the sexes differ in the coloration of bills and bare areas on the face. Many other seabirds develop colourful or ornamented bills, and bare facial patches. Ornamentation of the bill and face makes sense for burrow or crevice nesters, because that is the first part of the bird that a potential mate or rival will see. In fact, all the auks that have heavily ornamented bills and heads (*Aethia*, *Fratercula* and *Cerorhinca*) breed in burrows or deep within boulder screes, whereas the surface-nesting *Uria* has very little ornamentation (a white line in *U. lomvia*). However, though many tubenoses breed in burrows, none has brightly coloured or ornamented bills, while some surface-nesting albatrosses do. Nor do the burrow-nesting penguins

Figure 4.2   Examples of plumage variation with age in Herring Gull (2nd year, 1st year, adult), Northern Gannet (1st year, 2nd year, adult) and Great Cormorant (1st year, adult).

(*Spheniscus* and *Eudyptula*) have ornamented bills, whereas the surface-nesting *Eudyptes* species all have bright bills and facial plumes. Overall, the coincidence between ornamented bills and burrow or crevice nesting is rather imperfect.

DIFFERENCES WITH SEX AND AGE

Sexual dimorphism in plumage is virtually absent, except in the seaducks and phalaropes—two groups that may be fairly new to the sea—and the frigatebirds, where plumage dimorphism is fairly modest (females have varying amounts of white on the throat and breast, and the male develops a red, inflatable throat pouch during breeding). Lack of obvious differences in plumage between the sexes is characteristic of colonial and group-living birds, and applies to herons and colonial and group-living passerines, but is also characteristic of the solitary-nesting loons and grebes and most Charadriiformes, including territorial sandpipers, plovers and oystercatchers.

Some seabirds display considerable plumage variation with age (some albatrosses, cormorants, frigatebirds and gulls) and some alternate between breeding and non-breeding plumage (loons, some cormorants and most Charadriiform seabirds). Among species that change from breeding to non-breeding plumage ('alternate' and 'basic' in the official terminology), it is striking that those which are all white below in non-breeding plumage frequently assume black or otherwise pigmented throats for breeding (many auks, penguins, loons and also grebes). Among gulls and terns a black head or crown in breeding is usually lost in non-breeding plumage, while those with white heads during breeding may acquire a brownish tint in winter. The tubenoses show no variation in plumage according to sex or breeding status and only some albatrosses change plumage with advancing age. The plumage of the Wandering Albatross takes longer to mature than that of any other bird, attaining its whitest appearance after *c.*20 years (Warham, 1996). This is fitting in the species that takes the longest time to reach sexual maturity.

POLYMORPHISM

As my introductory comments on the fulmars of Prince Leopold Island indicated, some seabirds appear in more than one plumage. In some cases this polymorphism is fairly discrete, as in the pale and dark morphs of the Wedge-tailed Shearwater, several gadfly petrels, Leach's Storm-petrel, Parasitic Jaeger and Southern Giant Petrel, where intergrades are far less common than the two extremes. In other species, including Northern Fulmars, there is a complete gradation, so that a precise definition of 'morphs' is impossible and individuals must be ranked along a scale of darkness or lightness. Albinos occasionally occur in all species, but these are not generally considered polymorphisms, because they probably derive from occasional mutations, rather than constituting a regular part of the species' gene pool.

Leach's Storm-petrels exhibit a gradation of rump colour with breeding latitude in the eastern Pacific, dark-rumped birds predominating in the south. However, those breeding on Guadalupe Island, Mexico, are unusual in having segregation between birds with light or dark rumps, with the dark individuals mainly breeding during summer and the light individuals in winter. This makes them virtually subspecies, separated in time, rather than space (Ainley, 1980).

All of the jaegers show plumage dimorphism of a fairly discrete kind, having dark morphs that are sooty-brown all over and pale morphs with pale chins and bellies. In Europe, dark-phase Parasitic Jaegers predominate in the south, while virtually all are light phase in the extreme north and in Siberia. In Canada, the trend appears to be in the opposite direction.

Compared with landbirds, polymorphism in plumage is rather common among seabirds, especially those of high latitudes. It is found in most seabird groups except loons, although among auks it is confined to the nestling and juvenile plumages (in murres and Razorbill) and to a single, rather minor, variant in the adult plumage of the Common Murre (the 'bridled' morph).

Some cases of plumage variation appear to be the result of recent re-mixing by previously separated populations. An example is the race of the Iceland Gull breeding in Baffin Island and wintering in the Atlantic (Kumlien's Gull), in which individuals range in plumage from the white wingtips typical of the nominate Greenland race, to black wingtips, as in the race that breeds across the central and western arctic of North America (Thayer's Gull regarded by some people as a separate species). Most Thayer's Gulls migrate to the Pacific in winter, though a few occur in the Great Lakes region. It seems most likely that Iceland and Thayer's Gulls became isolated during the Pleistocene glaciation by the Laurentide ice sheet that covered eastern North America. During this period they developed separate migration routes. When they recolonised the Arctic during one of the interglacials they met and interbred in Foxe Basin and central Baffin Island, giving rise to Kumlien's Gull (Weir *et al.*, 2000).

Most cases of polymorphism show some variation in the relative frequencies of morphs across the species' range. These could derive from situations similar to that described for the Iceland Gull, where populations evolved towards different morphs while isolated, but subsequently came into contact again and interbred. Alternatively, plumage variation can arise from mutations within a single population that spread because they confer some advantage, at least in parts of the species' range. If a species varies from light to dark plumage morphs, with the ancestral light predominating in the north, and dark in the south, then it would be natural to assume that the original dark mutation arose in the south. However, this would be true only if the mutation was too recent to have reached equilibrium in the population. Otherwise the opposite could be true, with a dark morph that was neither advantageous nor harmful in the north spreading by chance to more southerly latitudes, where it conferred an advantage and spread faster.

In reality, few cases of polymorphism show clear-cut trends that offer clues to the origin of polymorphism or how it spread. Trends with latitude and temperature are frequently contradictory (white-phase Northern Fulmars are commoner in the south in eastern Atlantic populations, the reverse is true in the Pacific; pale Parasitic Jaegers predominate in southern parts of the North American range and vice versa in Europe). In fact, the distribution of colour morphs among Northern Fulmars is highly irregular (Figure 4.3), suggesting that ratios of dark and light are mainly colony specific, rather than adhering to any trend or regional norm. This mishmash of morphs suggests that no simple correlation with temperature or feeding ecology can explain the geographical variation. It also implies that the colonies are very ancient, with little interchange for hundreds, perhaps thousands of years.

At Prince Leopold Island, there is no indication that the proportions of different colour types are changing, so presumably all plumages work equally well at the demanding task that is being a high-arctic fulmar. This implies either that their appearance has little adaptive significance for fulmars or that being variable confers some advantage. There is little information to indicate that birds with different plumage colours differ in any measurable way in their reproductive abilities, except that experience seems to have a greater influence on the breeding success of dark birds than on that of others (Hatch, 1991).

Brown or grey?

A comparison of gulls, terns and auks with terrestrial Charadriiformes (shorebirds and coursers) suggests that the main difference in plumage between the two groups is in the relative prevalence of

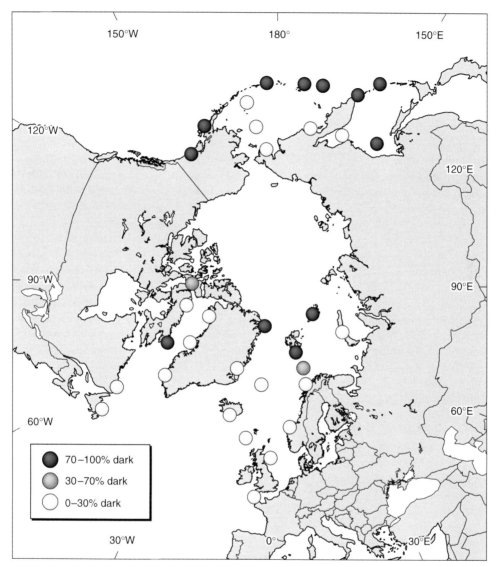

Figure 4.3 Distribution of dark and pale morphs in the Northern Fulmar, according to Van Franeker & Wattel (1982); Hatch & Nettleship (1999).

grey and brown tones, with the former predominating among marine species and the latter among terrestrial species. Many shorebirds are browner, sometimes reddish, in the breeding season, when they are found in marshes or on arctic tundra, than they are in winter, when they frequent the seashore. The phalaropes form a particularly interesting case, being brown and red in summer, when they are terrestrial, and grey in winter, when they remain entirely at sea. The *Brachyramphus* murrelets are mottled brown in summer, clearly a cryptic garb in their inland breeding locations, but revert to a typical auk pattern of black above and white below during winter. Perhaps the most striking proof of the cryptic nature of the brown plumage is provided by the fledgling Marbled Murrelet, which remains clothed in mottled brown down until just before leaving the nest site, whereupon it plucks off its down and makes its exit in the black-and-white plumage of a winter adult (Nelson, 1997).

Camouflage — aggressive

A very elegant series of observations and experiments carried out by Phillips (1972) demonstrated that fish could detect dark objects more easily than white objects against the bright sky. He suggested that, for birds that search for food in flight, having white underparts reduces the likelihood of detection by prey. That fish may detect terns flying above them and take avoiding action to reduce the terns' success in catching them was proved by Dunn (1973a), so obviously a degree of 'aggressive camouflage' could be beneficial to fish-eating seabirds.

All plunge-divers except the Brown Booby are predominantly white, as are most surface gleaners. Among the terns, all those that regularly plunge-dive are white below, but the noddies, which do not, are dark all over. Several inland terns that feed mainly by taking insects are also black below and some of these that winter at sea become white outside the breeding season. All of these observations seem to accord well with Phillips' experiments and the hypothesis that white underparts make birds less visible to potential prey as they descend on them from above (Simmons, 1972; Cowan, 1972).

Bottom-feeding seabirds tend to be either black all over (cormorants, scoters and, in summer, guillemots) or black below and white above (eiders), which may help conceal them when approaching prey horizontally, as they do if they are swimming along the bottom (Siegfried *et al.*, 1975; Cairns, 1986). Virtually all penguins and auks, which are mostly mid-water feeders, are black above (or dirty brown) and white (sometimes off-white) below in non-breeding plumage, as are some cormorants. The plankton-eating auklets that feed in mid-water are black or brown all over in summer, suggesting that being hard to detect may be less important when feeding on the small, slow-moving prey which they normally favour.

Camouflage — defensive

Both the broader comparison and the cases of the phalaropes and murrelets suggest that the dominance of monochrome and the lack of brown in the plumage of marine birds are to some extent adaptive, presumably making the average seabird less easy to see against the average seascape. Few seabirds have plumage patterns that are clearly cryptic (compared, for instance, to nightjars or grouse), but we may have a rather incomplete understanding of what is cryptic among the constantly varying light and wave conditions that characterise the seascape. Moreover, we must keep in mind that birds have very different colour perception from our own; they can see well into the ultraviolet frequency range and having four types of cones in the retina, they can perceive more and different primary colours. There is a possibility that these differences in visual capabilities make seabirds look rather different to other seabirds than they do to us.

Löfgren (1984) suggested that the grey upperparts exhibited by many seabirds were cryptic, because they converge with the 'battleship grey' of naval camouflage. Using the same logic, Murphy (1936), suggested to the US navy that the grey of prions' upperparts would provide good camouflage for warships. His advice was ignored, but after a series of tests, the colour finally chosen by the navy was an exact match for the plumage of the Antarctic Prion.

Bretagnolle (1993), who made the most extensive study of the adaptive significance of seabird plumage to date, also considered that the pattern and hue of the prions and Blue Petrel, pale grey with darker grey forming an indistinct W on the upper surface, was cryptic and adapted to reducing predation from larger seabirds (skuas and giant petrels). Some of the smaller gadfly petrels share this patterning, which also appears on some juvenile gulls, especially kittiwakes. The appearance of this plumage in unrelated groups of seabirds, especially among potentially more vulnerable juveniles, does argue for some functional significance and any ship-based observer can attest that prions are hard to pick out in all but the calmest seas, especially when you are looking down on them.

Thus far the idea that plumage is mainly camouflage, either defensive or aggressive, appears to hold up well. However, female eiders, which are brown and cryptic in their breeding habitat, do not adopt male plumage outside the breeding season, casting doubt over whether the black belly of the male eider has anything to do with foraging. Moreover, there are some cormorants that are black above and white below (many of the subantarctic shags), and these are not known to feed more in mid-water than the all-black cormorants (Siegel-Causey, 1988). Among boobies, those that generally plunge from low altitudes and at oblique angles (Brown and Blue-footed Boobies) are darker than those that specialise in vertical dives, but all the juveniles, except Abbott's Booby, are basically dark. In addition, some petrels, shearwaters, albatrosses, gulls and the dark morphs of Northern Fulmars and jaegers, are dark all over (mostly sooty-brown, rather than pure black). There could be special explanations for many of these plumages (e.g. these species may depend less on actively swimming prey and more on offal or slow-moving prey). However, the association between plumage and feeding technique is by no means sufficient for us to regard it as a rule of nature.

CORRELATIONS WITH ECOLOGY

The dark upperparts of most surface divers makes them rather hard to detect from above while they are sitting on the sea. Conversely, the white underparts of most surface gleaners and their generally pale plumage means that most of these species can be readily detected in flight by an observer above the sea surface. Many plunge divers, shearwaters, gulls and terns feed in flocks on shoaling fish that concentrate at the surface for only brief periods. It is possible that the easy detection of white plumage helps birds to keep track of others even when far away, allowing them to home-in as soon as they show signs of having detected food. The presence of many predators may help to break-up and disorient the fish schools, prolonging the availability of food for all individuals. However, the evidence for such an effect is weak. An alternative hypothesis would be that conspicuous patterns, attracting other members of the species from a distance, could evolve through reciprocal altruism ('I will help you now if you will help me tomorrow'), in a situation where the cost of competition caused by attracting other birds is very small. Both processes may contribute to the development of conspicuous plumage.

David Ainley (1984) has pointed to a tendency for all-dark storm-petrels to be less migratory and to forage closer to their breeding colonies than species with white rumps. It appears that this difference may apply to the two colour types of Leach's Storm-petrel as well, but the adaptive significance remains unknown.

GEOGRAPHICAL DISTRIBUTION OF COLOUR

As noted by Warham (1996) for tubenoses, there seem to be more all-dark seabirds in the tropics than at high latitudes (Figure 4.4), although there are also some striking exceptions (in the arctic, Black Guillemot in summer, and dark-morph Northern Fulmar). In birds as a whole there is a tendency for species found in the moist tropics to be darker than those in temperate zone or in the dry tropics (Gloger's Rule). Ellis (1984) showed that seabirds with dark plumage have lower metabolic rates than those with light plumage. However, the dark birds tend to do less flapping in flight than light birds, at least in the tropics. Hence, it is unclear whether the difference in metabolic rate has

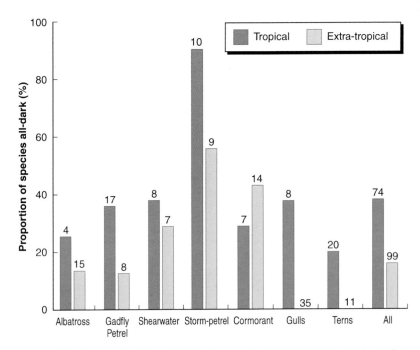

Figure 4.4   Proportion of predominantly dark seabirds in relation to latitude (classified on the basis of pictures and plates in Harrison, 1983, 1987).

anything to do with plumage colour. As Ellis himself stated: "no causality has been experimentally demonstrated".

Bergmann (1982) argued that heavy pigmentation in gull feathers conferred protection against damage from ultraviolet light. That desert birds, with some exceptions, tend to be rather pale appears to contradict the idea that dark plumage is protection against damage to feathers by sunlight, and suggests that improvement to camouflage is the main cause of selection for this tendency among landbirds. However, for seabirds, the strong tendency for the wingtips to be darker than the rest of the wing (very common in gulls, terns, pelicans and boobies, and frequent in tubenoses) may function to reduce wear on these, most susceptible and aerodynamically important feathers.

Several of the dark seabirds in the tropics (noddies, frigatebirds and Wedge-tailed Shearwater) are gregarious species (Bretagnolle, 1993) which could take advantage of being visible in the way that has been suggested above for white wings. The presence of all-dark flocking species inevitably damages the hypothesis that white plumage functions to attract other birds. It is difficult to argue that both pale and dark colorations are adaptations to making yourself more visible or, for that matter, less visible. Yet all the possibilities could be true under certain light conditions. Perhaps the best that we can offer is that some feeding behaviour is definitely enhanced by being pale below, but that if you are not a plunge-diver, or your prey is either rather immobile or totally dead, there may be more options available.

Perhaps surprisingly, in view of the prevalence of white in seabird plumage, there are very few all-white species: the tropicbirds (nearly), the white morph of the Southern Giant Petrel, Snow Petrel, White Tern, Ivory Gull and immature Iceland and Glaucous Gulls being the only exceptions. The polar regions seem to have a slight excess of such plumage, with the all-white Snow Petrel of the Antarctic being neatly balanced by the Ivory Gull of the Arctic. The coincidence of snowy plumage and snowy landscapes argues for the white plumage to act as camouflage. Similarly, the Greenland race of the Iceland Gull (*Larus g. glaucoides*), which remains in snow and ice-affected areas year-round, has all-white primaries, whereas the central North American Thayer's Gull, which winters from British Columbia to California, where snow is rare on the coast, has dark wingtips.

White underparts, the commonest pattern among all types of seabirds except seaducks, may make birds resting on the water less liable to detection from below by potential predators, such as fish and seals. It is noteworthy that among the very ancient penguin lineage, perhaps the most susceptible of all seabirds to predation by underwater predators, all species are white below. Notice also that the parts of penguins, auks and loons that turn black in summer (the throat and neck) are those that are held above the water when swimming at the surface, though penguins travel partially underwater when 'porpoising'.

The importance to seabirds of mortality caused by avian predators is difficult to assess, because only anecdotal observations are available. Most published accounts are of predation occurring opportunistically within mixed feeding flocks. In this situation, camouflage may be of little use. Consequently, the value of camouflage at sea is not evident. However, on land, where predation by land-based mammals and hawks is a definite possibility, being hard to see presents obvious advantages and might well cause selection against bright colours. Flocks of gulls or terns roosting on pebble beaches can be very hard to pick out, as can cormorants against dark, kelp-strewn rocks. However, the same gulls, seen on the wing with their white underparts flashing, are visible from a long distance, and have been considered to be actively advertising their presence.

For seabirds as a whole, white underparts (to avoid detection from below by prey or predators) and dark upperparts (to reduce detection from above by competitors or predators) is the default option. The modifications on this pattern for a range of species may be caused by less-obvious factors that we have not yet identified. I return to the issue of predation on seabirds and its possible consequences for their distributions in the next chapter.

Pigeon Guillemot doing a running take-off: unlike murres, it keeps its wings clear of the water while taxiing. (John Piatt)

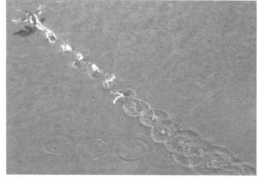

A Thick-billed Murre taking off: the large ripples at the start of the run show where the bird was rowing with its wings, the last six, smaller ripples are from the feet only. (Timothy J.F. Lash)

CHAPTER FIVE

Distributions and communities

While in New Zealand in 1990, I took a morning's trip with Sandy Bartle in a small fishing boat based at Kaikoura, near the north end of South Island. Kaikoura is famed as a whale-watching spot, as well as being the site of a long-running study of Red-billed Gulls. The snowy mountains that brood over the coastline are the sole breeding site of Hutton's Shearwater, one of only two oceanic seabirds that nest on the main islands of New Zealand. Given its reputation for whales and the proximity of the Hutton's Shearwater colony, I was prepared to be impressed, but what transpired in those few hours convinced me that New Zealand truly is the capital of the seabird world.

We left harbour before dawn and it was only just light when we reached the fishing ground. While Dave, the boat's owner went about hauling in the longlines that he had set the evening before, Sandy tossed a little chum into the sea and we stood gazing over the gently undulating Pacific swells. I had already spent a month on an island in Cook Strait, so I was fairly familiar with the range of seabirds that occurred locally. First to arrive, in fact already around us before we anchored, were the Cape Petrels, fulmarine petrels with jaunty black-and-white patterns on the wings; they were joined almost instantly by bullying shoemakers (White-chinned Petrels) and hulking Northern Giant Petrels. Soon, the great shapes of albatrosses came soaring and banking upwind towards us: Shy Albatross, Black-browed Albatross and an immature Royal Albatross. A large, quarrelsome Westland Black Petrel followed, while a steady stream of gadfly petrels passed us, rising and falling on their long wings and apparently unmoved by our chum.

We saw 21 species of seabirds that day, including 14 tubenoses. Fifteen species showed an active inter-est in the boat, while the rest either flew on past, like the gadfly petrels, or were seen close to shore on our return journey (Fluttering and Hutton's Shearwaters, and Red-billed Gulls). A similar trip to the equally rich inshore fishing grounds off Newfoundland or Britain in summer would probably yield a maximum of 12 species, of which only three would be tubenoses. Why is the diversity of seabirds so variable and, given their mobility, why do tubenosed birds not dominate the northern hemisphere oceans as they do in the southern hemisphere?

ZOOGEOGRAPHY

Seabirds are ubiquitous; they have enormous powers of dispersal, but despite this, many of them have very restricted breeding distributions. Zoogeography is the science of why animals live where they do. This chapter deals with the zoogeography of seabirds. First, I want to look at the patterns and then at the concordances with geographical and historical factors. Lastly, I shall speculate about why seabirds are distributed as they are.

I am going to discuss the diversity of families and genera and this involves making some choices about which classification to adopt. Fortunately, the choice of classification probably has little effect on the broad generalisations that I want to make, but it does affect the numbers, in some cases rather strikingly. Unless otherwise stated, I have followed the species list of Monroe & Sibley (1993), but for the albatrosses I use the generic classification of Nunn *et al.* (1996), and among auks I recognise the Long-billed Murrelet as a species. This does not imply any particular taxonomic preference for other groups—I just know less about them and therefore have found it convenient to stick with a single source.

Monroe & Sibley (1993), following Sibley & Ahlquist (1990), used a very distinctive ordering of families (see Chapter 2) and their classification tends to reduce most taxonomic categories above the level of genus by at least one rank compared to earlier classifications (e.g. gulls, terns and auks became tribes of a single subfamily, instead of subfamilies within a family). In terms of phylogeny, Sibley & Ahlquist may be correct, but in ecological terms, treating the auks, gulls and terns as a single grouping is awkward, because they behave very differently. Here, I treat the following groups as equivalent to families: penguins (Spheniscidae), loons (Gaviidae), albatrosses (Diomedeidae), petrels (Procellariidae), storm-petrels (Hydrobatidae), pelicans (Pelecanidae), frigatebirds (Fregatidae), trop-icbirds (Phaethontidae), boobies (Sulidae), cormorants (Phalacrocoracidae), phalaropes (marine Scolopacidae), skuas (Stercorariidae), gulls (Laridae), terns (Sternidae) and auks (Alcidae). I have omitted snakebirds (Anhingidae) because they are wholly fresh water and skimmers (Rynchopidae) because they occur mainly on lagoons or large rivers, although the Black Skimmer *Rynchops niger* occurs in sheltered inshore marine waters in places. Each of these groups is very distinct in their mor-phology and ecology and has been recognised as some kind of higher (supra-generic) grouping for many years. Whether they are tribes, subfamilies or families probably makes little difference to the arguments that I present.

In discussing seabird distributions, I have divided the world's oceans into five realms: southern cir-cumpolar (subantarctic and antarctic); Pacific, Atlantic and Indian tropical (tropical and subtropical of both hemispheres); and northern circumpolar (subarctic and arctic). The northern circumpolar can be further subdivided into Pacific and Atlantic cold realms, with many species confined to one or the other. Many species in the southern circumpolar realm are also limited to only a portion, sometimes a very small portion, of the realm, but seabird distributions suggest no obvious division within that realm and what divisions there are do not correspond with the southern boundaries of the tropical oceans, so I have left the southern circumpolar realm undivided.

Another problem in defining seabird zoogeography is that quite a few species occur close to the boundaries of the realms that I have defined, especially in the New Zealand region. I have, somewhat arbitrarily, defined those species that breed only around North Island as Pacific tropical (e.g. Buller's Shearwater and Pycroft's Petrel), while those around only South Island I consider southern circumpolar (Hutton's Shearwater and Yellow-eyed Penguin). The line had to pass somewhere and on this definition lies approximately where, passing towards the south, you might want to put on a wet suit to go snorkelling.

Because of their endurance, seabirds, especially the large tubenoses, are capable of breeding in one oceanic region, while at the same time doing much of their feeding in another. For example, during chick rearing, the Wandering Albatrosses of South Georgia may feed in waters off Brazil (Prince *et al.*, 1992) and some Yellow-nosed Albatrosses from subantarctic Amsterdam Island forage in tropical waters of the Indian Ocean (Weimerskirch & Guionnet, 2002). Likewise, Waved Albatrosses breeding on the Galápagos Islands may feed in the cold upwelling zone off the Peruvian coast (Anderson *et al.*, 1997). This mobility makes it hard to assign some species to a particular oceanic realm. I have done this solely on the basis of breeding site distribution simply because, for most species, this is much better known than feeding areas.

The discussion of seabird distributions will involve the frequent mention of remote islands and archipelagos with which some readers may be unfamiliar. I have not provided a gazetteer here, but many of those in the northern hemisphere were described by Gaston & Jones (1998), while many of the southern ocean islands are well described by Lance Tickell (2000) in his excellent book on albatrosses.

DIVERSITY

Compared with terrestrial birds, there are relatively few species of seabirds. This is true even on the most optimistic splitting of species and it accords with the general observation that marine animals tend to be less diverse than their terrestrial counterparts. The low diversity of species, considering the extent of the ocean, may be because the marine environment offers less opportunity for reproductive isolation or for differentiation of ecological niches.

While water is a barrier to landbirds, it is a dispersal highway for seabirds. The rails or reed-warblers that arrive on a remote oceanic atoll evolve thereafter in almost complete isolation from their kind, under selection from the unique combination of environmental factors that characterise that particular island. The storm-petrel or tern that arrives on the same island is likely to be joined at regular intervals by other colonists. At the same time, the huge areas over which seabirds forage, especially before they begin to breed, may overlap extensively with those of birds from other breeding colonies, making the whole population subject to similar selection pressures.

To make comparisons of species diversity more explicit, Table 5.1 presents a few examples of the number of species comprising seabird communities that occur within a given area at a single season, and the size of forest bird communities on continental landmasses at the same latitude. The contrast is greatest in the tropics, where the maximum diversity of landbirds coincides with a relatively low diversity of seabirds (e.g. the Maldives and Cape Verde Islands) and least in Western Europe, where a somewhat depauperate terrestrial avifauna meets a rather diverse marine one. Once we move to the Antarctic continent the picture reverses completely, with the avifauna totally dominated by seabirds.

The difference in diversity between seabirds and landbirds is even more striking if we consider genera, because seabird genera on average contain more species than landbird genera. However, these differences in numbers are created largely by the existence of several very large seabird genera,

Table 5.1 Numbers of breeding seabirds compared to numbers of landbirds (forest and scrub only) breeding on comparable continental areas at the same latitude

Breeding area	Seabirds (A)	Land area for comparison	Landbirds (B) (forest and scrub)	Ratio (A/B)
Britain	24	Northern France	68	2.8
Gulf of St. Lawrence	18	Gaspé, Quebec	99	5.5
Queen Charlotte Islands	12	Northern British Columbia	81	6.7
Iceland	20	Finland	95	4.7
Falklands	16	Patagonia	94	5.9
Maldives	13	Kerala, South India	225	17.3
Cape Verde Islands	9	Gambia	251	27.9
Tristan da Cunha and Gough	21	Cape Province	130	6.2
Central Pacific	23	North Queensland	190	8.3
Arabian Gulf	13	Somalia	154	11.8

Phalacrocorax, Leucocarbo, Pterodroma, Larus and *Sterna* all having more than 15 species apiece. These are all genera with extremely large global ranges, and found in every ocean, as well as occurring in fresh water (except *Pterodroma*). If these 'mega-genera' are eliminated from our analyses, the numbers of species per genus among seabirds is similar to the non-passerine landbirds. In any case, it is unwise to place any emphasis on taxonomic levels, as these are liable to change, subject to the whims of scientific fashion (e.g. Siegel-Causey, 1988 suggested that cormorants and shags comprise two subfamilies with nine genera, none containing more than seven species).

DISTRIBUTION OF FAMILIES

As far as breeding distributions are concerned, only the terns and petrels can be stated to be truly cosmopolitan. Storm-petrels, cormorants and gulls come close, being distributed over most of the world's oceans. However, storm-petrels do not breed in the Arctic, although they reach 65°N in Norway. Cormorants are missing from large parts of the tropical Pacific and from most remote, oceanic islands (except those around New Zealand). Gulls, like cormorants, are missing from many oceanic islands, especially in the tropical Pacific, as well as from a large part of the Indonesian archipelago.

Other families are entirely missing from large areas of one or more oceans. Albatrosses do not breed in the Indian or Atlantic oceans, outside subantarctic waters, or in the Pacific north of southern Japan. Penguins are restricted to the southern hemisphere, although they reach the equator at the Galápagos Islands. Frigatebirds and tropicbirds are restricted to the tropics and subtropics. Boobies and gannets are similar, but in the Atlantic, they reach subpolar waters off Newfoundland. As breeders, they are absent from the North Pacific outside tropical waters, although they apparently occurred in California in pre-Pleistocene times (Warheit & Lindberg, 1988). Auks occur mainly in subarctic and arctic waters of the northern hemisphere, except for a few in subtropical waters, and skuas have a unique bipolar range, but do not breed anywhere in subtropical or tropical areas.

There are some rather striking anomalies in seabird distributions, especially in tropical oceans. Tubenoses, in the form of shearwaters, gadfly petrels and storm-petrels are found on oceanic islands throughout the tropical Pacific, but they are completely absent from the islands of Wallacea, the

Philippines and Indonesia (White & Bruce, 1986; Dickinson *et al.*, 1991). The waters of the Sunda Shelf that surround the Indonesian archipelago are uniformly shallow, perhaps making them unattractive to some oceanic birds, but the seabed just east of the Philippines descends abruptly to one of the deepest abysses on the planet, so water depth cannot be the sole explanation.

Fossils of albatrosses are not uncommon in Pliocene and Pleistocene deposits from South Carolina and Europe (Olson, 1985). Although this does not prove that they bred in the North Atlantic in prehistoric times, such evidence does strongly suggest it, because no modern albatross makes regular trans-equatorial migrations. Their disappearance from the North Atlantic coincided with the Pleistocene glaciations, when a lowering of sea levels would have connected many previously isolated islands to larger landmasses, perhaps leading to a spread of terrestrial predators. Subsequent high sea levels, during interglacial periods would have inundated some existing landmasses. These adjustments would have been especially hard for North Atlantic breeders because of the paucity of potential breeding islands (Olson & Rasmussen, 2001).

The petrels and penguins appear at first glance to be replaced in the northern hemisphere by the gulls and auks, but this comparison is slightly misleading. Petrels are predominantly offshore feeders, many being truly oceanic, whereas most gulls are coastal or inshore. The contrast between penguins and auks is less clear. Most penguins, when not breeding, are offshore or oceanic, whereas most auks are confined to continental shelf waters. However, the puffins appear to be oceanic outside the breeding season. In fact, the ecological niches occupied by auks in the northern hemisphere appear to be split, in the southern hemisphere, among penguins, diving-petrels and shearwaters. The latter, for birds with relatively long wings, have surprising powers of underwater swimming (Chapter 6).

TROPICAL FAMILIES

The occurrence of small, but very distinctive, families in the tropics, with higher latitudes being dominated by large cosmopolitan families, is a common pattern among birds. Among landbirds, high latitudes are dominated by the passerines, while the tropics support a bewildering diversity of non-passerine landbirds (motmots, rollers, broadbills, toucans, etc.). During the tertiary era, the globe enjoyed a tropical climate for far longer than the brief intrusions of the glaciations. Warm, stable conditions allowed mature, specialised families to persist. When conditions began to change rapidly, during the Pleistocene, these families survived only in the tropics and more recently evolved and more adaptable families occupied higher latitudes. A similar scenario can be used to account for the persistence of boobies, frigatebirds and tropicbirds at tropical latitudes.

NORTHERN FAMILIES

The occurrence of the loons and auks as isolated and specialised families confined to high latitudes of the northern hemisphere is unusual, as they comprise 14% of the total number of seabird families worldwide (14, as I have defined them). The only landbird families or subfamilies unique to high latitudes are the waxwings (Bombycillinae), the grouse (Tetraonidae) and the sandpipers (Tringinae—qualifying only if we ignore the Tuamotu Sandpiper). This is less than 5% of families represented in northern temperate latitudes and a much smaller share of those found worldwide. Both loons and auks were in existence prior to the Pleistocene glaciations, and may have occurred south of their current ranges at that time (Emslie & Morgan, 1994). Hence these families are not a peculiar product of the ice age. Their restricted distributions emphasise the substantial barrier to seabird dispersal presented by tropical waters.

DISTRIBUTION OF GENERA

Dividing the oceans into six regions, on the basis of some restrictions on contact between them (Table 5.2), we find that the maximum number of seabird genera (29) occurs in the cold waters of the southern hemisphere. The cold waters of the North Atlantic and North Pacific support 21 genera. Tropical waters are less diverse, with 22 genera in the Pacific, 14 in the Atlantic and 12 in the Indian Ocean. In the tropical Pacific, three genera are confined to the cool waters of the Humboldt Current system and cormorants are almost absent in saltwater (outside the Humboldt Current). If these genera are ignored then the tropical Pacific supports just 19 genera.

The division of seabird families into genera suggests that some families are richer in diversity than others. This impression may depend somewhat on the opinions of systematists, but it is sufficiently striking to raise some questions. For instance, the very distinctive pelican, tropicbird, and frigatebird families are all comprised of single genera, with variable numbers of species; skuas/jaegers and cormorants comprise just two genera, while boobies comprise three. At the other end of the scale of diversity, the petrel family includes at least 13 genera, the auks 11 (12, prior to the Great Auk's extinction), terns ten and gulls and storm-petrels seven each. All these families are rich in species. On the other hand, the relatively small penguin and albatross families contain six and four genera.

The distribution of the number of species per genus is highly skewed, with most families containing one very large genus. All but seven of the 50 species of gulls are normally placed in the genus *Larus* (and some of the others are sometimes lumped in *Larus*; e.g. *Xema*), and 24 of the 43 species of terns belong to *Sterna*. Among tubenoses, the two large genera *Pterodroma* and *Puffinus* make up 54 of the 79 species of petrels and more than half the storm-petrels belong to *Oceanodroma*. Among the families comprising more than a single genus, only the penguins, albatrosses and auks show a fairly even distribution of species among genera. All these families belong predominantly or exclusively to cold waters. Pelicans, tropicbirds, frigatebirds and cormorants, families that are poor in genera, are all found mainly in warm water.

Table 5.2 Distribution of seabird genera in six oceanic regions

Family	Southern cold	Pacific tropical	Pacific north, cold	Atlantic tropical	Atlantic north, cold	Indian tropical
Penguins	6	1				
Loons			1		1	
Albatrosses	3	1				
Petrels	11	4	2	3	3	3
Storm-petrels	4	3	1	2	2	
Tropicbirds		1		1		1
Frigatebirds		1		1		1
Pelicans		1		1		
Cormorants	1	1	1	1	1	1
Boobies/gannets	1	1		1	1	2
Skuas/jaegers	1		1		2	
Gulls	1	2	4	1	5	1
Terns	1	5	1	3	1	3
Auks		1	10		5	
Totals	**29**	**22**	**21**	**14**	**21**	**12**

Unlike landbirds, few genera of seabirds are confined to small geographical areas; most being represented on several island groups or continents. Only Abbott's Booby (*Papasula*), which is confined to Christmas Island in the Indian Ocean, and Swallow-tailed Gull (*Creagrus*), found only on Galápagos, qualify as having really restricted ranges. The Inca Tern (*Larosterna*) has the smallest range of any seabird genus breeding on a large landmass. None of these genera is as distinctive as many highly localised landbird genera (e.g. New Zealand wrens Acanthisittidae [New Zealand]; todies Todidae [Caribbean]; Hawaiian sicklebills Drepaniidae [Hawaii], false sunbirds Philepittidae and cuckoo-rollers Leptosomidae [Madagascar], lyrebirds Menuridae [southeast Australia] or Ibisbill [Himalayas]).

TRENDS IN SPECIES RICHNESS

AREAS OF HIGH DIVERSITY

The species is the typical unit of choice in measuring biodiversity. As we noted earlier, seabirds are generally less diverse than landbirds, perhaps because of a lack of structure in the marine environment. As with genera, the centre of gravity of seabird species diversity lies in the southern ocean: 34 species of seabirds breed on the Crozet archipelago (Jouventin *et al.*, 1984), 28 on the Prince Edward Islands (Williams, 1984), not too far away, and 31 species on the Kerguelen group (Winterbottom, 1971). South Georgia supports 27 species (Croxall *et al.*, 1984), the Auckland Islands and Campbell Island, south of New Zealand, support 29, from a total of 70 seabird species breeding within the greater New Zealand region (Robertson & Bell, 1984). Although the tropics tend to support fewer species than colder waters, the relatively small archipelago of the Seychelles has 19 breeding seabirds and ten species nest on the tiny Aldabra Atoll alone (Stoddart, 1984).

In contrast to the southern ocean, Britain, a similar-sized island group to New Zealand, at a similar latitude but at the opposite end of the globe, supports only 24 species, the most diverse of the smaller islands being Foula, with 17 Species (Lloyd *et al.*, 1991); Britain nevertheless supports a greater diversity of seabirds than anywhere else in Europe. Iceland, perfectly positioned in terms of biological productivity and variation in oceanography, at the boundary between the Arctic and the warm waters of the Gulf Stream, supports only 20 species. Newfoundland, with a huge area of continental shelf and cold currents providing rich marine productivity, has only 17 species (or 18, if Ring-billed Gull, which is mainly an inland species, is included).

Of course, it is important to note that not all the species breeding on a single island feed in the same area, making the diversity of species occurring within given marine areas lower than those observed at breeding islands. Conversely, under some conditions, assemblages found at sea may be more diverse than those breeding in the area. Examples are the Grand Banks of Newfoundland, where in fall the local breeders are joined by Great and Sooty Shearwaters from the southern hemisphere, as well as two phalaropes and Little Auks from the Arctic, and Great Skuas from the eastern Atlantic (Brown, 1986). A similar mixture, plus Sabine's Gulls and the smaller jaegers occurs at the same season off western Britain.

'HOTSPOTS'

Outside of the southern ocean islands, there are few 'hotspots' of seabird diversity. Most of these, like the Galápagos, the Hawaiian chain, the Juan Fernández group or the Mascarenes, are remote island groups far from the continental shelf. A few do not fit this pattern, especially the Arabian Sea coast of Arabia and associated inlets (five endemics), the Benguela coast of South Africa and Namibia (five endemics) and the Gulf of California and nearby parts of the eastern Pacific with 11 endemics. Some other areas stand out as having an abundance of islands, but a relatively small number of endemic seabirds: Britain, with many islands, but only a single species (British Storm-petrel) the Caribbean (two gadfly petrels), Indonesia (two endemics on Christmas Island, but none in political Indonesia), the Japanese archipelago (two storm-petrels, Japanese Murrelet), the Aleutians (no endemics; one [Red-legged Kittiwake], if we include the Pribilof and Commander islands).

. . . AND 'NOT-SO-HOTSPOTS'

If we think of hotspots, we must also consider 'coldspots': areas where the seabird fauna appears especially poor in species. The huge inland sea of Hudson Bay and Foxe Basin supports only eight seabirds: two loons, three gulls, a tern and two auks (this is not counting tundra-feeding species, like jaegers and phalaropes), though non-breeding Little Auks and Northern Fulmars also occur (Gaston, 1991). Accessible to seabirds only since the last of the Wisconsin ice sheet melted, *c*.8,000 years ago, and patrolled by the world's densest population of Polar Bears, it may be a difficult area to colonise.

On the other side of the world, the myriad islands of Indonesia and the Philippines are surprisingly bereft of seabirds. They muster a list of 13 species, including a tropicbird, a frigatebird, three boobies and eight terns, but the numbers of birds involved are very low (White & Bruce, 1986, Dickinson *et al.*, 1991). Outside of oceanic Christmas Island, some 400 km south of Java, there are no major seabird colonies. I sometimes wondered why Joseph Conrad, the novelist who wrote so eloquently and accurately on maritime topics, made no mention of seabirds. Most of Conrad's personal maritime experiences were in the Far East and the omission of seabirds from his literary seascapes may tell us something about the dearth of seabirds in those waters. The same applies to the ecologically similar Andaman Islands, in the Bay of Bengal, which support no seabirds except four species of terns. In fact, the entire Bay of Bengal is virtually a desert for seabirds, certainly when compared with the Arabian Sea.

COMPARING OCEANS

In addition to the north–south imbalance, the Pacific has greater diversity than the Indian or Atlantic oceans. Comparing the tropical central Pacific (from 160°E to 140°W) with tropical latitudes in the other two oceans, the central Pacific supports 29 species, compared to 19 in the Atlantic and 23 in the Indian Ocean. In the North Pacific, the subpolar waters of the Bering Sea support 35 species, while similar waters in the North Atlantic support 22; only one more species than breeds on Buldir Island, a single small island in the western Aleutians (Byrd & Day, 1986). Moving into real Arctic waters, the Chukchi Sea, at the northern boundary of the Pacific, supports 20 species, compared to 15 in the Barents Sea (these numbers omit loons and phalaropes, but numbers of species in these families are similar in both oceans).

EFFECT OF LATITUDE

Seabirds are one of the few groups of organisms that disobey the common generalisation that species diversity decreases from the tropics towards the poles. In the Atlantic, in both hemispheres, the diversity of seabirds in the tropics is similar to that at higher latitudes. Diversity peaks at about the latitude of the subpolar boundary (Figure 5.1). In eastern Canada, the diversity of breeding seabirds remains unchanged from the Bay of Fundy, a little over 40°N, to Ellesmere Island, at 80°N. This is especially striking, as fishes and bivalves show the usual decrease in diversity further north (Figure 5.2). However, marine mammals, like seabirds, show constant diversity over the same range. In winter, the situation is quite different, with most seabirds leaving high latitudes because of ice cover, so that only Ivory Gull and Black Guillemot remain north of 70°N, compared with at least 12 species wintering on the Newfoundland Banks.

SPECIES WITH RESTRICTED RANGES

It is a commonplace of biology that some species are extremely widespread, while other, very similar, species, have very small ranges. BirdLife International has a category for the latter, 'restricted-range species', which are defined as those with global ranges of less than 50,000 km². This criterion is a little harder to apply to seabirds, because most breed only in a slim line along coasts. On the other hand, if we apply the criterion to feeding areas, most offshore species would be excluded, however small their breeding areas. To look at 'restricted range' among seabirds, I have used two criteria: for inshore species, those occupying less than 2,000 km of coast, and for offshore and oceanic species, those confined to two or fewer islands or archipelagos. In fact, most restricted-range seabirds are confined to single small islands or island groups.

When we examine the geographical distribution of restricted-range seabirds, we find that they are overwhelmingly concentrated in the tropics and the southern ocean. There is only one species that breeds in the cold waters of the northern hemisphere, the Red-legged Kittiwake, and the inclusion of even this species is marginal, depending on how we define 'island group'. The extinct Spectacled Cormorant, confined to the Commander Islands, would certainly have qualified, had it survived.

Many restricted-range seabirds occur in the 'hotspots' of seabird diversity mentioned above. There are no fewer than eight restricted-range cormorants on islands around New Zealand, as well as three penguins and four albatrosses. The Baja California region and the Gulf of California support two restricted-range gulls, two auks, a storm-petrel and a tern, while the Arabian Peninsula has a restricted-range gull and a cormorant. As endemism requires a restricted range, this coincidence is unsurprising.

One consequence of the absence of restricted-range species in northern cold oceans is that families heavily represented in the northern hemisphere tend to have fewer restricted-range species than those confined to the southern hemisphere. Only three auks have restricted ranges, all murrelets (*Synthliboramphus* spp.) breeding at the extreme southern limit of auk distributions. Among gulls, ten species (of 50) have restricted ranges, but only Saunders' Gull, breeding in China, reaches temperate latitudes in the northern hemisphere: the rest are found in tropical or subtropical regions. Unusually, the gulls with restricted ranges include seven species that occur along continental coasts, one in China, one in southwest Africa, two in Baja California and three in South America.

Among families widespread in the southern hemisphere, restricted-range species are abundant among albatrosses (13/25 species), cormorants (13/28 marine species) and gadfly-petrels (11/*c*.34 species). They are less common among frigatebirds, boobies and tropicbirds (only two species for all groups combined), fulmarine petrels (0/7) and terns (2/42).

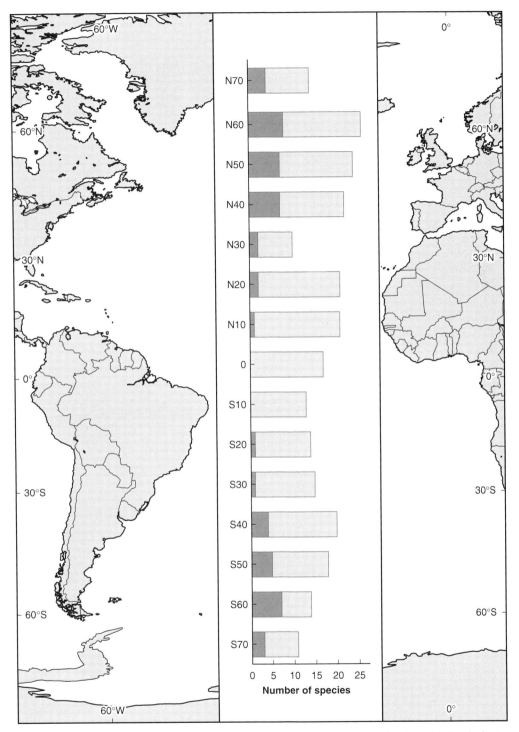

Figure 5.1 Trends in species diversity with latitude in the Atlantic Ocean: note that surface divers (darker shading) are relatively uncommon in low latitudes and their representation is the main factor creating high diversity at the polar boundaries. Phalaropes, pelicans, sheathbills and predominantly inland species are omitted.

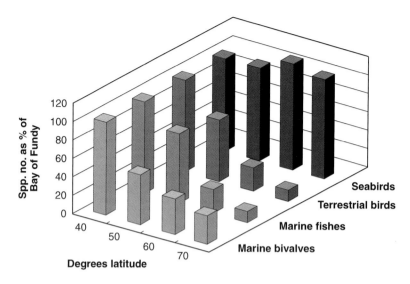

Figure 5.2   Trends in the species diversity of seabirds and other marine organisms in waters off eastern Canada.

EXPLAINING THE PATTERNS

It is tempting to relate the richness of seabird species breeding in cold-water regions to the greater productivity of cold continental shelf waters, compared to the clear waters of the deep tropical oceans. It is certainly true that enormous areas of the tropical oceans, being deep and strongly stratified, without significant sources of nutrient recycling, have a very low productivity and that the continental shelf waters, such as those off Britain, Newfoundland, the Pribilofs and the Falklands are immensely productive. However, the central Pacific supports more seabird species than the cold waters of the North Atlantic and the Prince Edward Islands, off South Africa, support as many breeders as the entire North Pacific.

Tropical coral reef systems and sea-grass beds are also highly productive, as are tropical estuaries and coastal lagoons. The continental shelf waters around Indonesia and in the China Sea support huge fisheries. The coasts of the Indian Peninsula, of Malaysia, Thailand, and Vietnam, are strung with lines of fishing villages where hundreds of thousands of people support themselves entirely from harvesting the sea. To a large extent, these coasts are barren of seabirds, except for some non-breeding terns and gulls. Overall, differences in productivity would seem to account for only a small part of the variation in diversity of breeding seabirds. If we set aside this explanation, there are a number of other factors that seem to be relevant.

1.   Geological and climatic history of the oceans.
2.   The distribution of potential breeding sites.
3.   Competition with and predation by other vertebrates, especially fish, perhaps to a lesser extent, marine mammals.
4.   Recent extinctions as a result of human colonisation.

I have listed human-induced extinctions last, but in fact we need to examine it first, because if the current distribution of species diversity is strongly affected by recent human activities, then any search for other causes based on current patterns would be futile.

POST-PLEISTOCENE EXTINCTIONS

About 10,000 years have elapsed since the end of the last major ice age. This is a relatively short period for extinctions. The background rate of species extinctions, outside of the periods of great extinctions, such as the end of the Silurian and Cretaceous periods, has been estimated at one per year for all plants and animals combined, or 0.00002% per annum. Hence, with a global diversity of only 300 species, we might have expected no more than one species of seabird to be extirpated in the 10,000 years. In fact, as with other birds, extinctions of seabirds since the Pleistocene have occurred at a much higher rate (May *et al.*, 1995).

The majority of birds that have become extinct since the end of the most recent glaciation, and most of those currently considered threatened with extinction, were or are endemic to one or a small number of island groups. They were killed off by introduced predators or competitors because, having evolved for a long time without them, they were unable to cope with the shock of their arrival. Cats, stoats, rats, pigs and tree snakes have been the most destructive introductions. With many seabirds confined to one or a few remote islands, and being similarly poorly adapted to coping with terrestrial predators, we might expect that seabirds would have been strongly affected by the same introductions. As well, most being edible and of a suitable size for human consumption, the impact of people themselves should have been substantial.

We actually know of four historically attested seabird extinctions (i.e. birds described by science before they disappeared): Great Auk, Labrador Duck, Spectacled Cormorant and Guadalupe Storm-petrel (the last could possibly still survive, but was not recorded in the 20th century). All had extremely restricted distributions when they became known to science. The most widespread was the Great Auk, which still existed in Newfoundland and Iceland (possibly Greenland) in the 18th century, at the time of its description by Linnaeus. The remainder were confined to smaller areas. The Great Auk and Labrador Duck were wiped out directly by human harvesting, while the Guadalupe Storm-petrel, confined to its eponymous island, was probably a victim of introduced cats and rats. The fate of the Spectacled Cormorant, known certainly only from Bering Island and the Commander Islands, off Kamchatka, is unclear, though harvesting by hungry seamen or fox-trappers seems the most likely cause.

We know about pre-historic extinctions only through finding fossils, or subfossil remains, but because many seabirds live on very remote, little-known islands, it is likely that our information on such extinctions is very incomplete. A few islands have been fairly well investigated and we need to extrapolate from these.

SOME ISLAND STORIES: ATLANTIC

In the Mediterranean islands, subject to human occupation for many thousands of years, the rather complete fossil records have revealed no unknown seabird species from the post-Pleistocene period (Alcover *et al.*, 1992), though Great Auks are known from at least two sites. Nor are any extinctions known from the Atlantic seaboard of western Europe or from other parts of the North Atlantic, except for at least one extinct shearwater among fossil remains in the Canaries (Walker *et al.*, 1990); all these are areas where a good deal of palaeontological research has been undertaken.

The more distant oceanic islands of the Atlantic were mainly uninhabited until the great age of European merchant voyages commenced in the late-15th century. Some subsequently became occupied by farming populations, while others were so small and remote that they never supported more than temporary groups of sealers or naval shore-stations. A sampling illustrates the evidence for human effects on seabirds.

The Azores, 38°N and 1,500 km from Portugal, were settled by the Portuguese in the 16th century and have been inhabited ever since. They have been subject to the introduction of practically all human camp-followers, including cats, dogs, rats and rabbits. Ten species of seabirds currently breed in the islands, mostly on small offshore islets. One other species may breed occasionally and one probably bred previously. There is no evidence for loss of species now extinct (Monteiro *et al.*, 1996).

Further south, close to the equator, the rather barren Ascension Island was famed for its seabird 'fairs' from earliest times. Discovered by the Portuguese in 1501, it supported rats and mice by 1775. It was permanently colonised by people in 1815, when cats also arrived. The island currently supports 11 seabirds, mostly on Boatswain Bird Island, a small islet 220 m from the main island, which has not been reached by rats or cats. Despite substantial investigation of subfossil remains, no species that are not currently present have been identified (Stonehouse, 1962).

The very remote island of St. Helena, at 16°S, was first visited by Portuguese merchant adventurers in 1502. From 1659, the island was permanently inhabited: goats, cattle, pigs, cats and rats all became established over time. Unfortunately, there are no records of birds from the island until 1817. Subsequently, there have been some rather thorough investigations of fossil and subfossil deposits on the island (Rowlands *et al.*, 1998). Three species of extinct seabirds that probably were endemic to the island have been identified: a shearwater (*Puffinus pacificoides*), a gadfly petrel (*Pterodroma rupinarum*) and a petrel (*Bulweria bifax*). In addition, a shearwater, a booby, two frigatebirds and a storm-petrel no longer breed, although present elsewhere in the Atlantic. The island retains nine species of seabirds, from an original complement of at least 17 species. At a similar latitude and 1,100 km from the coast of Brazil, Isla Trindade is a much less disturbed island. Being far from most trade routes and sometimes without permanent surface water, it has never been inhabited and still supported large numbers of seabirds into the 20th century. There has been little ornithological investigation, but it seems likely that the eight species of seabirds found by Murphy (1915) in 1912 were representative of the original avifauna.

In contrast with the rather drastic changes that occurred at St. Helena, the Tristan da Cunha group, further south in the South Atlantic, suffered much less. The islands were again discovered by the Portuguese, in 1506, but though some sealers spent a long time ashore from 1790, there was no permanent settlement until 1811, and then only on Tristan itself. The first scientific collection of birds was made in 1816. The outlying islands of Inaccessible and Nightingale, and more distant Gough, were never colonised by people. As far as is known, no mammals made it ashore on Nightingale and only House Mice *Mus musculus* on Gough (Wace & Holdgate, 1976). In consequence, the island group supports 22 species of seabirds and there is no evidence that any have been lost.

SOME ISLAND STORIES: PACIFIC

The Hawaiian archipelago is very rich in seabirds. Prior to the arrival of people, the islands also supported a rich fauna of endemic landbirds, many of which are known to have become extinct subsequent to the arrival of Polynesians, and thereafter the Europeans. However, among 32 species of extinct non-passerine birds described from Hawaii by Olson & James (1991), only one, a small gadfly petrel *Pterodroma jugabilis*, was a seabird. At Henderson Island, in the Pitcairn group, at least five seabirds that no longer breed there occurred and apparently bred prior to human colonisation. However, all were species that still breed on other islands of the group: no extinct endemics were reported (Wragg, 1995).

In New Zealand, there has been extensive investigation of middens created by the bird-hunting Maori colonists soon after their arrival in the islands, as well as other fossil deposits. They provide good evidence that many species now restricted to offshore islands bred on the main islands prior to the arrival of people and their commensal animals. On North Island, these included two shearwaters, a diving-petrel, a *Procellaria*, a prion, two gadfly petrels and at least three storm-petrels. The list for South Island is similar. Most of the losses from North Island took place prior to the arrival of Europeans (5/8 species), whereas most of those on South Island (6/9 species) took place since European contact. However, only one species found from post-Pleistocene deposits, the shearwater *Puffinus spelaeus*, became globally extinct.

New Zealand is remarkable in having two species of tubenosed birds still breeding inland on the main islands. This situation was originally possible because of the absence of any mammalian predators before the arrival of the Polynesian colonists. The two species still breeding on the main islands, the Westland Black Petrel and Hutton's Shearwater, are both decreasing and listed as threatened by BirdLife International (2000). Otherwise, the only tubenoses breeding inland on large continents or islands do so in the Atacama Desert of South America or in Antarctica.

SOME ISLAND STORIES: SUBPOLAR

The great seabird citadels of the subantarctic islands have never been permanently colonised by people, though sealers, whalers and later scientists, have constructed semi-permanent bases on some. Their winter climates are inimical to most terrestrial vertebrates so that, although the huge breeding populations of seabirds may provide inexhaustible food resources in summer, predator populations may be prevented from becoming truly established by the problem of winter survival.

Unfortunately, on some islands, rabbits were also introduced. These excellent grazing machines survived on Marion Island and the Crozet archipelago, providing alternative food for cats and allowing the cats to sustain high numbers, with very adverse consequences for the seabirds. Rats, which got ashore on most islands as a result of sealing activities, also provide an alternative food for cats (e.g. on the Auckland Islands). Despite all these problems, extirpations on the subantarctic islands seem to have been few. No seabird species are known to have become extinct since the arrival of Europeans. King Penguins, extirpated from some subantarctic islands by sealers, have subsequently recolonised most. On Amsterdam Island, ten out of 19 breeding seabirds were extirpated (Worthy & Jouventin, 1999), but none has become globally extinct. In the Aleutian Islands, deliberate introduction of Arctic Foxes *Alopex lagopus*, a very hardy and adaptable predator, for fur farming, led to the local extirpation of many seabird populations, but again, no species are known to have become extinct as a result (Bailey & Kaiser, 1993).

In addition to actual extinctions, several species came very close, especially the two gadfly petrels, the Chatham Island Taiko and the Cahow of Bermuda. Both were considered extinct before being rediscovered in the past 50 years. Both remain extremely vulnerable, with populations of fewer than 200 birds. Another two gadfly petrels, MacGillivray's Petrel and Beck's Petrel are known from birds collected and sighted at sea, but their breeding areas have not been located. Both occur in the western tropical Pacific, from where little archaeological or palaeontological evidence is available. There appears to be a strong likelihood that some, perhaps many, seabird species disappeared from this area during the original human colonisation, 3,000–4,000 years ago. The same may apply to the myriad islands of the Southeast Asian archipelagos, although sea-level changes during the Pleistocene connected most islands making them accessible to terrestrial mammals, so extinctions may have occurred early in the Pleistocene.

Overall, the evidence available from post-Pleistocene fossils suggests that, while losses of island populations were widespread, there may not have been many species extinctions. Probably some seabirds of remote Pacific islands became extinct in the wake of the Polynesian expansion, especially in the southwest Pacific. Unnoticed extinctions following the arrival of Europeans are less likely. Early European explorations in the Pacific were generally accompanied by naturalists (e.g. Steller with Bering, and Banks, the Forsters, father and son, with Cook) and thus most species would have been recorded prior to there being much European impact. Though seabirds of the Pacific undoubtedly suffered some losses that have not yet been (and may never be) identified, it seems that they were probably not sufficient to account for current patterns of variation in species numbers. In addition, it seems that the composition of the post-Pleistocene seabird fauna in cold waters of the northern hemisphere is pretty well represented by current and recently extinct species.

GEOLOGICAL HISTORY OF THE OCEANS

The distribution of land and sea has changed enormously during the Earth's history, as has the global climate. However, most extant seabird groups date back only as far as the early Tertiary, roughly the past 60 million years, and we probably need to look no further than this in assessing the impact of geological and climatic changes on seabird distributions. Three dramatic changes during the Tertiary must have had profound effects on seabird distributions: the disappearance of the extensive Tethys Sea that stretched from the Mediterranean through the Middle East to northern India for the first half of the Tertiary; the opening and subsequent closure of connections between the Atlantic and Pacific through Central America; and the fluctuations of sea level that exposed large areas of the Bering Sea, the North Sea and the Sunda Shelf during parts of the Pleistocene, and hugely increased the area of certain offshore islands, later drowning some when sea levels rose beyond their current position.

When considering seabird distributions, the most important geographical distinction among islands is whether or not they ever had land connections to continental areas. Continental shelf islands, such as Britain, the Japanese archipelago, Sri Lanka and Tasmania were connected regularly with adjacent landmasses during periods of lowered sea levels in the Pleistocene. Consequently, they support a diverse fauna of mammalian predators, as well as raptors, corvids and other potential predators of seabirds. On the other hand, island groups like Hawaii, New Zealand, the Galápagos and the Seychelles were never connected to continents during the Pleistocene. Although New Zealand is a fragment of the original Gondwana continent, it separated prior to the appearance of the first mammals, creating a separate zoological realm in which, until the arrival of the Polynesians, birds were kings.

When we examine the distribution of those seabirds that breed only on a single island or archipelago, we find that the majority are restricted to islands that were never connected to continents, especially those remote from other islands, such as the Galápagos, the Hawaiian archipelago, Tristan de Cunha, the Mascarene Islands, or the Juan Fernández group (Figure 5.3). The remoteness of these archipelagos allowed their breeding seabirds to maintain discrete populations continuously through the Pleistocene, when the species of continental shelf islands were being shunted from place to place by changes in sea level.

It is certainly the absence of land bridges, rather than remoteness itself, that has determined the existence of seabird endemics. Where non-land bridge islands occur close to continents (e.g. some of the Channel Islands of California, islands in the Sea of Cortez) they may support endemics, whereas islands further offshore but connected by Pleistocene land bridges do not (islands in the Gulf of Panama, Trinidad and Tobago, islands off Guinea Bissau, etc.). The absence of endemic seabirds from Indonesia can be contrasted with the occurrence of two species on tiny Christmas Island, only 500 km from Java, but separated from it by the deep Java Trench. On the other hand, off New Zealand,

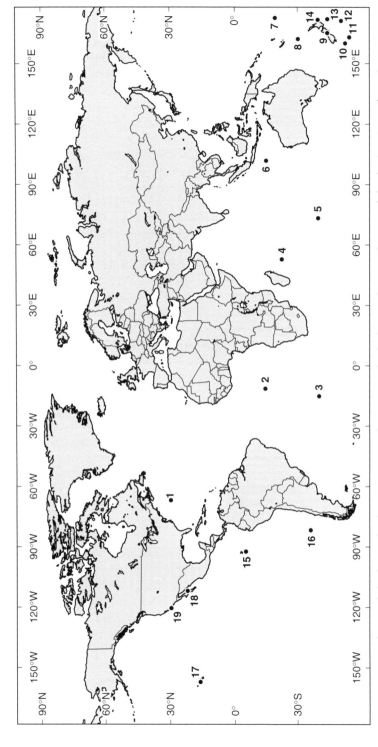

Figure 5.3   Distribution of islands or archipelagos supporting endemic species of seabirds (never known to have nested elsewhere): 1: Bermuda; 2: Ascension; 3: Tristan da Cunha; 4: Mascarene Islands; 5: Amsterdam Island; 6: Christmas Island (Indian Ocean); 7: Fiji; 8: Norfolk Island; 9: South Island: New Zealand; 10: Auckland Island; 11: Campbell Island; 12: Antipodes Island; 13: Chatham Islands; 14: Little Barrier Island and Mercury Islands; 15: Galápagos Islands; 16 Juan Fernández Islands; 17 Hawaii; 18: Sea of Cortez; 19: California Channel Islands.

many islands connected to the main islands during the Pleistocene continue to have endemic seabirds (Little Barrier Island, the Mercury Islands), because New Zealand supported no mammalian predators.

Looking at a map of the oceans, it is clear that the tropical Pacific, at least in parts, is dotted with many more island groups than equivalent areas of the Atlantic and Indian Oceans. The mobility of seabirds makes isolation on different islands less conducive to speciation than it would be for landbirds, but there is no doubt that being dispersed over more islands in the Pacific gives greater potential for speciation there than in the other tropical oceans.

The cold northern oceans are dotted with many island groups, but the huge transformations that occurred during the Pleistocene, which included a land bridge connecting Asia and North America, also connected most islands in the Bering Sea, the Sea of Okhotsk, the Aleutian chain and the Gulf of Alaska. This reduced the isolation of many potential breeding sites, while allowing access to them for many potential predators. Through an accident of the relationship of sea level to the continental margins, the number of islands connected to continents or larger islands by lowered sea level during the Pleistocene greatly exceeded the number created by the same changes. Islands off Britain, Norway and eastern North America, where not connected by land bridges, were in any case glaciated and rendered uninhabitable at some point during glacial maxima.

In contrast with the northern cold oceans, few of the islands of the cold southern ocean were connected to continents during the Pleistocene. The relative stability of the land–ocean configuration in the southern ocean during the Pleistocene seems to explain at least part of the greater seabird diversity observed there. This is also supported by the fact that pre-Pleistocene seabird faunas in the North Atlantic seem to have been substantially more diverse than they are at present.

COMPETITION WITH AND PREDATION BY OTHER VERTEBRATES

All pelagic birds, from albatrosses to phalaropes . . . necessarily rest and sleep on the water. Beneath the surface are hidden various predators, from barracuda to killer whales. What means do seabirds have, if any, for coping with the danger these underwater predators present?

Louis Halle, *British Birds*, 1971

If there had been polar bears in the Antarctic, as in the Arctic, there would surely not be penguins there . . .

Louis Halle, *The Sea and the Ice*, 1973

We can obtain evidence on the role of recent extinctions in seabird distributions by looking at the archaeological and fossil records, and the role of island distributions can be assessed merely by inspecting a map. The influence of competition and especially predation is much harder to judge. This is true for most birds, but especially so for seabirds. A small gull taken by a large fish could vanish in a second, leaving nothing but a spreading ripple. No trace might ever be visible of a penguin swallowed underwater by a shark. Halle's question remains largely unanswered. We do not know what action seabirds take to protect themselves or how often their evasion fails. Individual incidents of predation may be observed, such as this anecdote by Murphy (1915) of shark predation off Isla Trindade: "A booby which we had shot and wounded, so that it fell in the water, first had its legs bitten off, and was then devoured in one morsel."

My own experience includes observations of a lone Walrus *Odobenus rosmarus* hunting Thick-billed Murres below the colony cliffs at Coats Island. The walrus swam rapidly (for a walrus) underwater at a depth of 1–2 m and surfaced beside unwary murres, bearing down on them with jaws agape. Most murres saw the walrus coming and apparently discerned its evil intent, presumably when they dipped their heads beneath the surface. Less than 5% of those at which the walrus took aim failed to escape. Of those taken, several were engaged in preening or bathing and hence presumably less vigilant than most. Yet with hundreds gathered in the confines of the cove, the walrus caught eight in 40 minutes, dismembering them and finally swallowing them. My colleague Kerry Woo had seen similar attacks the previous year, but the animal involved was different. How often do walrus take murres? It is impossible to know, but dense feeding aggregations of murres occur frequently in summer within reach of walruses.

Many accounts suggest that predation by sharks and other predatory fishes, by Killer Whales *Orcinus orca* and by seals and sea lions is widespread and may be important, at least locally (e.g. Randall & Randall, 1990; Williams *et al.*, 1990). The Leopard Seal *Hydrurga leptonyx*, in particular, takes a great diversity of seabirds and specialises in penguins (Riedman, 1990). However, the ocean is so large, the potential predators and competitors are so diverse and seabirds are potentially so long-lived, that determining the population consequences of a scattering of such observations must be highly speculative.

THE ABSENCE OF PURSUIT DIVERS FROM THE TROPICS

The most compelling piece of evidence that interactions with fish, either as predators or competitors, or both, has played a significant role in the distribution of seabirds, is the remarkable lack of surface-diving seabirds in the tropics. The two pre-eminent families of underwater swimmers, the auks and the penguins, are pinned against the poles in their respective hemispheres. Auks comprise approximately 30% of seabird biomass in the Chukchi Sea and the waters of the Canadian high arctic, while penguins comprise more than 90% of seabird biomass breeding on the Antarctic continent. These families have only slight representation in tropical and subtropical waters, with three species of auks breeding in Baja California and one in the Yellow Sea of China, but with very small populations. Penguins reach the Galápagos, where a single threatened species exists, and the Humboldt Penguin comes close to the equator in Peru in the cold waters of the Humboldt Current.

Cormorants, likewise, though well represented in tropical freshwater habitats, are absent from the marine environments off the Atlantic coast of Brazil, from the Bay of Bengal and from much of Southeast Asia, from almost the entire east coast of Africa and from the whole coast of tropical West Africa. It is striking that marine cormorants *are* present in all areas occupied by the *Spheniscus* penguins. We could argue that the areas where cormorants are absent must be areas where fish are difficult to find, but if that is the case, we need to explain why these same areas support an abundance of terns (ten marine species in Southeast Asia, for example). We could also argue that the clear waters of the tropics make it difficult for cormorants to sneak up on their prey: it may be that very clarity that makes conditions so suitable for the plunge-diving or surface-snatching terns. However, many cormorants feed in waters very close to shore, where wave action stirs up sediments: visibility there will be no better than in similar subpolar waters.

As I mentioned at the outset, there is no definitive test of whether food, competition or predation accounts for the exclusion of auks and penguins and the near exclusion of cormorants, from tropical seas. It may well be a combination of all three. As Cairns (1992) pointed out, the 'burst speed' (short-distance escape speed) of fishes increases with water temperature, making them more difficult for pursuit divers to catch, and making predatory fish (sharks, tuna) more formidable threats. Seals are similarly absent from large areas of the tropical oceans, perhaps for the same reasons. Certainly sharks pose a significant threat both to penguins and seals. Whatever the cause, the disadvantages of life in the tropics for pursuit-diving seabirds have been sufficient to prevent auks, for 25 million years, and penguins, for 50 million years, from establishing themselves in the opposite hemisphere: no fossils of either family have yet to be discovered outside their respective ranges.

THE EFFECT OF MAMMALIAN PREDATORS

Louis Halle's comment on polar bears, at the head of this section, is just as unverifiable as my own speculations concerning tropical absences, but it is very striking that the habit of breeding on low, flat islands exhibited by Common Murres in places like Newfoundland and that the California Gull is entirely absent within the range of the Polar Bear. Instead, murres of both species breed exclusively on cliffs, as do all other surface-nesting colonial seabirds in those regions.

The wisdom of breeding on cliffs in the arctic was vividly illustrated a few years ago when a female Polar Bear and her cub arrived at a colony of Common Eiders on a small, flat islet off Southampton Island. In a few days, under the horrified gaze of the three women who had been hired to observe the breeding of the eiders, the bears proceeded to eat 3,000 eider eggs, before wandering off in, one presumes, a constipated stupor. According to my colleague, Grant Gilchrist, this is a common event at arctic eider colonies.

Nor is it sufficient to nest on any old cliff. Polar Bears are amazingly agile, for such large animals. For years, we observed Thick-billed Murres on a breeding cliff at Coats Island in northern Hudson Bay. We sat in our little wooden blinds wedged against the cliffs, believing ourselves secure from the bears. Then one year Kerry Woo arrived at the colony to find a small Polar Bear (and small is relative here, it would have been very large if it had been a Black Bear *Ursus americanus*!) comfortably ensconced on the cliff and systematically harvesting murre eggs and chicks. This experience taught us that any cliff where we could descend without ropes was also accessible to bears. It came as quite a shock.

It is equally noteworthy that the flightless Great Auk, confined, inevitably, to breeding areas accessible from the water on foot, did not breed within the normal range of Polar Bears. Moreover, Atlantic Puffins breeding in bear-prone areas tend to occupy crevice nests, rather than burrows, perhaps as an insurance against being dug out. In Arctic Russia, Polar Bears have been observed actively digging for Little Auks nesting in rocky screes (Stempniewicz, 1993).

At the other pole, it is noteworthy that obligate cliff-nesting species are absent. The great aggregations of murres and kittiwakes, clustered on precipitous cliffs, that are such a striking feature of the arctic, have no counterparts in the southern hemisphere. Antarctic Fulmars and Antarctic Petrels do breed on cliffs in places, but often they occupy slopes that would be easily accessible to mammalian predators, were any to occur. These birds, like all southern ocean seabirds, are confined to islands free of terrestrial predators and to the mammal-less Antarctic continent. Penguins, being flightless, cannot make use of precipitous cliffs. This fact alone would seem to exclude them from many parts of the northern hemisphere currently dominated by the ecological counterparts, the murres.

CONVERGENCE AND CO-EVOLUTION

A long-standing argument among evolutionary biologists concerns the relative importance of adaptation and chance historical events in determining the composition of a given community of animals. Some researchers consider that adaptation has been dominant, pointing to the convergent similarities between communities that evolved under similar ecological conditions (e.g. penguins in the southern hemisphere, auks in the northern hemisphere). Others are more impressed by differences among such communities and consider that chance historical events will usually obscure the effects of convergent adaptations. This argument has other implications, because if co-existing animal communities are just chance assemblages of species, competition among species cannot have played an important role in their formation.

Seabirds provide some excellent examples of communities concentrated in well-defined marine areas of comparable ecology situated far apart. Their great powers of flight and the nomadic habits of many species suggest that they are a group very unlikely to be affected by barriers to dispersal. Hence, they provide a good potential illustration of the adaptation versus chance debate and I shall attempt to illuminate it using three 'boundary upwelling' zones created by the predictable offshore winds of the trade-wind latitudes off the coasts of California, Peru and Namibia (Figure 5.4).

The boundary upwellings cause a regular enhancement of biological production in the surface waters by bringing deeper, nutrient-rich water into the zone where sunlight enables phytoplankton to make use of it. Hence, food for seabirds in upwelling zones tends to be highly concentrated compared to most marine areas and the boundary upwellings support very large seabird populations, both residents and non-breeding visitors. Table 5.3 shows the composition of the seabird faunas found in these three boundary upwelling areas.

The lists certainly have some notable similarities. However, most continental coasts with suitable breeding sites would support at least one gull and cormorant species and the cold upwelling accounts for the presence of the otherwise polar penguins and auks. Moreover, California and Peru are not far

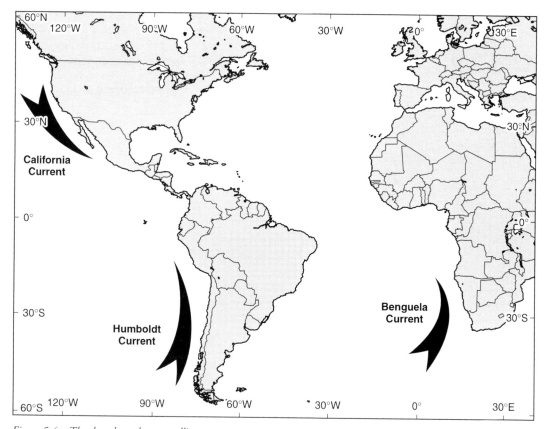

Figure 5.4   The three boundary upwelling zones.

Table 5.3   Seabird species characteristic of the boundary upwelling zones (i.e. those occurring in much greater abundance than in nearby non-upwelling areas)

Species	California	Humboldt	Benguela
Resident	Common Murre	Humboldt Penguin	African Penguin
	Brandt's Cormorant	Guanay Cormorant	Cape Cormorant
	Pelagic Cormorant	Red-legged Cormorant	Bank Cormorant
	Cassin's Auklet	Peruvian Booby	Cape Gannet
	Western Gull	Peruvian Diving-petrel	Kelp Gull
	Brown Pelican	Brown Pelican	
		Band-tailed Gull	
Non-breeding	Black-footed Albatross	Waved Albatross	Black-browed Albatross
	Sooty Shearwater	Black-browed Albatross	Red Phalarope
	Pink-footed Shearwater	Sooty Shearwater	Hartlaub's Gull
	Phalarope spp.	Red-necked Phalarope	Sabine's Gull
	Bonaparte's Gull	Franklin's Gull	Long-tailed Skua
	Pomarine Jaeger	Pomarine Jaeger	
	Rhinoceros Auklet		

apart and in years of strong upwelling (La Niña) the cold waters of the Humboldt Current virtually connect with those of the California Current, so similarity in fauna is unsurprising. The most convergent features of these communities appear to be that all three areas have endemic cormorants (Guanay, Bank and Brandt's) and all three are principal wintering areas for northern-hemisphere phalaropes and jaegers. All are commonly visited by non-breeding albatrosses, otherwise uncommon at those latitudes. My own opinion is that these lists provide modest, but useful, support for the hypothesis that similar oceanographic features will support similar seabird faunas, but you decide.

CONCLUSIONS

Given that different continents frequently support different families of birds, it should not surprise us that the proportional representation of the different seabird families varies among oceans. Perhaps, given their great mobility, we should be more surprised that all seabird families are not ubiquitous. However, the relative distribution of surface and sub-surface feeders, especially the virtual absence of surface-diving birds from the tropics, raises a more interesting question and one that can only be answered with speculation. In my opinion predation by fishes must play a role in their absence.

Halle's comment about bears and penguins cannot be turned around to explain the absence of penguins from the northern hemisphere, because Polar Bears evolved only in the Pleistocene, so there were tens of millions of years in which they posed no threat to ground-nesting seabirds. Can a fleet of sharks, patrolling the tropical seas, have denied penguins access to the rich feeding grounds of the northern hemisphere for the whole of the Tertiary epoch? It hardly seems possible, yet despite their mastery of the aquatic medium, the penguins never came, leaving us with further opportunity to exercise our imagination. It is the license to speculate that makes zoogeography such a fascinating playground for the scientist who is not totally wedded to the experimental method.

CHAPTER SIX

Feeding behaviour

As touching our first signs, the nearer we came to Africa the more strange kinds of fowls appeared, insomuch that when we came within no less than thirty leagues (almost a hundred miles) as we thought from any island, as good as three thousand fowls of sundry kinds followed our ship . . . A marvellous thing to see how God provided so that in so wide a sea these fowls are all fat and nothing wanteth them.

Thomas Stevens, on a voyage to Goa, 1579,
from *Hakluyt's Voyages* (David, 1981: 127)

I have not been privileged to be part of any great scientific discoveries. Even the trifling new knowledge that my own research has brought to light has generally emerged painstakingly through the gradual accumulation of facts that eventually resolved themselves into some pattern that had not previously been evident. Seabird ecology does not provide many Eureka! moments.

If there was an exception to this generalisation, it would have to be the day that Don Croll downloaded the first time-depth gauge that he deployed on a murre. Actually, it was the first time-depth gauge deployed on any auk that would give full details of individual dive profiles.

The bird involved, like all of the birds that Don used, was selected for the convenience of its breeding site and its apparently equable temperament. Indeed, these birds had to have a very sweet disposition, because the process of attaching the gauge required shaving the feathers from a section of their backs, then gluing on the device that weighed nearly 30 g with epoxy glue, which generates heat in setting. The entire process took more than ten minutes. Once released, the bird returned to its breeding site for several hours before being relieved of brooding duty by its mate. It left immediately and was away from the colony for about 12 hours. Don recaptured it as soon as it returned and removed the gauge.

The device was potted in solid acrylic. To expose the terminals and extract the depth information stored on the memory chip, Don had to saw off the end of the block with a hacksaw. Fine wires were then attached to the terminals and the information was downloaded to Don's laptop. However, we had no way to read out the binary code in which the information was stored. To do this, we had to print it, and a minor glitch occurred because Don could not remember the DOS command to print a file. Luckily, being from an older generation of computer users, I did.

The Eureka moment came as the data began to spill off the printer in hexadecimal code. The device had been programmed to switch on when it first submerged below two metres, so the data began immediately with the first dive profile. As the little battery-driven dot matrix printer clicked out the codes, Don translated them into numbers: 20m, 23m, 27m . . . 82m, 86m . . . . As the depth of the dive approached 100m, Don turned to us and used a word of which his mother would hardly have approved. "This is so . . . hot!", he said.

It was true. Our views of the diving abilities of auks and of murres in particular, were forever changed in that moment and Don's information remained the only detailed data on dive profiles in auks for nearly a decade: a rather small step for mankind as a whole, perhaps, but a significant step for seabird science. Even today, how seabirds locate their food and how they pursue and capture it, is one of the areas where least is known. It is also one of the most fascinating parts of the seabird story.

SPACE AND TIME

The distribution of food can be patchy in space and in time. In either case it may be more or less predictable, depending on the way in which patches are formed. An idea that has appeared frequently in discussions of those adaptations that constitute the seabird syndrome is that seabirds' food may be patchier and less predictable than that of typical landbirds. The argument is that food is more difficult to obtain because of patchiness and seabirds therefore must spend longer to find the same amount, reducing their provisioning abilities and constraining the number of chicks that they can rear. But if food is difficult to obtain, how is it there are so many seabirds?

In reality, it is very hard to compare patchiness in marine and terrestrial environments. How many trees must a woodpecker drill to find a grub? How often does a hornbill find a fruiting fig? How often does the crop of spruce cones fail, leaving the crossbills to range far and wide? The likelihood that a woodpecker encounters a grub in any particular tree may be no more predictable than the likelihood that a gannet will find a school of mackerel in any particular bay along the coast. The assertion that resources for seabirds are patchier or less predictable than those for landbirds really needs to be qualified in terms of the scale in time and space. What is certainly true is that a gannet will travel farther than a woodpecker between successful encounters because fish schools are much more dispersed than trees in a forest (put another way, woodpeckers do not live in areas where trees are as sparse as fish schools). That travel takes time.

Another difference between the woodpecker and the gannet is that trees stand still, at least relative to the lives of woodpeckers. Conversely, the fish schools that gannets seek move. The place where they were abundant yesterday may be barren today, so gannets have to adjust their search hour by hour, day by day, whereas woodpeckers know that the tree where they succeeded yesterday will be there again today.

Hence, compared with terrestrial environments, the availability of prey in the marine environment varies much more over short periods of time and tends to be much less predictable (Haury *et al.*, 1978; Gaston & Brown, 1991). The herding of large predatory fishes and marine mammals may cause aggregations of forage fishes to form and disperse on a scale of minutes (Safina & Burger, 1988). For marine predators, this puts a premium on mobility.

Many seabirds travel constantly, in response to changes in weather and food supply. The fact that food patches are frequently far apart requires them to search enormous areas to be sure of finding them. Hence, many specialised seabirds, especially the petrels and albatrosses, travel long distances in search of food. Their highly efficient soaring and gliding flight enables them to do so at little more cost in energy than they would expend sitting on a log going nowhere. Minimising flight costs has been an essential strategy in allowing birds to exploit the broad expanses of the ocean beyond continental margins (see Chapter 3).

However, when a patch, such as a shoal of fish at the surface, or a dead whale, is located, the food may be very easy to obtain and the birds gorge themselves until they can scarcely take off. Compared to many landbirds, therefore, seabirds are more accustomed to alternations between feast and famine.

FOOD REQUIREMENTS

Warm-blooded marine animals, especially those inhabiting cold waters, need to find a great deal of food daily to satisfy their basic metabolic needs. Among auks, Common Murres need to find *c*.40% of their body weight in fresh weight of food daily. The Least Auklet needs to find about 75% of body weight.

Moreover, compared to marine mammals, seabirds do not carry large energy reserves relative to their rate of expenditure. Thick-billed Murres wintering off Newfoundland were estimated to have only 3–4 days of energy reserves in peak condition (Gaston *et al.*, 1983b); Common Murres during breeding carry only 1.5–2.5 days of energy reserves (Gabrielson, 1994). Because they are larger and do not need to fly, penguins can store much more fat then auks. They frequently fast for weeks while breeding or moulting. Accounts of Great Auks stress how 'excessively fat and oily' they were (Hardy, 1888), suggesting that the elimination of flight in the species allowed it to maintain much larger fat reserves than those of flying relatives.

If their prey was evenly dispersed at sea, many seabirds might have a hard time making a living. Simple calculations suggest that prey densities of at least 100x the average are necessary for profitable foraging by auks (i.e. energy gained in foraging exceeds energy expended; Brown, 1980). Seabirds have developed several strategies for dealing with this problem. Those that are less mobile, or those for which flight is energetically expensive, cannot forage everywhere in the ocean, but must concentrate in areas where their prey is suitably clumped. This accounts for why cormorants and auks are mainly confined to continental shelf waters, where marine productivity is generally an order of magnitude higher than in deeper oceanic waters. They are especially associated with areas of predictably high prey availability, such as tidal upwelling zones.

PREDICTABILITY

Inshore-feeding penguins, auks, cormorants and diving-petrels, generally forage in predictable feeding areas from day to day. Cairns (1987b), studying Black Guillemots in northeastern Hudson Bay, found that birds regularly returned to localised feeding areas throughout the chick-rearing period. In the Quoddy region of New Brunswick, the pattern of foraging Black Guillemots was similarly predictable and determined by tidal cycles (Nol & Gaskin, 1987), while in waters around Haida Gwaii, British Columbia, Marbled Murrelets occur in the same nearshore waters annually.

The need for predictable food supplies means that many seabirds take advantage of permanent food concentrations, in the form of current rips (turbulence, upwelling, convergence, etc.) that concentrate prey, or bring slow-swimming organisms closer to the surface than usual. Such features occur especially off headlands, among islands, and in areas of very uneven bottom topography, and in association with strong tidal currents (Schneider *et al.*, 1990). Examples of multi-species concentrations at this type of upwelling occur among the Aleutian passes, especially Akutan and Baby passes, where up to 12 species of seabirds occur, including hundreds of thousands of Short-tailed Shearwaters and similar numbers of auklets (Hoffman *et al.*, 1981); aggregations of tens of thousands of Thick-billed Murres in the Nuvuk Islands of northeastern Hudson Bay (Cairns & Schneider, 1990) and off Cape Upright, St. Mathews Island (Hunt *et al.*, 1988); and of Ancient Murrelets in winter among the islands of the Strait of Juan de Fuca (Gaston *et al.*, 1993).

On a larger scale, the aggregation of Little Auks at the edge of the Newfoundland Banks in winter may result from similar upwelling processes (Brown, 1985) and the large numbers of seabirds breeding in boundary upwelling systems of California, Namibia and Peru discussed in Chapter 5, appear dependent on the enhanced productivity created by the cool upwellings. In years when the upwellings fail, as a result of the El Niño phenomenon, reproductive success is lower than normal (e.g. Ainley & Boekelheide, 1990) and in the case of the Peruvian upwelling, frequently fails completely (Duffy *et al.*, 1988).

Apart from the patchiness of their prey, how easily can seabirds locate those patches that are within their range? Hunt (1990) demonstrated that seabird abundance and the availability of prey, as measured by various acoustic methods, are not necessarily correlated at relatively small scales. This seems to be truer of planktivores than of fish-eaters (Russell *et al.*, 1992), though Woodby (1984) found little relationship between concentrations of murres and of patches of their potential prey in the eastern Bering Sea.

Given that people tend only to write about those studies that demonstrate some kind of effect (or journals only accept such papers), we may anticipate that the real relationship between seabird distributions and the abundance of their prey is weaker than published data suggest. In addition, studies matching the distributions of seabirds and prey depend on our ability to identify all the relevant prey and it is hard to be certain that this is always the case. Despite much time and effort devoted to mapping offshore seabird distributions, our ability to predict where and when seabirds will form dense concentrations away from predictable tidal upwellings is still poor. This means that, except in very limited areas, we may never know enough to be able to confidently predict in advance the consequences of an oil spill at a particular time and place.

HOW WE STUDY SEABIRD FEEDING

With most terrestrial birds it is possible to follow them to their feeding areas and observe them capturing and handling their prey. For those seabirds that capture their prey underwater, even if we can follow them to their feeding areas out at sea, we have very limited means of studying what they eat and how they capture it. Consequently, some consideration of the methods at our disposal is essential to understanding the limitations of current information.

Apart from their distributions, the behaviour of seabirds at sea has not been much studied. Most surveys from boats have concentrated on describing where different species occur, rather than what they are doing. Data on the type of behaviour being performed is hard to collect if you need to keep scanning the horizon as the ship moves forward. Because of this, observations of the proportion of time spent feeding and the length of time spent underwater have seldom been compiled for species that occur far offshore. Although information on numbers of birds seen flying and on the water has routinely been collected as part of most surveys at sea, it has not often been published.

The application of radio-telemetry (e.g. Wanless *et al.*, 1988) and especially satellite telemetry (e.g. Weimerskirch *et al.*, 1993, Jouventin *et al.*, 1994; Hull *et al.*, 1997, Weimerskirch & Guionnet, 2002) has recently begun to supply some of the missing information about how birds behave at sea. Another approach that has supplied information on behaviour at sea is the attachment of devices that record the accumulated time spent underwater, and on the surface, so that the time spent on different foraging activities can be determined (Cairns *et al.*, 1987; Cairns & Schneider, 1990; Falk *et al.*, 2000). However, the strategies and behaviour of birds at sea, especially in the deep ocean, is still an area that invites further research.

What diving seabirds do once they submerge was, for a long time, something of a mystery. It is easy to watch auks or penguins swimming in a large aquarium, but this is not likely to tell us much about the tactics that they adopt for foraging in the wild. This is a subject where wildlife photographers seem to have been ahead of researchers. Until recently, popular wisdom held that gannets used their plunge directly to secure prey, diving straight down on a fish and bobbing back to the surface immediately. It was only after someone put on scuba gear and went down with a camera that we realised that gannets swim actively and strongly once the momentum of their dive has petered out, like rather ungainly shearwaters. In films that I have seen, at least, they catch most fish after swimming some distance (this has now been described by Garthe *et al.*, 2000). Likewise, off Japan, sport divers brought back pictures of Streaked Shearwaters swimming underwater after making shallow plunge-dives: something not previously known to occur (Oka, 1994).

A National Geographic film on arctic wildlife showed a sequence of Thick-billed Murres rising to the surface after feeding at considerable depth. The birds came up towards the surface at amazing speed, their wings held against their sides, trailing streams of bubbles, which made them look like little rocket ships. Only later, using devices that monitor wingbeats, could we confirm that murres hardly swim as they return to the surface, apparently making use of buoyancy almost entirely. Unfortunately, filming is restricted to shallow depths where there is adequate light. What goes on at typical feeding depths for auks and penguins, where light levels may be very low, has not been observed.

In the last 20 years there has been much progress in developing devices that can record the depth and duration of dives. The simplest of these devices, a plain rubber tube open at one end and coated on the inside with icing sugar, records only the maximum dive depth (Burger & Simpson, 1986; Burger & Powell, 1990). An ingenious mechanism constructed from a small syringe used a light emitting diode, sliding backwards and forwards in response to water pressure, to fog a small patch of 35–mm film. The proportion of time spent at different depths could then be assessed on the basis of the density of fogging on the developed film (Wilson *et al.*, 1989). More recently, gauges have been developed using a combination of a depth transducer and a microchip to record depth at pre-set intervals after submersion, giving a detailed profile of each dive (e.g. Croll *et al.*, 1992; Watanuki *et al.*, 1993; Falk *et al.*, 2000). Such gauges are now available commercially and have become a routine research tool.

Recording devices attached to birds have the advantage that they make it possible to take a more random sample than might be obtained from birds drowned in nets, or shore-based observations. However, the attachments certainly affect the performance of the birds selected, in most cases to an unknown degree (Wilson *et al.*, 1986; Croll *et al.*, 1996). Moreover, thus far it has only proved feasible to deploy them on breeding birds that return regularly to their colony. This applies especially to devices that must be removed to be read. A consequence of all these restrictions is that, despite recent technological advances, much of what can be said about the underwater foraging of seabirds is by necessity based on inferences, rather than on direct observations.

HOW PREY IS LOCATED

SENSE OF SMELL

That tube-nosed birds can locate their food by smell has been known for a long time. Murphy (1936) relates this anecdote of the indefatigable bird collector, Rollo Beck:

> When Mr Beck was collecting for the American Museum of Natural History in Peru . . . he sailed several days' journey off shore. One quiet, gray morning, Beck remarked that he would like to lower a boat for birds.
> "But there are no birds here, señor", said the skipper . . .
> Nevertheless, a skiff was sent down and Captain Charlie manned the oars. For two miles he pulled straight ahead, while Beck methodically tossed flecks of oil and grease and scraps of meat in the boat's track. They then doubled on their course, and to Charlie's amazement the long food line was soon dotted with unfamiliar, dainty sea-sprites which skipped and danced like butterflies along a blossoming hedgerow. A series of many birds, including specimens of Hornby's Petrel was brought back to the sloop and displayed before the doubting crew.
> "But we have never before had such birds as these in Peru, señor", insisted the captain. And his men unanimously agreed. (Murphy, 1936: 8)

This anecdote illustrates two things about storm-petrels that strike anyone that looks for them: they are very thinly spread and hard to find, but they assemble quickly when any oily refuse is put overboard.

As referred to in Chapter 3, there is plenty of evidence that tubenoses, especially petrels and storm-petrels, can detect oily smells at sea and home in on them (e.g. Hutchinson & Wenzel, 1980). Tubenoses observed homing-in on a potential food source (usually a sponge soaked in cod-liver oil) by smell tend to exhibit a characteristic pattern of behaviour. Like hunting dogs, they zigzag backwards and forwards across the downwind scent trail, flying closer than normal to the sea surface and gradually reducing the zigzagging as they approach. Storm-petrels seem to be able to home-in from as far as 8 km away (Verheyden & Jouventin, 1994). Other species that have been shown to react to the scent of cod-liver oil include fulmars, giant petrels, shearwaters, Blue Petrel, Cape Petrel and White-chinned Petrel. No cormorants, gulls, terns or auks have exhibited an interest in cod-liver oil, but whether this means they do not smell it, or they just don't like it, we cannot be sure.

SOME CONSTRAINTS

BIRDS OF PREY AS SEABIRD PREDATORS

The firm determination of most oceanic seabirds, especially small species such as storm-petrels, to remain a minimum of several kilometres from land suggests that the threat from land-based falcons and eagles is considerable. Most seabird colonies along continental coasts are subject to predation or harassment by land-based birds of prey. The effect of this source of mortality is hard to gauge because raptor populations in many areas have been much depressed by human activities, either active extermination policies, as in the Scottish highlands, or pollution by organochlorine pesticides. However, there are many examples of heavy predation by raptors on breeding seabirds.

The Peregrine Falcon, a species found in every continent except Antarctica, takes birds up to nearly 1 kg in size and commonly hunts in open, coastal habitats. Coastal breeding Peregrines take seabirds throughout the species' range (e.g. Paine *et al.*, 1990), but the race *pealei*, found in the northern Pacific, specialises in capturing seabirds while it and they are breeding. In British Columbia, most breeding sites are situated in the Queen Charlotte Islands, the main breeding area for its most favoured prey, the Ancient Murrelet (Gaston, 1992). In the Aleutians, too, seabirds constitute the bulk of its diet in summer. Most Ancient Murrelets appear to be taken by Peregrines over open water. If, as sometimes happens, the murrelet is struck, but not gripped, in the first attack, the Peregrine has to pluck it from the sea. This is a much more difficult job than taking off from land with a carcass and probably limits the size of prey that can be attacked over the ocean.

Also in the North Pacific, Bald Eagles and Steller's Sea Eagles (Lobkov & Neufeldt, 1986) take many seabirds, including loons, auks, gulls and cormorants. Their presence may also deny seabirds many feeding opportunities. When herring shoals appear in the Hecate Strait, Glaucous-winged Gulls do not settle on the water to take the fish when eagles are present. If many eagles gather over a shoal (more than 20 is not uncommon), gulls stay well clear until the eagles have all obtained a fish and flown ashore to eat their catch. Only then do the gulls move in.

PIRATES

Birds that specialise in waiting for others to find food and then robbing them of it are known as kleptoparasites (they parasitise by stealing). This method of feeding is among landbirds, but is well developed in seabirds, with the frigatebirds, skuas, jaegers and some petrels resorting to the technique very frequently. In addition, many other seabirds, especially large gulls, are occasional kleptoparasites, with some individuals specialising in this type of behaviour. Some examples of kleptoparasitism show the range of parasites and victims (Table 6.1).

Kleptoparasitism makes sense in a situation where the victim can be quickly robbed of a substantial meal that might otherwise take a long time to find. There is no sense in devoting time and energy to chasing another bird if the reward is a grass seed. Many seabirds take fish, which are relatively large, high-energy, food packets, so chasing after them makes sense, even if it consumes lots of energy. Moreover, the lack of cover in the marine environment, means that victims cannot escape by hiding. Even swallowing the prey is not sufficient to deter a pursuer, because the extra weight reduces flight performance. In order to escape harassment, the victim must disgorge its stomach load, at which the parasite not only receives the meal, but has it pre-heated, not a negligible benefit in cold climates.

Table 6.1   Examples of kleptoparasitism on seabirds at sea

Parasite	Victim	Area	Success rate	Reference
Waved Albatross	Peruvian Booby	Peru	high	Duffy, 1980
Brown Pelican	Guanay Cormorant	Peru	?	Duffy, 1980
	Peruvian Booby	Peru	?	Duffy, 1980
Great Frigatebird	Red-footed Booby	Galápagos	12%	Nelson, 1975
Christmas Island Frigatebird	Red-footed Booby	Christmas Island	63%	Nelson, 1975
Roseate Tern	Common Tern	England	7%	Dunn, 1973b
Parasitic Jaeger	Black-legged Kittiwake	High Arctic	30%	AJG, pers. obs.
	Hartlaub's Gull	South Africa	25%	Furness, 1983
	Common Tern	South Africa	17%	Furness, 1983
	Common Tern	Scotland	5% (single attacking bird)	Taylor, 1979
	Sandwich Tern	Scotland	18% (single attacking bird)	Taylor, 1979
	Thick-billed Murre	Northern Hudson Bay	10% (only attempted over sea-ice)	AJG, pers. obs.
South Polar Skua	Blue-eyed Shag	Antarctic Peninsula	5% (>3.5 km from colony)	Maxson & Bernstein, 1982

SEABIRD PREDATORS

Although most seabirds are predators on fish and other marine life, few are regular predators of other seabirds, principally the large gulls, the skuas and the giant petrels. Moreover, even these regular predators confine most of their predatory activities to land. Predation by seabirds on other seabirds at sea appears to be unusual and opportunistic (e.g. in a scrum of birds behind a trawler), rather than systematic. However, we have to consider that predation events, especially on small seabirds such as auklets or storm-petrels, may be very rapid and therefore under-represented in typical seabird observations. Many albatrosses, especially sooty albatrosses, have been reported to eat small tubenoses, such as prions and diving petrels, although whether captured alive is not always known (Cherel & Klages, 1998).

At first sight, the apparent lack of predation at sea appears surprising, because most seabirds are built for endurance, rather than speed and some, especially the larger petrels and shearwaters, appear to lack manoeuvrability. In addition, the ocean affords nowhere to hide for species that cannot dive below the surface. It seems that there is a golden opportunity here for some seabird to give up fishing for a living and take to eating its fellow seabirds.

Part of the answer to this puzzling absence of offshore predators may be the difficulty that the predator would experience in dismembering prey at sea. Gulls open up a carcass on land by a series of vigorous pecks to the abdomen, interspersed with periods when the corpse is gripped and shaken to loosen the skin. At sea, the force of pecks delivered to a floating victim would be substantially reduced by the bobbing of the corpse, while partial immersion of the corpse would hinder vigorous shaking, unless the victim was small enough to be lifted clear of the water—in which case it could probably be swallowed whole. In my own experience, floating corpses attract young gulls, rather than the adults that could presumably displace the immatures. Adult Glaucous Gulls are adept at opening up carcasses on the water, but this species is exceptionally predatory in its habits. The difficulty experienced by scavenging gulls in feeding on seabird carcasses may be a major reason why so many seabirds wash ashore virtually intact, rather than as hollowed shells.

Another factor limiting predatory behaviour in the tropics would be sharks. These predators respond to the smell of blood. Once a floating carcass had been opened, any sharks in the vicinity would be alerted and a shark might not be choosy about whether it swallowed prey or predator. Some hawks devour small prey on the wing, tearing at the carcass while gripping it in the talons and this behaviour would certainly eliminate the risk from sharks. Such a strategy would seem a likely one for a frigatebird, which can soar aloft easily, but the poor frigatebird is handicapped by having webbed feet, not nearly as useful as talons for manipulating prey. What with one thing and another, the absence of avian predators at sea may not be as hard to explain as it appears at first sight.

DIET

The ocean contains an amazing diversity of organisms. Life first evolved in the sea and many early experiments in animal and plant design have persisted in the sea, although they never made the transition to land. Consequently, in the marine environment, organisms almost unchanged in half a billion years, such as corals, sea urchins and annelid worms, exist side by side with recent evolutionary products such as whales and seabirds. The sea supports fewer species of organisms than the land, but marine life is far more varied in its structure and relationships.

Given all this diversity, we might expect seabirds to eat a very wide range of marine organisms, but this is not the case . . .

No seabird feeds on kelp, or sea-grass, and only a few feed on benthic or sessile organisms of any kind (these are the speciality of the seaducks). The majority of seabirds concentrate on fish, especially teleost fish (cod, smelt, sculpins and the like) and large mobile zooplankton, the small, mainly crustacean, organisms that browse the oceans primary producers, the phytoplankton. They tend to be very catholic in their diet, taking a wide spectrum of different sizes and types of prey. However, while rearing chicks they may be more selective. Murres and puffins, for instance, take a very diverse diet, but feed their chicks almost exclusively on fish. In some situations a particular species of fish may become very dominant in the diet. In the northwest Atlantic, the capelin *Mallotus villosus*, a small schooling smelt, is very important to most seabirds, as well as to Atlantic cod *Gadus morhua* and marine mammals (Brown & Nettleship, 1984). Another fish, the sand eel or sand lance *Ammodytes*, comprises a large proportion of the diet for many seabirds in northwest Europe and throughout the temperate waters of the North Pacific (a different species from the Atlantic, but almost identical in appearance; Sanger, 1987). In the Arctic, the Arctic cod *Boreogadus saida*, a small relative of the Atlantic cod that occurs in enormous shoals in arctic waters, is the main prey of many seabird species. In tropical waters, flying fish (Exocetidae) are extremely important in the diet of boobies, tropicbirds, frigatebirds, noddies and Sooty Terns (e.g. Ashmole & Ashmole, 1967).

PREY SIZE

Prey size among predators in general is related to body size. In seabirds, it seems to relate especially to the size of organism that can be swallowed whole. Few seabirds dismember their prey, possibly because of the difficulty of doing so in a medium where the prey cannot be pinned down, and possibly because of the danger of being pirated by other birds. Both gulls and large petrels have exceptionally large gullets that allow them to consume food items up to one-quarter of total body weight in a single gulp. I make this comparative statement on the basis of MacGillivray's (1852) comments on the subject. The auks and penguins swallow most of their food underwater, making it possible to obtain more than one food item at each dive. This is essential where a bird must dive deep to find abundant small prey. It also eliminates the danger of kleptoparasitism by non-diving jaegers and frigatebirds. Cormorants often surface with prey, but these may simply be large items difficult to swallow underwater. Pelicans have to come to the surface, because they must expel the water in their pouch before they swallow.

For many seabirds, the median size of prey taken is much smaller than the maximum, probably because the size distribution of prey taken by any individual tends to follow a distribution typical of many biological phenomena, with many small and few large items. If we regard the size of the throat as being a major factor constraining the upper size limit for prey (depending on the cross-sectional area of the prey), then we might expect prey mass to be proportional to the body weight of the bird, as both prey and throat cross-sectional area are proportional to the square of linear dimensions. This appears to be approximately true when the maximum size of prey is considered, but less true when we consider the most important size for energy intake. We might anticipate this from the observation that larger predators can take a greater range of prey size than their smaller relatives and this appears to be true. However, the smallest seabird prey items, the copepods, are taken mainly by the smallest seabirds (small auklets, storm-petrels). They may be too small to be worth going after for larger seabirds.

PREY SELECTION

The degree to which seabirds specialise in their choice of prey is hard to know unless we know the abundance and accessibility of the potential prey species. Most species take a wide variety of the invertebrates and fishes available in their foraging habitat. In addition, most examples of apparent specialisation involve exclusively taking a prey species that is extremely abundant (e.g. krill among Antarctic and subantarctic penguins, capelin among puffins in Newfoundland). There are some exceptions: Leach's Storm-petrels wintering in tropical waters take large numbers of sea striders (a marine insect; Ainley, 1984), and Thick-billed Murres in Labrador mainly took daubed shannies *Lumpenus maculatus*, whereas other auks in the same area (Atlantic Puffin, Razorbill, Common Murre) fed on capelin (Birkhead & Nettleship, 1987). Conversely, certain types of prey that are common seem to be avoided. Jellyfish and comb jellies appear to be rare in the diets of most seabirds, except fulmarine petrels and Parakeet Auklets (and perhaps some albatrosses (Tickell, 2000)), though they occur in suitable sizes and are common throughout the world's oceans. Comb jellies were abundant in surface waters within an area heavily foraged by murres studied by Hunt *et al.* (1988), but the murres ignored them, swimming deeper to take euphausiids.

Because these gelatinous animals are very fragile, we might expect them to be under-represented in diet studies, due to their rapid disintegration after ingestion. However, the fact that they have rarely been reported at all in seabird diets suggests that they are generally ignored as prey. Likewise, pteropod molluscs and arrow worms, very abundant in arctic waters, are rarely reported as dietary items for seabirds, and then usually only in small numbers, although they have a similar energy density to some crustacea commonly taken. Norderhaug (1980) specifically noted the prevalence of comb jellies, pteropods and arrow worms where Little Auks foraged in Spitsbergen, but did not find them in the birds he examined. These organisms may present difficulties in handling, may be less digestible, may be distasteful, or may be more difficult to locate underwater. More information on what seabirds do not eat would be highly desirable.

As noted above, despite the wide variety of fish and zooplankton of a suitable size available in the boreal and arctic waters of the northern hemisphere, a small number of prey species make up a large proportion of the diets of most seabirds. This reflects, in part, the predominance of a small number of dominant species in marine food webs, but this explanation is not sufficient to account for all of the uniformity of diet observed. It is likely that certain species of fish and crustacea exhibit behaviour that make them especially useful prey for seabirds, either because they happen to come in just the right size package (*c.*10–30 g suits most seabirds very nicely), by forming dense swarms or by approaching the surface. Capelin, for instance, enter shallow, coastal waters in dense shoals to spawn in summer. The breeding cycle of many seabirds in Newfoundland is timed to coincide rather exactly so that chicks are being fed during this spawning period (Brown & Nettleship, 1984). Likewise, the dense shoals formed by sand eels, which may be corralled and herded by Rhinoceros Auklets (Grover & Olla, 1983) and Marbled Murrelets (Mahon *et al.*, 1992) appear to provide especially suitable foraging targets. Very large, dense schools of Arctic cod that form in shallow waters in the arctic are described later.

Euphausiids (shrimp-like crustacea, usually less than 4 cm long) are an important constituent in diets of many North Pacific seabirds, the species of euphausiid involved varying with region and season. The Antarctic krill *Euphausia superba* is a staple food of many seabirds in southern polar waters, especially penguins. The euphausiids' habit of aggregating into dense swarms apparently makes them more attractive as prey than other common crustacea of a similar size; mysids fill a similar role in Arctic waters.

FEEDING BEHAVIOUR

BEHAVIOURAL TACTICS

Despite the exploitation of some predictable food sources, many seabirds do not appear to rely on the type of food concentrations created by permanent tidal upwellings. Where they are confronted with finding an ephemeral and unpredictable prey their problems can be divided into two: (a) locating the whereabouts of a suitable prey concentration and (b) actually pursuing and capturing the prey. During the breeding season the first problem is particularly acute, because birds must periodically depart the feeding area to relieve mates or feed chicks. By the time their colony shift is over (as much as a month for the large albatrosses and penguins), the location of food may have changed, forcing them to search for a new feeding area. Both of these problems pose challenges to seabirds.

Seabirds may fly directly away from their colony until they encounter a suitable large aggregation of prey and then remain in that area until they have acquired enough food to return (e.g. Thick-billed Murre), or they may cruise about until they find a small food source, eat it and then continue elsewhere (e.g. Wandering Albatrosses—rather appropriately named, it appears). These are the extremes and probably most seabirds adopt a strategy that is somewhat intermediate, using several feeding areas on a trip, and perhaps lingering at each for some time.

FLOCKING

The degree to which seabirds are aggregated while foraging depends very much on the scale of measurement (Haney & Solow, 1992). All species will appear aggregated on the scale of the whole planet, because none is distributed evenly throughout the world's oceans. At the other end of the scale, we might find that individuals within a feeding flock are actually rather evenly dispersed on the scale of a few tens of metres. However, from a practical point of view, if we are looking at several square kilometres of sea, as we usually do when perched on a fishing boat or ferry, and most of the birds in sight are within a radius of 100 m, then we consider that they are flocked. Most people have little doubt about what is or is not a flock and this is the sort of aggregation that I will be discussing.

Flocks at sea may consist of just one species, but it is much more typical for several species to be involved, and in many areas it is unusual for any seabirds within sight of the flock to ignore it. Some examples, from my own experience follow.

Off the west coast of Haida Gwaii, mixed flocks of Pacific Loons, Pelagic Cormorants, Black-legged Kittiwakes, Glaucous-winged Gulls, Tufted Puffins and Rhinoceros Auklets occur at shoals of smelt and herrings in summer. Of the seabirds present in the area, only Common Murres stand aloof, although even they sometimes participate. These flocks are highly ephemeral. If a shoal disappears (presumably by going deep), birds sit about on the water, gradually drifting apart.

Generally, kittiwakes, the most mobile species, are the first to discover a new shoal (or the old one surfacing again), while the cormorants are often the last to shift from the previous patch, perhaps because they can dive deep enough to continue feeding after other species have been forced to stop.

Observations of Rhinoceros Auklets attacking sand eel shoals show that the auks mainly approach the fish from below, trapping them against the surface. Bite-marks on fish delivered to auklet chicks suggest that this is a common tactic (Burger *et al.*, 1993). The behaviour of the auklets may benefit the surface-feeding gulls and kittiwakes by keeping the fish where they can reach them. Hence the auklets may benefit from the activities of the kittiwakes in locating the shoal, while the kittiwakes benefit from the auklets tactics in keeping the prey from going deep. Notice that the white kittiwakes are very easy for the auklets to locate. In addition, their behaviour in fluttering and wheeling close to the surface clearly indicates the presence of prey. The auklets, on the other hand, which acquire no benefit from the arrival of kittiwakes after they have located prey, are among the more cryptic seabirds (see Chapter 4). Similar flocks off Vancouver Island were described by Porter & Sealy (1981, 1982).

In the high-arctic waters of Resolute Bay, enormous swarms of Arctic cod attract large aggregations of Northern Fulmars, Black-legged Kittiwakes and Glaucous Gulls (Welch *et al.*, 1993). Arctic Terns, for which the cod are too large and Thick-billed Murres, though common in the region, are not normally present. The size of these cod schools is much greater than the fish schools described from Haida Gwaii and they are correspondingly much less common. For the murres, the effort of searching out these very localised prey schools may not be worth the effort: they can obtain cod in much deeper water than the other species.

Off North Brother Island, between the North and South islands of New Zealand, a characteristic feeding assemblage occurred each day when the tide was right. It consisted of Fairy Prions, Common Diving-Petrels and Red-billed Gulls, with smaller numbers of Fluttering Shearwaters. This aggregation needed no searching and no advertisement. It occurred throughout the day, except at slack tide, and depended on a reliable source of tidal upwelling bringing food organisms to the surface. The position of the aggregation changed between the ebb and flow. Different species took up different stations, depending on their feeding method, with the gulls and shearwaters occupying the centre of the upwelling, prions displaced somewhat downstream and diving-petrels even further downstream (Gaston & Scofield, 1995).

These anecdotes illustrate some of the range of flock types that may occur, from those forming over permanent sources of food concentration, as in the case of the tidal upwelling near North Brother Island, to the highly intermittent aggregations over vast Arctic cod schools in the high arctic. The latter type provide a good illustration of a situation where food is, briefly, limitless. The birds have no need to compete and can even be choosy about their prey: the fulmars tear open the cod and take just the livers. Interactions among birds in the more regular, but none the less somewhat unpredictable, situation of the Haida Gwaii flocks may be more subtle and complex, with individuals and species playing different roles, resulting in different costs and benefits.

Species with the same ostensible feeding potential may adopt very different strategies towards food finding. Least, Crested and Whiskered Auklets choose to feed mainly in limited areas of strong currents and tidal upwellings, necessitating feeding in dense aggregations. However, Parakeet Auklets breeding on the same islands feed solitarily, grazing on widely dispersed zooplankton. A similar offshore dispersal is characteristic of zooplankton-feeding Thick-billed Murres in many parts of the arctic, whereas Common Murres, which concentrate on schooling fish, generally feed in much denser aggregations (Piatt, 1990).

At permanent upwellings, behaviour may be determined by feeding preference. Detailed investigations by Hunt *et al.* (1995) around the Delarof Islands, Alaska, showed that Least Auklets fed on copepods concentrated in near-surface convergences on the downstream side of a pass, whereas Crested Auklets fed on euphausiids where water upwelled at the upstream entrance. The two species switched places when the current reversed.

In the eastern tropical Pacific, Lisa Ballance and co-workers (Ballance *et al.*, 1997) found they could define three types of seabird flocks: those comprised mainly of Sooty Terns, those in which Juan Fernández Petrels and Wedge-tailed Shearwaters were co-dominants, and those where boobies and noddy terns comprised the majority of the birds. The Sooty Tern flocks occurred mainly over waters of low productivity, where potential food was scarce, whereas booby flocks were found in places where food was abundant. Petrel/shearwater flocks occurred where productivity was intermediate. They suggested that Sooty Terns, having the lowest flight costs, were best able to exploit sparse food supplies, while the boobies, being large and aggressive, could appropriate food where it was dense and competition was therefore fierce. The shearwaters and petrels, being less efficient fliers than the terns, and less competitive than the boobies, predominated where conditions were intermediate. The distributions were independent of colony locations and their observations emphasise the importance of flight efficiency in determining seabird lifestyles.

THE ROLE OF HERDING BY PREDATORY FISH AND DOLPHINS

Most observers who have watched seabird feeding behaviour in the tropics have emphasised the importance of predatory fish and marine mammals (e.g. Harrison *et al.*, 1983; Au & Pitman, 1986). Large predatory schooling fish, especially tuna, tend to corral schools of smaller fish by encircling them and driving them towards the surface where, unable to escape, they mass together. The tuna then plunge into the dense swarm of food, dispersing it in the process. Similar tactics are adopted by dolphins, especially Pantropical Spotted *Stenella attenuata*, Spinner *S. longirostris* and Common Dolphins *Delphinus delphis* (Au & Pitman, 1988). When the school of bait fish or squid is pinned against the surface, it forms a perfect target for frigatebirds, boobies, terns and shearwaters. In the clear oceanic waters of the tropical oceans these predator-driven surface swarms are a major source of food for seabirds and some species appear to be virtually dependent on them: Sooty Terns and frigatebirds in particular.

The herding tactics of tropical tuna and dolphins may be an important factor in the development of short aerial escape flights by flying fish and flying squids, tactics presumably encouraged by the more rapid acceleration available to fish and squid in warm waters. A consequence of these escape flights is that some food becomes available to seabirds without contacting the water and this type of aerial foraging has been noted for tropical gadfly petrels, shearwaters, frigatebirds, terns and the Red-footed Booby (Ballance & Pitman, 1999). Such opportunities are not available to cold-water seabirds.

DO SEABIRDS HERD FISH THEMSELVES?

Cooperative herding of prey by dolphins and Killer Whales *Orcinus orca* is well known (Evans, 1987), but evidence for this type of behaviour in seabirds is poor. The corralling behaviour of Rhinoceros Auklets, described above, may be one example. In fresh water, both cormorants and pelicans use cooperative drives to herd fish (Anderson, 1991), but this is generally in shallow water where the fish cannot escape by diving. Herding of the sort seen in marine mammals would seem possible for penguins and auks, but perhaps the need to return frequently to the surface to breathe makes the technique inefficient in deep water. For whatever reason, cooperative 'pack hunting' feeding does not seem to be characteristic of seabirds.

FISHERIES WASTES

The gatherings of scavengers around a fishing boat hauling nets or lines, or disposing of bycatch, form a special type of seabird flock. In the North Sea, these flocks tend to be dominated by large gulls and Northern Fulmars, sometimes with gannets and skuas in attendance. Access to the resource is determined by size, with the largest species, gannets and Great Black-backed Gulls, getting the first choice and the smallest, usually kittiwakes and Black-headed Gulls picking up scraps left over by the larger species (Camphuysen *et al.*, 1995).

Seabirds learn to use the sort of man-made opportunities such as fisheries wastes very rapidly. In Sierra Leone, in 1968, I watched Common Terns roosting on sandy beaches. Every now and then there was a distant explosion and the birds would all rise and fly directly towards the noise, returning a few minutes later. Later, I found that the bangs were small charges of dynamite being detonated by inshore fishermen to stun fish. The terns presumably had learned to associate the noise with food floating at the surface.

FEEDING UNDERWATER

LOCATING PREY

How seabirds locate their prey once underwater is even more of a mystery. The role of 'head-dipping', periodic submersion of the head for 1–2 seconds while swimming on the surface, in locating underwater prey has been proposed, but not confirmed. An alternative explanation for this behaviour is that the birds are looking for potential predators. It is quite possible that such periodic underwater observations serve both functions.

No one has been able to detect any acoustic mechanism by which seabirds could locate their prey underwater, (evidence that certain penguins produce ultra-sound 'clicks' underwater has been described, but not confirmed) and chemical detection (e.g. smell, taste) seems very unlikely, because water is excluded from the olfactory membrane. Consequently, we have to assume for the moment that vision is the universal detector. As discussed in Chapter 3, seabirds are good at seeing underwater and, penguins at least, have some special adaptations towards the peculiarities of vision in water. However, the real limiting factor is the size of the eye. A study by Cannell & Cullen (1998) showed that Little Penguins, a medium-sized diver, abandoned foraging for fish when light levels approached those of half an hour before sunrise or after sunset. However, the similar-sized Thick-billed Murre continues foraging throughout the night in August in northern Hudson Bay, including the period of full darkness (Croll *et al.*, 1992). The difference may simply relate to depths at which prey is available—if prey is mainly at depth, feeding will cease at higher light levels than if the prey is close to the surface.

At the maximum depths to which seabirds, especially large penguins and murres, typically dive, very little light penetrates. Even in highly transparent water, the intensity of light at 100 m is less than 5% that at the surface and in typical coastal waters, with high phytoplankton density it may be only 0.1% (Valiela, 1995). Moreover, some seabirds feed in water of high turbidity (e.g. cormorants and loons feeding in or close to the surf zone along sandy shores) where visibility may be obscured at much shallower depths. Kittlitz's Murrelets sometimes forage in fiords made turbid by glacial melt-water and although they may be feeding in saline water below the freshwater inflow, light must be very much reduced. Guillemots and cormorants often forage among kelp and other seaweeds and on rocky or boulder-strewn bottoms where prey is likely to be extremely cryptic (Cairns, 1987b). In addition, Black Guillemots may winter as far north as 80°N (Renaud & Bradstreet, 1980), where, even at midday, there is little light at the surface, let alone where they feed, under the ice. All this evidence suggests that diving seabirds have exceptionally good vision in low-light conditions, though in some cases they may be aided by the bioluminescence of their prey. For King Penguins foraging at 300 m, bioluminescence is almost certainly important—their preferred prey is lanternfish (Myctophidae), a family well equipped with light-emitting skin cells.

BEHAVIOUR UNDERWATER

Most foraging dives can be divided into three stages, a descent phase in which the bird dives rapidly and in most cases rather vertically (Figure 6.1, A), a feeding phase, when the bird is actively searching for and pursuing prey (bottom phase, Fig. 6.1, B), and an ascent phase, when the bird rises rapidly to the surface (Figure 6.1, C).

The speed of ascent is usually faster than that of descent, because while going down, birds must fight against their own buoyancy, whereas the same buoyancy gives them a boost on the way up. However, once the degree of compression of air in feathers and air sacs has reached the point where

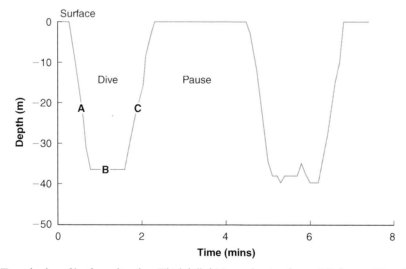

Figure 6.1   Time-depth profile of two dives by a Thick-billed Murre, showing descent (A), bottom (B) and ascent (C) phases (K. Woo and AJG, unpubl.).

the bird's density is the same as that of the water, any further descent will be aided by increasingly negative buoyancy: this point is reached by a Long-tailed Cormorant at *c.*5 m, but a more buoyant Thick-billed Murre reaches it only at 40 m.

Buoyancy determines where foraging can be accomplished with the least effort, because birds foraging at above the depth where they are neutrally buoyant have to keep swimming to stay down, while those below the depth of neutral buoyancy have to work to prevent themselves from sinking. As the volume of air halves with each doubling of pressure, the effect of equal increases in depth on buoyancy diminishes with depth. A bird that floats at the surface with one-third of its volume out of the water because of the air in its lungs, feathers and air sacs, has a density 77% that of water. If it has a minimum (incompressible) volume of 70% of its initial volume and none of the air escapes as it dives, it reaches neutral density at *c.*50 m depth (5 atmospheres pressure). However, if 20% of the air in its plumage at the surface is expelled as it dives, it becomes neutrally buoyant at about 40 m. This would be an advantage in certain circumstances, but a disadvantage in others, because a bird that has expelled air will be more dense than one that has not, once it reaches below the depth of neutral buoyancy (Figure 6.2).

We might expect that birds which habitually dive below their neutral buoyancy depth would prefer to retain air trapped in their plumage to reduce the negative buoyancy experienced below the neutral point and to assist in returning to the surface by increasing buoyancy on the way back up. The bubble trails behind murres rising towards the surface suggest that some air trapped in the plumage escapes as pressure decreases during the ascent. This air must have been retained during the descent by some physical process, perhaps involving a muscular arrangement of the feathers. Its loss during the ascent, when close to the surface, suggests that by this stage it is no longer necessary. Management of buoyancy in diving birds is still a subject about which little is known.

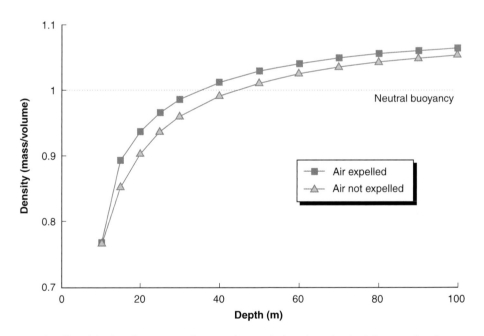

Figure 6.2   The effect of depth and pressure on the mean density of a hypothetical seabird during a dive. In one case the bird retains all the air in its plumage, lungs and internal air sacs, and in the other a proportion of the air is expelled as it begins to dive.

Birds feeding in shallow water have a choice of remaining in mid-water, or descending to the bottom and searching there for prey. Those diving in water beyond their maximum diving depth may also choose to forage at a particular depth, rather than searching down as far as they can go and then returning to the surface. Dives in which ascent begins as soon as descent has ended are known as 'V-shaped' or 'bounce dives' and those in which the descent and ascent are separated by a period at a fairly constant depth are 'U-shaped', or 'flat-bottomed' dives. V-shaped dives suggest either that the bird is looking for a feeding horizon, but does not find it, or that it secures a large food item while still descending and returns to the surface to swallow it.

For most diving birds, U-shaped dives are the most common, presumably indicating that a concentration of prey was either located or suspected at a given depth, where the bird therefore concentrated its foraging time. Most diving seabirds make a series of dives fairly close together (a bout), followed by a prolonged rest. The length of inter-dive intervals (pauses) tells us something about the time needed by the bird for recovery and respiration and is often standardised in relation to the length of the dive by expressing it as the 'dive-pause ratio'. As this ratio decreases, the bird is taking longer to recover between each dive. The ratio varies with the length of the dive, being highest for brief immersions. This effect occurs because, as the length of dives increases, so does the proportion of the dive during which respiration is anaerobic, causing the build-up of lactate in the blood. The lactate must be cleared by aerobic respiration at the surface before the next dive.

DIVING IN THICK-BILLED MURRES

To illustrate diving behaviour I have used some data that Kerry Woo and I obtained from Thick-billed Murres breeding at Coats Island, in 1999. Our data were based on time-depth gauges placed on 11 different individuals foraging for chicks, a bigger sample than in most studies. Also, the diving depth was sampled for only 20 minutes in each hour, spreading the results over a longer period than usual. Hence, our data should be particularly useful for summarising the 'average' behaviour of the population.

Both U-shaped and V-shaped dives were observed, but U shaped predominated. Figure 6.3 shows samples of dive profiles for a single bird on two different foraging trips. Trip one included periods of repeated shallow dives to 10–20 m depth (6.3 A), with very short pauses between dives, as well as deeper dives to more than 50 m (6.3 B). In both cases the dives were U shaped with approximately the same bottom time of 30–60 seconds but, as predicted, pauses between the deeper dives were longer (Figure 6.4). During trip two, dives were more V shaped in profile, suggesting more exploration and less predictable prey.

Overall, birds spent about the same amount of time in the bottom phase, irrespective of depth (Figure 6.5). Consequently, the time spent in the bottom phase, presumably a measure of the actual feeding time, fell from *c.*70% of total dive time in dives to depths of 10 m to only 20% of dive time for dives below 50 m. Because the duration of the surface pause increases with dive duration and hence with depth, the bottom phase becomes an even smaller proportion of total foraging time as dives get deeper, falling from 40% for 10-m dives to less than 10% of the time involved in dives to depths greater than 50 m (Figure 6.6).

Despite the predictions from buoyancy changes outlined above, our Thick-billed Murres appeared to maintain a fairly uniform rate of descent of 1.2–1.5 m/second (Figure 6.7). Presumably the murres adjusted their swimming effort to maintain a fairly uniform speed, perhaps maintaining the optimum speed for the amount of turbulence created. However, the rate of ascent followed predictions rather well, accelerating from *c.*0.8 m/second below 40 m, where they were fighting negative buoyancy,

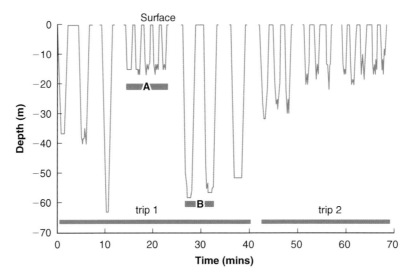

Figure 6.3   Dive profiles of several dive bouts on two consecutive foraging trips by a single Thick-billed Murre during the incubation period (mid-July) at Coats Island (data courtesy of Kerry Woo).

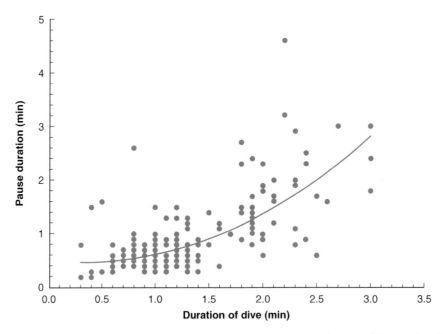

Figure 6.4   Duration of surface intervals between dives in a bout in relation to the duration of the preceding dive (same bird as in Fig 6.3).

to reach nearly 2 m/second just before they reached the surface, in the zone where their buoyancy would have been most positive (Figure 6.8).

The above figures applied to birds diving deeper than 50 m. Birds diving to shallower depths generally descended and ascended more slowly. Those diving only to 30 m rarely exceeded 1 m/second

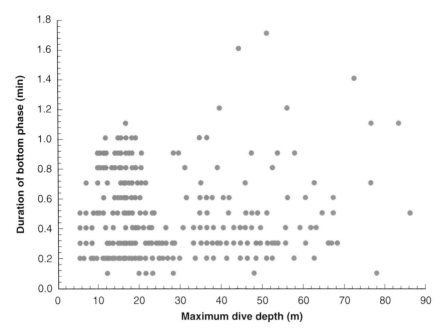

Figure 6.5   Time at probable feeding depth (bottom phase of the dive) in relation to the maximum depth attained (same bird as in Fig 6.3).

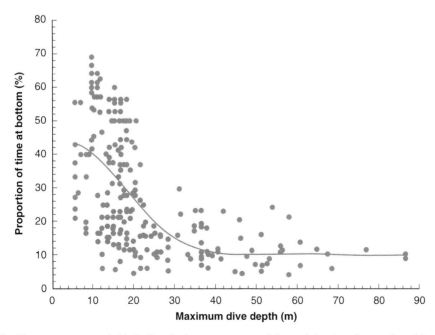

Figure 6.6   The time spent at probable feeding depth as a percentage of the total time in a foraging bout (dive time + pause), in relation to the maximum depth attained (same bird as in Fig 6.3).

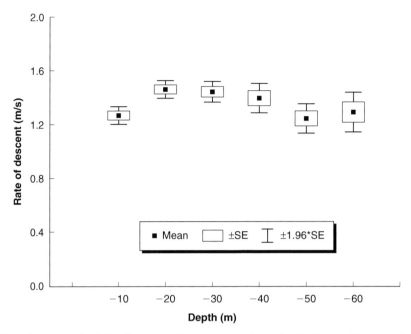

Figure 6.7   Rate of change in depth (similar to actual swimming speed assuming bird is travelling approximately vertically) of birds descending at different depths: only birds diving to >50 m (sub-sample of birds in Fig 6.3).

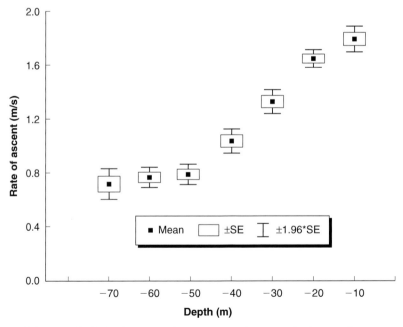

Figure 6.8   Rate of change in depth (similar to actual swimming speed assuming bird is travelling approximately vertically) of birds ascending at different depths: only birds diving to >50 m (sub-sample of birds in Fig 6.3).

in their descent, whereas deeper divers were travelling 20–50% faster at the same depths. Likewise birds ascending from a maximum depth of 30–40 m were ascending at only 1 m/second when they reached 20 m depth, whereas birds that descended below 60 m were ascending half as fast again at 20 m (Figure 6.9). That murres travel at different speeds when diving to different depths suggests that they have a good idea of how far they are going and how long they will spend underwater when they begin the dive. A similar effect was seen for King Penguins (Kooyman *et al.*, 1992). This is hardly surprising, given that many bouts consist of many dives with almost identical profiles. However, it does emphasise that there may be an advantage in knowing where you are going in order to devote the correct amount of energy to swimming.

Another result of the variation in descent and ascent rates with depth is that the total dive time does not increase linearly with depth as Douglas Dewar (1924) suggested many years ago. Instead, the deeper dives do not last as long as one would expect based on the shallow dives (Figure 6.10). As the energy expended in swimming increases rapidly with swimming speed, it seems likely that deep dives are considerably more costly than shallow dives. When this is added to the fact that a much smaller proportion of time during deep dives is spent at feeding depth, we have to assume that the prey density made accessible by deep dives is much greater than that available near the surface, otherwise murres are making a big mistake.

Diving depth

Our knowledge of the depths at which seabirds may forage has increased considerably in the past two decades, due to the deployment of Maximum Depth Recorders (MDR) and Time-depth recorders (TDR; Table 6.2). Large birds, having a lower metabolism and cost of propulsion (because

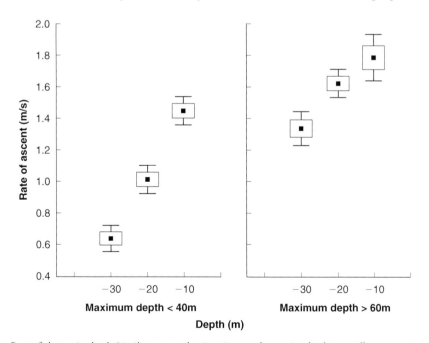

Figure 6.9   Rate of change in depth (similar to actual swimming speed assuming bird is travelling approximately vertically) of birds ascending at different depths: comparison of birds swimming to maximum depths <40 m with those reaching below 60 m (sub-sample of birds in Fig 6.3).

of lower drag per unit weight), but similar oxygen storage capacities per unit mass, should be capable of diving for longer than small birds (Wilson, 1991). Given similar or greater underwater swimming speeds, that should permit larger birds to dive to greater depths than small birds. Such a correlation can be seen for the maximum diving depths of both penguins and auks (Figure 6.11). A similar correlation for the maximum length of time spent submerged was reported by Boyd & Croxall (1996; see Figure 6.12).

The diving performance of auks, in terms of duration and depth of dives, is rather good when compared with that of penguins. Such comparisons are inevitable for auk biologists because penguins, with their very long specialisation in aquatic life, should be the best avian diving machines. Certainly, the performance of King and Emperor Penguins, which regularly dive below 200 m, cannot be matched among auks. However, the normal diving depths of murres are greater than those measured for penguins several times as large (Burger, 1991; Fig. 4.5) and may indicate exceptional physiological abilities relating to anaerobic respiration (Croll *et al.*, 1992). This may not apply to other auks, e.g. anaerobic respiration appears to be rare in Rhinoceros Auklets (Burger *et al.*, 1993).

Many cormorants, especially freshwater species, typically forage at shallow depths (Cooper, 1986). As noted, their wettable plumage allows them to remain submerged at shallow depths with less effort than would be necessary for auks or ducks. However, some marine cormorants are deep divers, especially the Blue-eyed (South Georgia) Shag, which dives below 100 m and can submerge for more than five minutes (Croxall *et al.*, 1991; Wanless *et al.*, 1992).

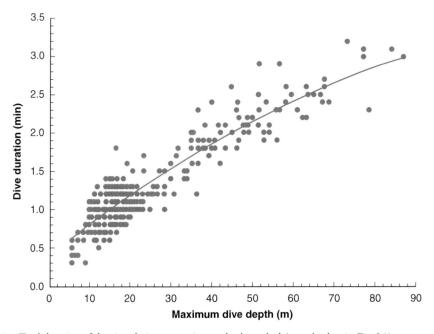

Figure 6.10   Total duration of dive in relation to maximum depth reached (same bird as in Fig 6.3).

Table 6.2   *Details of some diving behaviour reported for seabirds, based on time-depth recorders*

	Maximum depth (m)	Maximum dive duration (sec)	Mean depth (m)	Mean dive duration (sec)	Reference
King Penguin	304	427	125–232	241–309	Kooyman *et al.*, 1992
Adélie Penguin	180	275	23	62	Watanuki *et al.*, 1993
Macaroni Penguin			27 (day), 5 (night)	90 (day), 54 (night)	Croxall *et al.*, 1993
Rockhopper Penguin	104	660	27	72	Hull, 2000
Royal Penguin	226	450	33	102	Hull, 2000
Japanese Cormorant	40 (male), 32 (female)	110 (male), 80 (female)	15 (male), 7 (female)	37 (male), 24 (female)	Watanuki *et al.*, 1996
Blue-eyed Shag	107	370	83	276	Kato *et al.*, 1992
European Shag	49	–	26	–	Wanless *et al.*, 1997
Thick-billed Murre	135	224	65	55	Croll *et al.*, 1992
Thick-billed Murre	–	210 (male), 240 (female)	–	116 (male), 84 (female)	Jones *et al.*, 2002
Rhinoceros Auklet	60	–	30	45	Burger *et al.*, 1993

FORAGING RANGE

While breeding, the area over which seabirds can forage is constrained by their need to return to the nest to relieve their mate or feed their nestling. This is more of a constraint for some birds than for others. Black Guillemots, which make up to ten trips/day to feed nestlings usually forage within 10 km of the colony (Cairns, 1987b). At the other extreme, Wandering Albatrosses may move as far as 3,600 km from the nest during incubation (Weimerskirch *et al.*, 1994b). As we shall see in Chapters 9 and 10, foraging range has been considered very important in the evolution of the distinctive life-history characteristics of marine birds.

Frustratingly, considering its importance, foraging range is extremely difficult to measure and to characterise for individual species. Distributions at sea can be only an imperfect guide to foraging range, because all seabird populations contain substantial numbers of pre-breeding individuals, not to mentioned failed breeders. The earliest studies of foraging range in seabirds were mainly based on deductions from the duration of absences from the nest and usually assumed that seabirds travelled to and from their feeding area in a straight line: 'as the crow flies', as we might say. It is only recently, with the advent of satellite tracking (e.g. Jouventin & Weimerskirch, 1990) and miniature navigation recorders (e.g. Benvenuti *et al.*, 1998), that we have been able to evaluate this assumption and measure actual foraging ranges. Even now, instrumentation is so expensive that, to date, only a few individuals of a handful of species have been tracked. Moreover, foraging range probably varies enormously between seasons, years and colonies, making generalisations even more fraught. It will

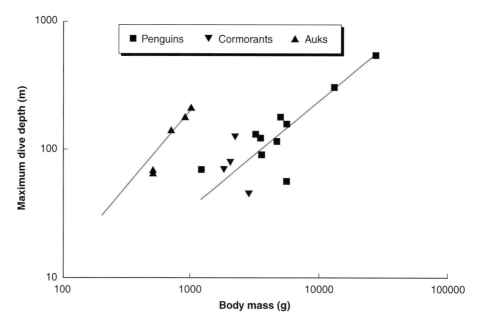

Figure 6.11   Diving depths of seabirds in relation to body size, showing the much greater depths achieved by auks, for their size, compared to penguins and cormorants.

probably take many years before we are in a position to make broad comparative analyses based on accurately measured foraging ranges. For the moment, we cannot do much better than Ashmole's 'inshore, offshore, pelagic' for most species.

Unsurprisingly, it transpires that species for which flight is expensive, such as the Thick-billed Murre, do travel direct to their feeding areas, but that species for which flight is cheap and food perhaps less predictable, such as albatrosses and fulmars, may wander a good deal between their nest and their feeding grounds (Prince *et al.*, 1992; Weimerskirch *et al.*, 1993, 1994a, 2001; Brothers *et al.*, 1998). However, while the duration of the trip does not yield a good estimate of the area over which the bird could have foraged, it does give a rather good estimate of the distance travelled (Weimerskirch & Guionnet, 2002). It appears that the large albatrosses spend much of the daylight period in flight and that ground speed, averaged over days, is fairly uniform. The same is true of the Northern Fulmar.

The same satellite data reveal how limited some species are by the need to return frequently to the nest. Birds brooding chicks are limited to half the foraging time that they have available once they have deserted the chick. At Bjørnøya, in the Barents Sea, this resulted in Northern Fulmars foraging over much larger areas between successive colony visits after they had ceased to brood the chick. Feeding rates in tubenoses tend to be rather uniform throughout the chick-rearing period, allowing parents to travel further once brooding has ceased. Among those auks that cease to brood their chick partway through the growth period (puffins, auklets), feeding rates in the post-brooding period are generally higher than during brooding, so there may be little adjustment in foraging range, the extra time being used in making more trips.

Compared with the duration of foraging trips to provision chicks, the duration of incubation shifts may provide an indication of foraging ranges that is less constrained by the need to return to the nest.

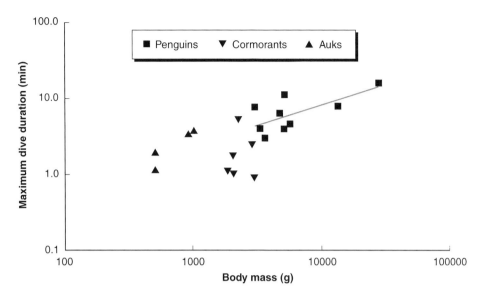

Figure 6.12   Maximum amount of time spent submerged in relation to body size. Here the auks seem to fall on the same line as the penguins.

Mean incubation shifts vary enormously in length, from less than half an hour in the inland-nesting marsh terns to 22 days in the Waved Albatross. As with other aspects of biology, inshore species tend to have short incubation shifts, usually less than one day, while offshore species nearly all undertake multi-day shifts.

Among tubenoses, all of which, apart from diving-petrels, have multi-day shifts, the gadfly petrels mostly average shifts of more than ten days, while those of fulmarines and shearwaters tend to be shorter. Shifts among albatrosses vary from less than ten days to 20 days. Storm-petrels average 2–5 days (Warham, 1990).

In the case of the Thick-billed Murre, we have found that incubation shift length varies widely among colonies and this relates to the distance that birds are travelling to the feeding area: at Coats Island, where most feeding takes place within 100 km of the colony, incubation shifts average 12 hours, whereas at the much larger Digges Island colony, birds travel well over 100 km to feed and incubation shifts exceed 24 hours (Gaston & Noble, 1986). Similarly, Northern Fulmars, which usually sit for 3–5 days, averaged shifts more than twice as long at Prince Leopold Island in years of poor food availability.

Given the evident advantage conferred by long incubation shifts in reducing the time spent in commuting to and from the colony, the observed variation among and within species raises the question of why birds should bother to change over frequently, even if their inshore lifestyle permits them to do so without a large penalty. For example, although most auks change over at intervals of 24 hours or less, the Ancient Murrelet averages three-day incubation shifts and may take up to six days. It apparently has no problem in doing so. Birds may take shorter shifts, where circumstances permit, because short shifts allow them to maintain lower energy reserves, making flight less costly. This strategy also enables them to live off their income and avoid the metabolic processes involved in storing energy and then breaking it down again.

LONG AND SHORT TRIPS

Once the foraging patterns of individual albatrosses and shearwaters had been studied, it became evident that, during the later part of chick rearing, parents tend to alternate short and long feeding trips. It seems probable that the short trips are solely for the purpose of provisioning the chick and that the long trips are for self-feeding, as well as to find food for the offspring. This type of strategy has been reported from albatrosses, shearwaters and fulmars (e.g. Weimerskirch *et al.*, 1994b). However, it seems likely that it is a rather common phenomenon, especially in species where the chick is fed on a particular subset of the adult diet (many auks). In that case, even the feeding strategy adopted may be different: murres may have to dive deeper to find fish to deliver to their chicks than to find amphipods to feed themselves (Kerry Woo, unpubl.).

NOCTURNAL FORAGING

Squid and deep-water fishes that appear at the surface only at night feature in the diets of many seabirds and have given rise to speculation that the birds actively forage after dark. As it is hard to watch birds at night, except when there are artificial lights—something that obviously creates a rather unnatural situation—information tends to be scattered and anecdotal. That gadfly petrels are seldom seen foraging by day suggests that they must do so at night, especially as their diet contains squid that come near the surface mainly at night (Brooke & Prince, 1991). However, Lipinski & Jackson (1989) reported that most nocturnal squid taken by seabirds belonged to genera that float after death, which raises the possibility that nocturnally rising squid found in seabird diets are actually scavenged. There was little confirmation of this until the recent deployment of technical gadgets that can record feeding behaviour throughout the birds' foraging trip. To date, it appears that Wandering Albatrosses, which feed commonly on squid that appear at the surface mainly at night, acquire most of them during the day, presumably by scavenging dead animals, rather than catching them alive (Cooper *et al.*, 1993). However, the activity patterns of the Black-browed and Grey-headed Albatrosses at night suggest that they may be feeding after dark. This is an area where more information would be useful, especially for smaller petrels.

Both auks and penguins are known, from continuous dive-recording data, to dive at night and must, presumably, be feeding when they do so. Nocturnal dives tend to be much shallower than those during the day (Croxall *et al.*, 1988; Croll *et al.*, 1992; Jones *et al.*, 2002). So far there is little evidence for nocturnal feeding in cormorants, which generally fly to roost well before dusk. Among gulls, Red-legged Kittiwakes and Swallow-tailed Gulls forage at night, but most gulls cease activity at dusk.

CONCLUSIONS

The physical uniformity of the marine environment leaves seabirds with relatively few feeding strategies to differentiate among species. In addition, there is much dietary overlap between species, at least during breeding (Diamond, 1983). Species feeding in mixed assemblages are common, especially outside the tropics. Consequently, the main segregating factor among seabirds is their foraging depth and their foraging range while breeding. The latter depends on an interaction between the energy they expend on flying, the amount of food reserves that they can lay down and maintain, and the amount of food that they can transport to their nestlings. Wing-powered underwater swimmers benefit from short wings and hence tend to have high wing-loadings, making the delivery of large nestling meals impossible. Conversely, frigatebirds and gadfly petrels, which have low wing-loadings, are highly efficient at travel and able to carry large loads, but are confined to feeding at the sea surface and must therefore search much larger areas to find the same amount of food. By the same token, they can never attain the densities that are achieved by auks and shearwaters. Further consequences of foraging range are discussed in Chapter 9.

An adult Glaucous Gull hovers on updraughts close to breeding Thick-billed Murres, ready to pounce on a momentarily exposed egg or chick. (Timothy J.F. Lash)

CHAPTER SEVEN

Migration, movement and weather

The lady comes to the gate, dressed in lavender and leather
Looking north to the sea, she finds the weather fine
She watches seagulls fly, silver on the ocean
Stitching through the waves, the edges of the sky.

Judy Collins, 'Albatross', 1967

Sadly, seawatching is not always conducted in such a genteel manner:

But what is a good sea-watch like? Throughout the night the wind and rain beat on the walls and windows of the observatory. Alarm clocks go off an hour before dawn and reluctant observers stagger out of bed and snatch a hasty breakfast, brew up flasks of coffee and don oilskins, while listening to the uninviting gale outside. It is still almost dark, the roads slippery underfoot, as the sea-watchers leave the observatory . . . Half an hour later a decision has to be taken . . . Blanan' it is and another 30 minutes will be spent climbing over slippery, dangerous rocks, some razor-sharp, with the sea crashing below. The air is filled with rain and salt spray, often blowing vertically upwards, the sea is foam-covered . . . It may be madness to go to such a place at such a time but every birdwatcher ought to visit Blanan' tip on a day like this once in a lifetime.

Tim Sharrock, *The Natural History of Cape Clear Island*, 1973

That pelagic seabirds adjust their behaviour in relation to normal weather events is apparent to anyone who has spent time seawatching. When the sky is clear and a gentle breeze is blowing (exactly the weather you want for sitting on the beach), there is usually little movement to be seen that cannot be accounted for by the daily comings and goings of local seabird populations. But let the wind rise to gale force, and the lowering clouds cast raindrops with the speed of bullets in your face, so that you must clean the lens of your telescope every half minute, then, as Tim Sharrock describes in The Natural History of Cape Clear Island, *things are very different.*

Reef Island, lies on the west side of Hecate Strait, the 100–km wide strip of sea that divides the Queen Charlotte Islands from the mainland. Bad weather nearly always comes with winds from the southeast. Large depressions arriving from the Pacific bump into the abrupt wall of the British Columbia coastal mountains. The topography entrains the winds into the trough of Hecate Strait and every few weeks (sometimes more frequently) the relatively sheltered waters of the strait are whipped into a fury of foam with the passage of a major low-pressure cell.

When Ian Jones and I began to work at Reef Island in 1984 we soon became aware that 'southeast weather' brought a characteristic seabird spectacle. From April, as soon as the wind speed rose to gale force (above 50 km/h), a steady stream of seabirds began battling southwards, into the teeth of the wind, about 1 km offshore. As the wind rose higher, and especially if, as was often the case, the gale was accompanied by low cloud and heavy rain, the birds came still closer inshore.

The exact composition of the passage varied somewhat between years, corresponding roughly to variation in the numbers of different species present in Hecate Strait. Sooty Shearwaters and Black-legged Kittiwakes were the most common species and their numbers varied enormously from year to year. In years when Sooty Shearwaters were abundant, they made up the vast majority of birds seen, frequently passing at rates in excess of 10,000 birds/hour. In other years, rates could be little more than 100/hour. Kittiwakes never amounted to as much of one-tenth of these numbers and in most years were uncommon after mid-May. Interspersed with these dominant species were Common Murres, Tufted Puffins, Fork-tailed Storm-petrels and Pacific Loons. Strangely, Cassin's Auklets and Ancient Murrelets, which both breed in large numbers in the region, appeared only in small numbers, sometimes being completely absent. Movements usually continued throughout the passage of the gale, sometimes for several days, and often for up to 12 hours afterwards, but once the sea state subsided, the movements ceased abruptly, almost as though someone, somewhere had turned off a tap.

We used to huddle in a crevice on a rocky headland, humped over our telescopes and shrouded in raingear; we always obtained our closest views when the weather was at its worst. We were very excited at first by these spectacular processions of birds, but gradually, we came to realise that they were a regular, actually rather predictable, feature of Hecate Strait. In later years, we did not pay nearly as much attention to them, though we would always sample a good storm to make sure what species were passing.

On a fine day in May, it was evident to observers on Reef Island that seabird movements in the Strait were minimal—perhaps the occasional Rhinoceros Auklet buzzing about its business or a small group of Pelagic Cormorants shifting from one feeding area to another would be all that was visible. On the other hand, if we took the time to cast off our boat and head out into the strait, we would often see a very different picture. At first, only curious local gulls, perhaps wondering if we had any fish to throw overboard disturbed the calm sea. Twenty minutes of steady eastward running would bring us 6–7 km from the eastern tip of Reef Island. Suddenly, birds would start to appear, sometimes just dozens, sometimes thousands. Again the mainstays were Sooty Shearwaters, but now we might see phalaropes, jaegers, terns and Pacific

Loons flying steadily north, and Ancient Murrelets and Rhinoceros Auklets dotted the sea. These offshore movements are totally beyond the ken of shore-based observers.

I was treated to another example of the vagaries of seabird migration in May 1988, when I took the coastal ferry that runs from Port Hardy, on the north coast of Vancouver Island, to Prince Rupert, near the Alaska/British Columbia border. As is my habit, I spent most of the daylight hours on deck, partly to watch for seabirds and partly to avoid the entertainment provided in the ship's saloons. The weather was fine and the trip is in any case through sheltered waters, so walking the decks was very pleasant.

Leaving Port Hardy, the ferry threads through a curtain of islands before cutting across the mouth of Queen Charlotte Strait towards the narrow canals that wind among British Columbia's coastal archipel-ago. This stretch of Queen Charlotte Sound is the only part of the trip where the horizon is not crowded by mountains and islands. As soon as we reached open water, I began to see compact flocks of small gulls flying north, low over the water. They were Bonaparte's Gulls which nest in the interior of northern British Columbia and Alaska, and winter in inshore waters of southern British Columbia south to California.

Each flock numbered 20–50 birds and they formed a regular stream, spaced several hundred metres apart. They overhauled the ferry, travelling at c.30 km/h, at a leisurely speed, perhaps 10–15 km/h faster than we were travelling. With the calm sea, I could observe 5–6 flocks ahead of us and as many behind us at any one time. Then the route of the ferry diverged slightly from their line of travel and the stream of gulls sank into the westward horizon. I counted more than 1,000 gulls while we travelled together. From their heading, I judged that they would pass close up the eastern shore of Hecate Strait.

Despite many days in many Mays spent seawatching at Reef Island, and despite our periodic boat trips into the strait, I never saw any flocks of Bonaparte's Gulls there. The route must be precise. This is the only occasion on which I have witnessed the migration of Bonaparte's Gull and it illustrates how cryptic these important movements may be.

Our Hecate Strait observations were quite typical of many visible from coastal vantage points around the world during bad weather. At Cape Clear Island, at the southwestern-most tip of Ireland, the story is the same. When gales move in, a seemingly endless stream of shearwaters, auks and kitti-wakes, flying low over the spray-drenched waves, forges steadily upwind. These events are a normal part of the lives of seabirds. They are especially prominent where there is some narrow strait or major embayment: the Irish Sea, the Kattegat or the English Channel. These movements are quite distinct from the migratory movements, such as the one that I described for Bonaparte's Gulls. True migra-tory movements can be seen from certain prominent headlands: Cape Verde, Cape Cod or Cape Wrath. They seem to occur more often in fine weather than in gales and they reverse their direction with the season.

Seabird movements related to weather conditions, or to birds commuting from colonies to distant feeding areas, often produce rates of passage far in excess of those developed by genuine migrations. The varied causes of seabird movements make this a very difficult topic to disentangle.

MIGRATION

MIGRATION AMONG SEABIRD GROUPS

With many seabirds breeding at high latitudes, where migration is a normal response to winter and with their enormous powers of flight, we might expect that migration would be exceptionally com-mon among seabirds. Moreover, as most seabirds migrate exclusively at sea, they have an opportunity to rest or feed whenever they feel like it: not an option for landbirds crossing water or deserts, which many of them do.

Despite these evident advantages, and the very spectacular travels of certain terns and shearwaters notwithstanding, true migration, by which I mean vacating the breeding area completely and shifting to a well-defined wintering area, is not particularly common among seabirds. Peter Berthold's (1993) excellent survey of bird migration makes almost no mention of seabirds. A surprising proportion of seabirds, even of those that breed outside the tropics, remain at their breeding latitudes throughout the year. This is especially true of cormorants: most are sedentary. A few, such as Brandt's Cormorant, actually move to higher latitudes in winter.

TRANS-EQUATORIAL MIGRATION

Among migrants, this is really the 'Grand Prix'; to go from temperate or polar summer in one hemisphere to the same at the other end of the world, and in so doing eliminate the need to suffer any sort of winter at the price of some very prolonged travel. Given their great powers of flight, this would seem to be a relatively small problem for seabirds, but in fact they are less given to crossing the equator than their cousins the shorebirds.

Among species that have most of their breeding range above 30° latitude, transequatorial migration is found in only a few families and is the dominant strategy only among phalaropes (all three species), skuas/jaegers, where 5/7 species cross the equator and the shearwaters (9/13 species). Other groups that include transequatorial migrants are the gadfly petrels (5/12 species), storm-petrels (2/9 species), gulls (2/36 species) and terns (6/17 species).

Given the much greater diversity of seabirds breeding in the southern hemisphere and the fact that they are especially abundant at latitudes south of 40°S, where winter weather can be very severe, we might expect that more southern hemisphere than northern hemisphere species would cross the equator. Surprisingly, there is a much higher proportion of transequatorial migrants among northern hemisphere seabirds. All of the northern hemisphere skuas and jaegers cross the equator, whereas only the South Polar Skua is known to move the other way. Likewise, all of the shearwaters breeding in the cooler latitudes of the northern hemisphere (three) are trans-equatorial migrants, whereas only six out of ten from the southern hemisphere do so. No southern gulls or terns move north, but Franklin's and Sabine's Gulls both travel in the opposite direction, along with three northern hemisphere terns.

One group of species that includes an especially high proportion of transequatorial migrants comprises species that breed on arctic tundra: the three jaegers, Sabine's Gull, Arctic Tern and Grey and Red-necked Phalaropes. Along the low, marshy coasts of northern Hudson Bay where I have worked a good deal, this assemblage of species (minus Red-necked Phalarope, which breeds somewhat further south) forms a characteristic community of seabirds that are largely terrestrial while breeding, though Arctic Terns may feed in shallow coastal waters, as well as tundra ponds.

In North America, the breeding habitat of these tundra-breeding seabirds consists almost entirely of land that has emerged from the sea during the past 8,000 years, owing to the slow rise of the Earth's crust after the crushing weight of the Laurentide ice sheet was removed. An inspection of the likely geography of North America during the height of the final (Wisconsin) glaciation suggests that little suitable habitat would have been available to these species at that period. Hence, they seem to represent opportunistic colonists that have taken advantage of a relatively novel ecological setting. We can speculate that their ranges and populations may have been much smaller during the height of the Pleistocene glaciations. In this respect they resemble their relatives, the shorebirds, which make up a high proportion of landbirds breeding above the treeline in the northern hemisphere, and many of which are also trans-equatorial migrants. It is not clear why breeding on the arctic tundra should be associated with trans-equatorial migration, but there does seem to be a strong correlation.

Many of the northern hemisphere breeders that cross the equator are associated during the non-breeding season with the upwelling zones of the Benguela and Humboldt currents. In addition, all of them feed by surface gleaning while at sea (jaegers, especially Parasitic Jaegers, also pirate food from other birds, but there is not a lot of profit in that when the other birds are not carrying food for their young). The need for these species to radically change their ecology between breeding and wintering is very evident, because the tundra is frozen solid for more than half the year, but the reason why they all choose to cross the equator is less clear.

Overland migration

Many seabirds migrate exclusively over the sea, a practise that keeps them safe from terrestrial predators and ensures that they can rest at any time. However, because of the shape of Eurasia and North America, many species breeding on the coasts of the Arctic Ocean and its adjacent seas can greatly reduce the distance they must travel if they cut across land. Some overland routes are well known, while others have been suggested but are not fully substantiated. The species most likely to follow inland routes are the tundra-nesting species, such as jaegers and phalaropes, and the gulls. Some examples follow.

It is likely that most northern seabirds shifting from northern Asia to winter in the Arabian Sea travel overland at least part of the way. Parasitic Jaegers are regularly seen on passage in the Black Sea, the eastern Mediterranean and in the Red Sea. This seems to form an obvious corridor for birds breeding in western Siberia to reach the Indian Ocean. Some Pomarine Jaegers, occasional visitors to the Caspian Sea, may also travel overland.

Red-necked Phalaropes are even more continental in their migrations, occurring on passage in large numbers on lakes in Kazakhstan, Iran and eastern Turkey. I vividly remember coming on several hundred in lovely breeding plumage on a small reservoir in the desert of eastern Iran one hot dusty day in May: a refreshing reminder of the cool of northern climes. They winter commonly offshore from the Arabian Peninsula (Bailey, 1966). Likewise, in North America, they follow the Mackenzie Valley in fall (Johnson & Herter, 1989) and are common on passage in the Canadian prairies and throughout the Midwest and Great Plains states. This habit of overland migration contrasts strongly with Grey Phalaropes, which are rare in the continental interior of Asia and North America.

In North America, both Long-tailed and Pomarine Jaegers have been observed travelling through the Brooks Range in northern Alaska to reach the coast of the Beaufort Sea (Dean *et al.*, 1976). Small numbers of Parasitic Jaegers appear annually on the Great Lakes, especially Lake Ontario. This is such an obvious shortcut for birds breeding in Hudson Bay that it is scarcely surprising. Whether they travel overland from Lake Ontario to the US east coast is not certain, but seems likely, as no migration is evident through the St. Lawrence Valley in fall. A lack of inland records in the prairies and the Mississippi Valley states suggests that a direct movement from northern breeding grounds to the Gulf of Mexico is unlikely. Most inland records of Parasitic Jaegers are in fall, suggesting that spring migration occurs mainly by sea.

Some mysteries

There is still a great deal that remains to be discovered concerning seabird migrations. Many of the problems concern species that are hard to identify by sight, especially those like gadfly petrels that tend to keep moving and do not follow ships. But even among more familiar species there are some strange riddles.

Take the Red-necked Phalarope. As I have explained, this little bird is quite happy to cross continental interiors, but it feeds mainly at sea. In North America it occurs as a passage migrant in millions in waters off Atlantic Canada, and off the coast of California. In winter, a few occur off Florida and California, but the main wintering area is in the upwelling zone of the Humboldt Current off the coast of Peru. In fall, large numbers occur on passage off the US east coast, but it is absent from, or occurs only as a vagrant in, the Caribbean, along the Caribbean coast of Central America and on the north coast of South America, as far south as Brazil. It seems that the millions that stage off Atlantic Canada in fall do not cross to the Pacific. However, no wintering area is known in the South Atlantic and the destination of the birds moving down the US east coast is a mystery. This is of more than academic interest, because the species is thought to have declined sharply in North America and it is hard to speculate about possible causes when we do not even know where the birds are for half the year.

Another mystery concerns the migration of Sabine's Gulls breeding in eastern North America. Many tens of thousands nest around Hudson Bay and Foxe Basin, but only small numbers are seen in fall in the Labrador Sea and the species is very rare off Newfoundland and further south on the eastern seaboard. A few occur on the Great Lakes, some even wintering, but not enough to account for more than a small fraction of the known population. In the eastern North Atlantic, Sabine's Gulls are common in late fall in the Bay of Biscay and there is a large concentration off Namibia and South Africa in winter.

Numbers breeding in the Barents Sea are very small and the nearest substantial Asian breeding area is the Kolyma: those birds could move east rather than west in fall to join birds from Alaska and western Canada that move through the Bering Sea to passage off California and winter in the Humboldt Current region. Do the birds from eastern Canada travel direct to Europe after leaving their breeding grounds, as has been suggested by Brown *et al.* (1975), thence moving south to the South Atlantic? Could they possibly make a huge loop around Alaska to join the Pacific wintering population? Or is there another unknown wintering concentration, perhaps somewhere in the Atlantic and perhaps occupied also by Red-necked Phalaropes? When we can put satellite transmitters on Sabine's Gulls (not far off, surely) we shall find out. Whatever the answer, their avoidance of the continental shelf areas off Newfoundland, a magnet for practically every other seabird visiting the North Atlantic, is unique, almost perverse.

NAVIGATION

I will not say much about how seabirds navigate from one part of the ocean to another. This is not because I do not regard this as an interesting subject, but because little research on this topic is available for marine birds. Moreover, after a century of investigations into bird navigation, we appear to be no nearer to learning how they do it. While celestial cues, landmarks, smell and magnetic fields have all been shown to play a role, none appears exclusively responsible: some birds appear quite capable of making do without any of them. There are some other cues that seabirds might use (water temperature, salinity) and smell appears a promising mechanism for the proven scent-followers, the tubenoses, but in reality the topic is shrouded in ignorance and there seems to be no reason to heighten the confusion by adding my own interpretations. For a scientist who relishes a real challenge, seabird navigation could provide just that.

WEATHER MOVEMENTS

Bad-weather movements raise many interesting questions: where were the birds before the storm arrived and where did they go? Why were they travelling at all in such difficult conditions? Why are some species very prominent, while others, common in the area at the same time, rare or absent? How important are these movements to the survival of seabirds? Considering how commonly these movements occur, it is surprising how little comment they have received from researchers. As Bill Bourne (1963) remarked:

> *The effect of storms on displacing seabirds from their normal range is well known, but the full consequences of these events on the birds that remain at sea has hardly been studied.*

Bourne's statement remains broadly true. Lack of information on the impact of weather on seabirds may persist because of the difficulty of studying the relationship, rather than because scientists regard it as unimportant. On the other hand, weather conditions that fall within the normal range encountered by a given species are unlikely to have obvious effects, especially on survival, because such frequent selection would soon result in adaptations enabling the species to cope; if it did not then the species would not occur in the area at all.

Apart from the sort of regular weather that I have described, seabirds also must contend with really big storms: hurricanes that develop wind and sea conditions in which ships have difficulty in remaining afloat, or exceptionally prolonged periods of adverse weather conditions, especially in winter, that can drain the birds' energy reserves, resulting in their being washed-up exhausted on beaches, or even driven far inland. Some species are famous for such periodic 'wrecks'. Unpredictable and highly dispersed events, such as major storms and hurricanes, are by their nature very hard to study because we have very little warning of when and where they will take place. On the other hand, because they often produce unusual visitations of otherwise rare species, and because they frequently involve very conspicuous meteorological phenomena, much has been recorded on their occurrence. We may be closer to understanding the consequences for seabirds of major storms than we are to determining the significance of variation within usual weather conditions.

In this section, I deal with the effects on seabirds of 'normal weather'; the kind of conditions that might occur several times a year within a species' normal range. I also consider the occurrence of seabird wrecks and what they tell us about seabird ecology. In the Pacific, and to a lesser extent in other oceans, multi-year fluctuations in the ocean–atmosphere system produce cyclical changes in oceanographic and climatic conditions that have important repercussions for marine ecosystems and may produce striking effects on seabird biology. Finally, I speculate a little on the effects of tropical hurricanes on seabirds.

RESPONSES TO 'NORMAL' WEATHER

Weather is an important feature of every bird's environment. However, though the habitat in which landbirds seek their food is usually affected only by extreme forms of weather (cyclones, major gales and floods), the habitat of seabirds changes continually in response to weather, especially wind. Consequently, weather forms a more significant part of the seabird's world than it does for landbirds. Atmosphere and the ocean form a closely integrated physical system. Hence, it is appropriate that seabirds, living on the interface between air and water, should be among the most weather-dependent of birds (with the possible exception of swifts).

Casual observation suggests that oceanic seabirds are amazingly unaffected by bad weather. As Norman Elkins (1988) noted, 'seabirds can easily tolerate weather conditions which man may find appalling'. The large albatrosses are actually dependent on strong winds to allow them to glide the enormous distances they must cover to find their widely dispersed food supply. At the other end of the scale, David Ainley (1984) gives an excellent description of storm-petrels' ability to survive bad weather at sea:

Storm-petrels twist and turn in moving troughs of waves with the crests towering far above them. Their wings are extended and they push themselves away from the moving green walls with out-stretched feet. Strong winds shear the crests from the tops above them, but far, far down in the troughs they are protected.

However, that we see seabirds gaily flapping along in what we regard as a howling gale, does not mean that they are unaffected.

Many of the large-scale movements of seabirds reported by land-based observers seem to be in response to particular weather conditions. It is rare to see birds actively feeding during such weather-related movements. Moreover, these movements clearly displace sizeable numbers of birds from their normal feeding areas. Hence they must have a two-fold effect, in costing the birds time away from feeding, and in the otherwise unnecessary expenditure of energy on flight, in many cases clearly expensive in terms of distance covered, because of the adverse wind direction.

The conditions under which pelagic seabirds, especially Northern Gannets, Northern Fulmars, Black-legged Kittiwakes and Sooty Shearwaters appear off Kullen, at the southern end of the Kattegat, were described by Blomqvist & Peterz (1984). None of the species involved was local to the area of observation, but the movements were rather frequent. They showed that the movements were in response to the passage of low-pressure systems moving across Scandinavia from the Atlantic that brought strong westerly (onshore) winds to their area. Most birds observed were moving south and east, making use of slope-soaring (Chapter 2) and keeping in the wave-troughs for long periods.

Blomqvist & Peterz suggested that these arrivals were the result of birds moving away from the path of the depression by simultaneously following wave alignments and making use of whatever tail-wind they could. The birds were able to do this because the alignment of the waves lags behind the wind direction, as it changes in response to the movement of the depression. This process leads to a clockwise movement of pelagic birds within the somewhat enclosed waters of the North Sea. Observations from the British and Dutch coasts support this interpretation. However, from the numbers of birds and time periods involved, we have to conclude that feeding was disrupted over a large area and for several days.

WRECKS

Abnormally large numbers of seabirds cast ashore or found inland are often referred to as 'wrecks', a term that is sometimes applied rather loosely. Both 'die-off' and wreck have been applied to events involving the mass mortality of seabirds. The term wreck has been especially associated with the inland occurrence in large numbers of birds that are otherwise strictly marine (e.g. auks, storm-petrels; Thomson, 1984). Die-off, in contrast, has been applied more commonly to events involving large numbers of beach-cast birds, where adverse weather was not an obvious contributory factor. They are occasionally used interchangeably.

To clarify things, I intend to apply the term **wreck** to events in which unusual numbers of seabirds occur inland, associated with periods of adverse weather, including strong onshore winds (e.g. Little

Auk wrecks in the UK, in 1895 and 1912, and Sabine's Gull occurrence in western France in 1993; see Table 7.1). I shall confine the term **die-off** to events in which uncommonly large numbers of seabirds come ashore dead or dying in the absence of any obviously adverse weather.

For events where birds occur in large numbers outside their normal range without any apparent adverse weather, it is proper to use the term **irruption,** which is applied to similar events for land-birds. This term was applied to the arrival in South African waters of large numbers of various species of southern ocean seabirds in the summer of 1984, culminating in many being involved in a wreck in August (Ryan *et al.*, 1989; Jury, 1991); also to the periodic events when Thick-billed Murres visited the Great Lakes in large numbers, flying up the St. Lawrence without any wind assistance (Gaston, 1988).

Wrecks and/or die-offs frequently follow irruptions, and this coincidence may occur because the displaced birds, having travelled a long way, and perhaps having left their normal range in poor condition, are confronted by unfamiliar marine habitat in which they may not be able to forage effectively, causing their condition to deteriorate further. Poor body condition would make them more readily susceptible to exhaustion in the event of adverse weather conditions, or might lead to starvation even without the intervention of storms. Some notable wrecks and die-offs that have been well described are listed in Table 7.1.

Table 7.1   Some examples of major seabird wrecks

Locality	Date	Principal species involved	Associated weather	Reference
(1) Around Wellington, New Zealand	Apr 1968	Royal Albatross, Soft-plumaged Petrel, Black-winged Petrel, Fairy Prion, Buller's Shearwater	Major storm—many birds, including some albatrosses, blown up to 150 km inland	Kinsky, 1968
(2) West coast of North Island, New Zealand	Sep 1981	Kerguelen Petrel, Blue Petrel	Major storm	Reed, 1981; Imber, 1984
(3) East coast of New Zealand	Jul 1984	Blue Petrel, Kerguelen Petrel	Strong southerly winds as far as 60°S	Jenkins & Greenwood, 1984
(4) New Zealand	Aug 1984	Kerguelen Petrel, Blue Petrel, Fairy Prion	Southwest gales in the Tasman Sea	Powlesland, 1986
(5) Southwest Western Australia, Victoria	Aug 1984	Kerguelen Petrel, Blue Petrel	Gale-force onshore winds, but not exceptional	Carter, 1984; Brown *et al.*, 1986
(6) Central Victoria	Aug 1985	Common Diving-petrel	Prolonged severe gales	Norman & Brown, 1987
(7) South Africa	Jul–Aug. 1984	Kerguelen Petrel, Blue Petrel, Antarctic Prion	Strong onshore winds, but not exceptional: many species present offshore in unusually large numbers earlier	Ryan *et al.*, 1989
(8) West coast of South Africa	May 1984	Black-browed Albatross	Major gales	Ryan, 1987

Table 7.1 continued

Locality	Date	Principal species involved	Associated weather	Reference
(9) Port Elizabeth, South Africa	Aug 1981	Blue Petrel, prions	Prolonged gales	Batchelor, 1981
(10) Sea of Cortez	Sep 1976	Least Storm-petrel	Hurricane 'Kathleen'	Stallcup, 1990
(11) Newfoundland, Nova Scotia		Laughing Gull, Black Skimmer	Hurricane Helene	Tuck 1968
(12) Great Lakes, northeast USA	Nov 1950	Thick-billed Murre	Strong easterly gale	Tuck, 1961
(13) Great Lakes, northeast USA	Nov–Dec 1962, 1963	Little Auk	Strong easterly gale	Audubon Bird Notes, 1962, 1963
(14) Great Lakes, northeast USA	Nov 1969	Little Auk	Strong easterly gale	Audubon Bird Notes, 1969
(15) Holland and Belgium	Sep 1963	Great Skua	Prolonged gales	Thomson, 1966
(16) Irish Sea	Sep 1969	Common Murre	Gales, but some birds cast ashore before onset of bad weather	NERC, 1971
(17) Irish Sea	Jan 1974	Common Murre, Razorbill, Great Cormorant, gulls, seaducks	Prolonged cold and stormy weather	Bogan *et al.*, 1974
(18) Britain and western Europe	Oct 1952	Leach's Storm-petrel	Prolonged westerly gales right across the Atlantic	Boyd, 1954
(19) North Sea coasts	Feb–Mar 1962	Northern Fulmar	Prolonged westerly gales, becoming very severe in mid-Feb	Pashby & Cudworth, 1968
(20) Portugal	Nov 1983	Leach's Storm-petrel	Strong southwest gale	Teixeira, 1987
(21) Western France	Sep 1993	Sabine's Gull	Extra-tropical depression, giving max. winds >150 km/h	Elkins & Yésou, 1998

Some species are especially susceptible to wrecks, which seem to be a regular feature of their ecology. The Little Auk is probably the best-known species in this respect, because most wrecks occur in densely inhabited parts of Western Europe and eastern North America. There are several features that seem to be common to most Little Auk wrecks in North America:

(1)   In years of wrecks, first sightings off Massachusetts were nearly always in late October or early November, well before wrecks occurred.

(2)   The actual wrecks nearly always occurred in late November or December, rather than after Christmas.

(3)   Years when large numbers were seen in the northeastern USA, whether or not involving wrecks, tended to be in runs (1930–32, 1948–51, 1962–70, although not 1964); in the 20th century there were four years of high numbers in the 1930s, three in the 1950s and seven in the 1960s. The other seven decades had only two big years among them.

(4)   Most inland records coincided with gales, but large numbers outside their normal range (e.g. off Cape Cod) were not necessarily associated with bad weather.

From the timing of arrival of birds off the northeastern US and the lack of association with weather events, it is clear that the birds had deliberately moved out of their normal wintering range. The non-random distribution of wreck years suggests some climatic or oceanographic process working over a scale of several years. Alternatively, there could be some relationship to population fluctuations or to inter-annual variation in breeding success, but we have no information on either for the huge Little Auk population in Thule District, Greenland, from which the birds presumably originated.

The concentration of wrecks in early winter, rather than in late winter when the birds might be expected to be in poorer condition, suggests that inexperience may be involved. Museum study would reveal whether, like murres, most Little Auks wrecked in the northeastern states are young of the year. A number of other major wrecks have involved mainly young birds, including the Kerguelen Petrels involved in the 1981 wreck in New Zealand, the Blue Petrels (but not the Kerguelen Petrels) wrecked in New Zealand in 1978 and Australia in 1984, Antarctic Fulmars wrecked in New Zealand in 1975 and 1978, and Great Skuas wrecked in Holland and Belgium in 1963 (Table 7.1).

WRECKS IN THE ABSENCE OF IRRUPTIONS

Though it is clear that many seabird wrecks follow irruptions of the species involved outside their normal range, some bad-weather incidents may be sufficiently violent and prolonged to bring ashore species that would normally occur in the area. An example is the New Zealand storm of 9–10 April 1968 (Table 7.1), with winds gusting to 160 km/h, which sank a ferry in the mouth of Wellington harbour. All of the species driven ashore were those that would have been present within a few tens of kilometres offshore. Likewise, birds coming ashore in the 1974 Irish Sea–Firth of Clyde wreck represented a cross-section of local wintering seabirds. It is evident that in this case the duration of adverse conditions was sufficient to cause mortality across a wide spectrum of ecologies. In contrast, in the Irish Sea wreck of 1969, Common Murres began to come ashore in starving condition under quite moderate weather conditions, though more were beached after storms. In this case, the event was probably triggered by a failure in the local food supplies; possibly a particular fish stock, as seaducks and cormorants (presumably bottom feeders) were not affected.

Susceptibility to being driven onshore appears to vary a great deal among species. One of those most commonly involved in wrecks is Leach's Storm-petrel, which is periodically sprinkled across Europe by weather that induces little mortality among other species. The events of a particularly spectacular wreck that occurred in Britain and adjacent parts of the European seaboard in October 1952 were documented in detail by my colleague, Hugh Boyd.

Probably more than 5,000 birds were found on beaches and inland in Britain, with records in nearly every county. Small numbers were seen at coastal stations in late September, which is not unusual, but the main wreck began on 19 October, with landings initially in southwest Ireland. By 23 October large numbers appeared in southwest England and, by 25 October, on the west coast of Scotland; the peak in Liverpool Bay came on 30–31 October. They were also reported from western France from 31 October, in Holland on 31 October–2 November and in Belgium on 5–11 November.

The meteorological situation prior to the first Leach's Storm-petrels coming ashore was characterised by a succession of strong westerly gales persisting over several weeks. Boyd suggested that the movements of fronts and their associated gale-force winds could have brought petrels across the Atlantic from the outer Newfoundland Banks area: the heartland of the species' distribution. Small numbers of British Storm-Petrels also came ashore during the same period, but most of the North Atlantic population had probably migrated out of the area by the time of the storms. A similar wreck was noted in Britain in 1895, and a smaller wreck occurred in Portugal in November 1983, the latter involving mainly first-year birds.

Another species that appears susceptible to being storm-driven is Sabine's Gull, a rather tern-like species that is perhaps remarked more closely than others because it is rather rare in Europe. Elkins & Yésou (1998) catalogued the appearance of this species in western France and southern England and demonstrated that several striking arrivals of the species, especially in western France, were associated with the arrival of exceptionally deep low-pressure systems in September or early October. One of these, known in southern England as 'the Great Storm', occurred on 15 October 1987, and brought 180 km/h winds to the south coast of Britain, felling many ancient trees across the southern counties. This storm brought many inland records of Sabine's Gulls. Elkins & Yésou considered that birds found inland may have been travelling in the eye of the storm, perhaps crossing the coast at night, after the storm centre moved inland, leaving them exposed to the violent winds surrounding the eye. The 1987 event constitutes the only widespread wreck of the species ever recorded in the British Isles.

The timing of Sabine's Gull influxes on the western European seaboard suggests that they are normally present in the western approaches to the English Channel and the Bay of Biscay during September and October. Some occasionally enter inshore waters without being gale-driven, but the major coastal events occur when they encounter exceptional onshore winds. It provides an example of a seabird that, despite regular occurrence in offshore waters, is little known to the birdwatchers of the region because it remains far offshore except under extreme circumstances.

HURRICANES

Hurricanes are abnormally deep low-pressure cells that form in tropical waters but sometimes reach temperate areas. They generate enormous wind speeds and huge clouds, and frequently cover hundreds of thousands of square kilometres of ocean. The average radius of a typical Caribbean hurricane, within which wind speeds exceed 100 km/h, is more than 500 km (nearly 1 million km^2).

Hurricanes are a familiar component of fall weather in the Caribbean and off the coast of the southeastern USA. Because the eastern seaboard of North America has many resident birders, we might expect the ornithological consequences of the frequent hurricane visitations to be rather well documented. In fact, little information has been published, presumably because most hurricanes do not produce obvious displacements of birds. Here are a few that did.

Murphy (1936) dealt in some detail with the consequences of six major hurricanes that struck the southeast coast of the USA in August or September between 1876 and 1933. To summarise the highlights, most resulted in tropical Caribbean species, such as Sooty Terns, Black-capped Petrels, tropicbirds and frigatebirds being recorded on the US east coast. Two, which originated as far east as the vicinity of the Cape Verde Islands, delivered Herald Petrel (perhaps Trindade Petrel) and Band-rumped (Madeiran) Storm-petrels to eastern North America, as well as large numbers of Wilson's Storm-petrels. The Band-rumped Storm-petrels, in particular, being characteristic of the eastern tropical Atlantic, were probably transported several thousand kilometres before being driven ashore.

In the fall of 1939 an initially typical hurricane moving off the US east coast met a strong frontal system off New England that drove it inland into the Connecticut Valley. There was widespread flooding and property damage along the storm track, but displaced seabirds mainly occurred in areas outside the zone of damage, with many Leach's Storm-petrels and smaller numbers of White-tailed Tropicbirds, Cory's Shearwaters and Great Shearwaters being found inland (Eliot, 1959).

In September 1976, Hurricane Kathleen blew up to 1,000 Least Storm-petrels north from their normal range in the Sea of Cortez and scattered them across southern California and Arizona (Stallcup, 1990). Because Least Storm-petrels have a very restricted range, it was possible to be confident of where the birds had originated.

Two large hurricanes on the east coast of North America, in 1958 and 1968, dispersed Laughing Gulls and Black Skimmers north at least as far as Newfoundland, with several thousands being observed out of range. Ringed birds that were encountered in eastern Canada during these incidents had been ringed in Florida, Virginia and the Carolinas. All were in their first or second year; no adults were encountered (Tuck, 1968). Until 1958, the Laughing Gull had not been recorded in Newfoundland; however, in the aftermath of the storm at least 1,000 were present in the Burgeo area alone, mostly in an exhausted condition.

A very severe hurricane (Hugo) struck the coast of South Carolina on 21–22 September 1989, with winds of c.200 km/h when it touched the coast, and still >100 km/h several hours later when it reached North Carolina. Pelagic seabirds, including 50 Cory's Shearwaters, a Leach's Storm-petrel, a White-tailed Tropicbird, an Audubon's Shearwater, dozens of jaegers, six Sooty and three Bridled Terns, and a Brown Noddy were scattered inland along the storm track, mainly on lakes and reservoirs (Le Grand, 1990). From the location of the inland sightings, which followed the storm track very closely, Le Grand suggested that the majority of birds were carried inland in the eye of the storm, rather than being blown inland by the surrounding winds.

Reports of hurricane-driven seabirds in the eastern US, where there are many active birdwatchers, suggest that most seabirds are able to evade hurricanes. Considering the size of the average hurricane and the enormous wind speeds involved, this is a rather surprising observation. Several facts seem to point to the possibility that those that do come ashore may be transported in the 'eye', the calm centre of the storm. In addition to the evidence suggested by Le Grand, based on the close relationship between the storm centre and the distribution of wrecked seabirds, there is the fact that, in many cases, the species coming ashore in large numbers are not those that would be expected to be just offshore of the area where the hurricane touched land.

It is difficult to imagine birds such as tropical terns, tropicbirds, or gadfly petrels simply moving in front of a hurricane, when they are capable of using the very strong winds on the periphery of the storm to outflank it and avoid it. This may be less true of hurricanes in the Gulf of Mexico, where the encircling land and restricted exits may force birds to choose between flying into the storm or crossing land. The lack of very large wrecks of oceanic seabirds on the American Gulf coast, or in western Florida, may indicate that seabirds tend to avoid these waters in the hurricane season. Hurricanes always seem to bring more birds ashore on the eastern US seaboard, where their landfall is less common.

What the relatively small seabird mortality caused by hurricanes and other very large storms does suggest is that marine birds are capable of detecting low pressure and its associated weather symptoms very early and moving away from it. As doing so will inevitably disrupt their feeding temporarily, perhaps for several days, they also need to be able to store sufficient energy to be able to make these movements, combined with temporary fasts, at short notice. This feature of the ecology of oceanic birds may have been significant in keeping them relatively large (Chapter 3) and in causing them to maintain an energy supply sufficient for several days' survival more or less throughout the year. The need to transport this enlarged fuel supply may have had a significant effect on the design of the average seabird.

THE WIDER CONSEQUENCES OF WEATHER

It is clear that major storms, or prolonged periods of bad weather, can result in the deaths of many seabirds. When some birds die, presumably others that survive do so in a weakened condition. Young birds are clearly affected to a greater extent than older birds by these events. What is less clear is the overall importance of bad weather in determining survival rates and other population characteristics of seabirds. On this point, there is little evidence, but I have tried to assemble a few pointers.

Bryan Nelson (1988) reported that cyclones blowing nestlings from their nests were an important cause of nestling mortality for Abbott's Booby on Christmas Island.

The mortality of first-year Great Skuas appears to be significantly affected by bad weather, with variation in the recovery rates of ringed birds being related to the occurrence of inland wrecks (Furness, 1978). More tellingly, there appears to be a tendency for cohorts that were recovered in large numbers as first-years due to bad weather to also suffer heavier mortality in their second year, possibly because they never reach the body condition that they might have attained in a more clement winter.

Thick-billed Murres at Prince Leopold Island sometimes have difficulty in landing on the breeding cliffs through a combination of fog, reduced visibility and high winds, making manoeuvring difficult. If these conditions persist for several days, as they sometimes do, birds may be forced to desert their eggs to seek food, resulting in losses of eggs to gulls. Conversely, at Coats Island, at the other end of the species range in the Canadian arctic, a combination of very hot weather and dense clouds of mosquitoes may cause the murres to suffer from dehydration, forcing them to leave their eggs or risk dying, which a few do (Gaston *et al.*, 2002). In both cases, birds are quite capable of enduring the most extreme conditions: the critical factor is their duration.

EL NIÑO AND THE SOUTHERN OSCILLATION

El Niño is a spectacular oceanographic event, recurring every 4–5 years. If it is a strong event, it generates lots of publicity. El Niño ('the child', a name assigned because the events in Peru, where the name originated, often begin about Christmas) was the name given to a periodic failure of the coastal upwelling system along the coast of Peru and Ecuador. This failure causes a catastrophic decline in local marine production, resulting in the disruption of local marine ecosystems, the deaths of billions of fish and the death or emigration of their associated avian and marine mammal predators.

Though the El Niño phenomenon has been known for many years, the larger atmospheric changes that bring about this and related oceanographic effects are only gradually being elucidated. As is frequently the case, we know a lot about the mechanisms by which El Niño is created. However, we do not know what triggers it, so we are little further ahead at predicting when such events will arrive than we were 50 years ago.

It transpires that El Niño is the result of an alternation of atmospheric conditions over the Pacific known as the Southern Oscillation. The Southern Oscillation is a periodic reversal of pressure imbalances, such that high pressure over the eastern Pacific and low pressure over Indonesia and the western Pacific is replaced with the opposite situation. This reversal reduces or eliminates the Northeast Trade-winds, causing a cessation of cold-water upwelling in the Humboldt Current system, along the coasts of Peru and Ecuador. The most obvious symptom is that, in the absence of cold upwelling, the surface waters of the eastern and central Pacific become much warmer than usual. One commonly used measure of the Southern Oscillation is the difference in atmospheric pressure between Darwin, Australia, and Tahiti (the Southern Oscillation Index; SOI). The relationship between the SO Index and sea surface temperatures in the eastern Pacific is shown in Figure 7.1. It is this surface water warming, with its associated die-off of fish, mammals and birds, which is the real El Niño. The whole atmosphere–ocean event is known as an El Niño Southern Oscillation (ENSO for short).

Very large ENSO events of recent decades were those of 1982–83 and 1997–98 (Figure 7.1). The 1982–83 event was the first large ENSO to be carefully monitored, and the results were summarised by Ainley *et al.* (1988), Ainley & Boekelheide (1990), Duffy *et al.* (1988) and Schreiber & Schreiber (1984, 1986). The most dramatic effects were seen, as usual, along the coast of Peru, where breeding of the 'guano birds'—the Peruvian Booby, Brown Pelican and Guanay Cormorant—failed entirely and the total population of the three species was decimated. Many birds moved outside their normal range, with large numbers of Peruvian Boobies seen in the Gulf of Panama in 1983, many of which died. Out of eight million guano birds present in Peruvian waters in July 1982, as the El Niño began, only 100,000 were present by June 1983. Including those that emigrated and then returned, only one million survived the El Niño episode.

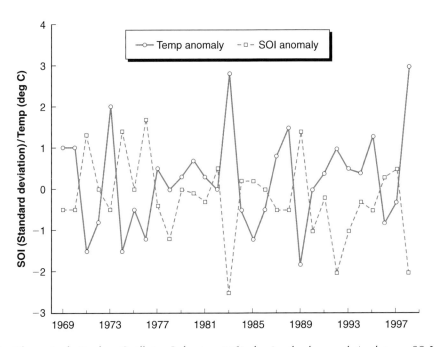

Figure 7.1   Changes in the Southern Oscillation Index since 1960, showing the close correlation between SO Indices and water temperatures: when SOI is high, water temperature is high and vice-versa.

Breeding also failed for the 18 seabird species nesting on Christmas Island, in the central Pacific (five tubenoses, one tropicbird, three boobies, two frigatebirds and seven terns). However, declines among these populations were less marked than those in Peru, except for Sooty Terns, which were reduced from four million to 100,000 birds. Elsewhere, from the Galápagos Islands, along the Pacific coast of the Americas north as far as Alaska, breeding of some species failed and dead and dying seabirds were reported. At the Farallon Islands, California, all species showed reduced breeding success except storm-petrels, and increased mortality was reported for Cassin's Auklets and Western Gulls. At French Frigate Shoals, in the Leeward Islands, many Sooty Terns disappeared, but other species were hardly affected.

The 1982–83 event also had repercussions in the Atlantic, where the upwellings of the Benguela Current, off southwest Africa, also failed, causing breeding failure for cormorants and penguins. This is a typical event in the Benguela Current system, affecting especially African Penguins and Cape Cormorants. Effects on seabirds were observed in 32 years in 1901–1983, with 27 breeding failures and seven mass-mortality events, most of which were associated with ENSO events (La Cock, 1986). However, Magellanic Penguins in Argentina showed increased breeding success in 1983.

Catastrophic mortality as a result of ENSO events occurs only in the largest events, when there appears to be a total breakdown of local food-webs. The widespread die-offs that were observed during the 1982–83 ENSO had a strong effect on ideas about seabird population regulation, because they made it clear that even such potentially long-lived organisms as seabirds could suffer abrupt population changes. This led many people to reject the concept of density dependence as a mechanism for controlling seabird populations. However, although die-offs of seabirds have been reported for many species and from a wide range of different marine areas, mortality on the scale seen in 1982–83 appears to be rare. Other cyclical or periodic changes in oceanographic conditions that affect seabird survival rates have been reported and more will certainly be identified. However, nothing creates the impact seen in a full-scale El Niño. On the other hand, breeding failures are frequent and widespread. The significance of these observations will be further discussed in Chapters 9 and 10.

CHAPTER EIGHT

Breeding, coloniality and its consequences

In 1983, I decided that it would be useful to initiate some studies of Pacific seabirds, which, in Canada, seemed to have received less attention than those of the Atlantic. I joined a field camp in the Queen Charlotte Islands, run by Gary Kaiser, Mike Rodway and Moira Lemon of the Pacific and Yukon Region of the Canadian Wildlife Service, to assess what type of research might be useful and feasible.

After spending several days based on the east side of the archipelago, the whole camp transferred to Hippa Island, off the west coast. We did not know much about Hippa Island then, but we did know that it supported a very large colony of Ancient Murrelets. I was anxious to see something of this obscure and little-known species, but because of other commitments I had only one day in which to do it.

After a long, rough voyage up the west coast of the Charlottes, during which seasickness was compensated by my first sight of Black-footed Albatrosses, we set up camp amid the striking mossy greenery that blanketed the whole of Hippa Island. The rest of the field crew were well exercised by the end of the day and everyone except myself retired early. As darkness fell, I forced myself to stay up, because I knew that the murrelets would not arrive until near midnight. I was reading in the cook tent, by the light of a Coleman lantern, when I heard the unmistakable piping of a young auk, sounding very much like a fledging murre. To my surprise, before I could move, two downy murrelet chicks ran in the door of the tent at amazing speed, scurried about at my feet and then exited under the side flap.

I dowsed the lamp, which presumably had attracted them, got out my flashlight, and stepped outside. All around me, I could hear the fluttering of wings and the sound of leaves and twigs snapping. The forest was alive with invisible creatures. I stood for some time in darkness, listening to the movements and the calls, faint at first, from birds flying above the forest, and then louder, as birds perched in the canopy and on the ground began to call. From time to time I switched on the flashlight to reveal small, grey, torpedo-shaped birds sitting on logs and stumps. Some flew, but as the night grew darker, some began to fly towards the light and I had to duck to avoid being hit. Some birds that had begun to sing in earnest seemed to take little notice of the light and continued to sit and call as I watched.

I must have spent several hours wandering slowly backwards and forwards, afraid to go any distance from camp, as I felt I could easily become lost in the surrounding forest. During that time, I saw several hundred birds in an area of no more than a hectare. I saw a few more chicks, but it was late in the season and most had left. From what I subsequently learnt, the birds I saw must have been mainly prospecting pre-breeders.

The cacophony was awesome, with an amazing variety of sounds coming from underground burrows and from birds on the surface and in the trees. It was impossible to make any sense of what was happening, but I was tremendously impressed with the spectacle. Whatever the reason for this strange behaviour, I knew it was something completely outside my previous experience. Unravelling the basics of who was doing what and why they were doing it took the following six years. The picture of Ancient Murrelet behaviour is still very incomplete and this is true of most seabirds that visit their breeding colonies at night.

'SEABIRD COLONIES'

In Chapter 1, I indicated that one of the salient characteristics of seabirds was their habit of breeding in colonies. This contrasts with landbirds, many of which defend breeding territories within which they do most of their feeding. The chain of cause and effect that has led to colonial habits in seabirds is well established and so self-evident that, fortunately, no one has bothered to build mathematical models to describe it. What more or less everyone agrees is that:

A. Adaptation for life in the marine environment (long wings, webbed feet set far back, etc.) reduces mobility on land and the ability to escape predators.

B. Their vulnerability to predation, especially by terrestrial mammals, places a premium on breeding on small offshore islands that terrestrial mammals have failed to reach.

C. The large area available for foraging means that many seabird populations are very large.

D. Many birds attempting to breed on a small island cannot avoid being conspicuous, if they nest on the surface, so clumping together is the most effective defence against avian predators (eagles, gulls, skuas and giant petrels) which are the inevitable camp-followers of large seabird aggregations.

E. Also, and the importance of this factor is not entirely clear, the practical problem of defending a feeding territory at sea appears insurmountable.

Of course, if you want to feed at sea, being on an island surrounded by potential foraging areas offers advantages that a mainland situation does not. However, it is very striking that, where an island close inshore or a prominent mainland headland offer similar breeding sites, the island is nearly always preferred, though there may be only a small difference in flying time to potential foraging areas.

Because many of the characteristics of seabird breeding behaviour are connected to the fact that they breed close together in colonies, I shall begin by considering the habit of colonial breeding.

What is a colony?

The application of the words 'breeding colony' to a group of nesting seabirds is somewhat surprising, in view of the etymology. In a non-ornithological context, a colony is not an aggregation of something, but a permanent settlement placed at a distance from the traditional area inhabited by the nation involved. This usage conforms to that of its Latin root, so it has a long history. The Oxford Dictionary does give a biological meaning for 'colony', but defines it as a group of animals that are attached together (e.g. coral polyps).

The dual meanings of the word colony lead to a certain amount of semantic confusion, which I will attempt to unravel for any readers who were not brought up with the vagaries of English. A colony of birds means a group of breeders: a colony of people means the Portuguese in Goa or the English in New Zealand. Birds arriving at an established colony do not *colonise* it, they merely re-occupy it; they are not *colonists*, just birds. On the other hand, non-colonial birds invading a previously unoccupied area (Savi's Warblers arriving in Kent) *are* colonists and are said to be colonising the new area; in this case the meaning is the same whether applied to birds, rabbits or people. The two phenomena are distinguished by different suffixes: coloniality (the state of living in a colony) and colonialism (the state of living in someone else's country). The former is absent from most non-technical dictionaries.

Despite the difference between seabird colonies and colonialist colonies of colonists, there is a sense in which the two concepts coincide. When a seabird comes ashore to its breeding colony, like the Dutch arriving in the Spice Islands or the English sailing up the Hooghly to Calcutta, it is entering a completely new environment. A young murre attempting to land for the first time on a narrow cliff ledge in a brisk wind may be just as ill-prepared, in its way, as the early Spanish conquistadors were for yellow fever and the many new diseases that they encountered in Central America. Like their human counterparts, many seabirds set about converting their colonial habitat into an environment more to their taste (digging burrows, building nests) and like their human counterparts, they sometimes end up destroying the whole place (dead trees, eroded soil).

In Britain, the term colony is mostly avoided for landbirds. Rooks breed in rookeries and herons in heronries. House Martins and swifts just breed in groups; only the highly aggregated burrows of Sand Martins are automatically referred to as colonies. However, in the literature of science, all these species are regarded as 'colonial breeders' and their breeding aggregations can properly be termed colonies.

When is an aggregation a colony?

I have suggested that one of the main reasons why so many seabirds nest in colonies is the shortage of prime breeding locations in the form of offshore islands. This seems to suggest a very passive process, with birds aggregating merely because there is nowhere else to breed. However, very few islands are completely covered by breeders of a given species. Usually the colony comprises one or more areas where the nests are concentrated, scattered in a matrix of unoccupied ground.

In some cases the reason for the concentration is obvious: at Funk Island, off Newfoundland, all the Atlantic Puffins nest in a small area because that is the only piece of the island that provides soil for them to burrow in (Plate 21). At Bonaventure Island, in the Gulf of St. Lawrence, Northern Gannets occupy sloping ground at the periphery of the island, rather than flat ground, because they can become airborne more easily on the slope. At Prince Leopold Island, Thick-billed Murres occupy the steepest, highest cliffs, because those that are less steep might be accessible to Arctic Foxes *Alopex lagopus* and because chicks might not succeed in gliding to the sea where the cliffs are not vertical.

That said, there are still many instances where the clumping of colonial-breeding seabirds appears much greater than the habitat requires. Returning to the example of Funk Island, while the puffins aggregate because of restricted habitat, the gannets and murres which nest on rocky areas create distinct patches not evidently necessitated by habitat requirements.

WHY COLONIES?

LANDBIRDS

Colonial breeding is a form of breeding dispersal in which a number of birds nest much closer together than a random dispersal on the landscape, or in the case of seabirds, the coast, would dictate. David Lack (1968) reviewed the main characteristics associated with colonial breeding in birds and concluded that it occurred mainly where the distribution of food, or of potential nest sites, made the maintenance of separate feeding territories unprofitable. Taking the cave-nesting swiftlets (*Collocalia*) as an example, their food supply of flying insects is highly mobile and very unpredictable in its distribution, while their preferred breeding sites, in caves, are scarce in most areas. There would be little value in trying to defend a cave breeding site, because additional swiftlets in your range will hardly affect the food supply. And, if you cannot defend your space, you might as well go the other way and pack together as tightly as possible. That way you may swamp the local predators (falcons, in the case of the swiftlets) by sheer numbers. Swiftlets can really do that: I once saw more than 100,000 emerge within less than ten minutes from a single cave in the Nilgiri Hills of south India!

Only a small proportion of landbirds breeds in colonies, mainly aerial feeders (swallows, swifts and the like), scavengers on large animals (vultures), some fruit and seedeaters (parakeets, weavers, silverbills) and some birds of open country that excavate nests in earthen cliffs (Bank Mynas and bee-eaters). However, many freshwater birds do so, especially herons, ibises, storks, pelicans, cormorants and some grebes and rails. Many colonial breeders feed in flocks, sometimes even cooperating to do so (many freshwater cormorants and pelicans), but some are solitary feeders, especially the larger herons, storks and cormorants: the association between colonial breeding and flock feeding seems coincidental rather than causal.

Why colonial breeding should be more common among freshwater birds than among those feeding in terrestrial habitats is not immediately obvious. Some wetlands are ephemeral: small ponds and streams may dry up, causing birds to shift elsewhere, but there are plenty of swamps, lakes and rivers that are permanent and the banks of which could be defended as feeding territories. The main cause seems to be the availability of secure nesting sites. Virtually all the colonial herons, ibises and storks, as well as freshwater cormorants, nest in tall trees (occasionally on cliffs), which confer protection from most terrestrial predators. In tropical areas, these trees must be isolated from continuous forests, otherwise the nests will be susceptible to predation by primates. But the primates themselves may be wary of crossing broad open areas, especially swamps or shallow water, so isolated clumps of tall trees in swamps or surrounded by water are the preferred nesting site, and such clumps are usually infrequent.

TUNDRA-BREEDING SEABIRDS

Turning to seabirds, most are colonial breeders, for the reasons advanced at the start of the chapter, so rather than looking at the colonial species, it may be more profitable to examine the ones that are not, to interpret the cause of these exceptions. Virtually all seabirds that feed at sea while breeding are colonial. However, those that switch to feeding in terrestrial habitat, such as jaegers, are dispersed, territorial breeders, as are their wholly terrestrial counterparts, Rough-legged Buzzards and Snowy Owls.

A few species are intermediate. Sabine's Gulls in the Canadian arctic feed mainly on small ponds on arctic tundra close to the coast. They breed either solitarily, or in scattered groups of up to ten, on small islands in lakes (Stenhouse *et al.*, 2001). This habitat and breeding distribution is shared with Arctic Terns, and many other inland-nesting terns and small gulls breed in a similarly dispersed fashion. However, Arctic Terns that feed at sea in the same parts of the arctic breed in colonies of up to several hundred pairs on small offshore islets or shingle spits.

LARGE GULLS

There are other species that adapt their breeding habits to suit their feeding ecology. Many Glaucous Gulls breeding in Thick-billed Murre colonies in the eastern Canadian arctic feed almost exclusively on the eggs and chicks of the murres. Compared to most predatory birds, they breed very close together, the nests sometimes within 10–20 m of one another. However, despite being packed very close together, they divide the murre colony into feeding territories with very precise boundaries (Gilchrist *et al.*, 1998).

That these territories are concerned with protecting an adequate food supply is clearly demonstrated by the behaviour of the Glaucous Gulls. With breeding sites mainly spread along the upper margin of the murre colony, the territories approximate vertical strips of cliff. Off-duty birds keeping watch for intruders frequently perch on a convenient lookout close to their nest. A foraging gull likes to fly into the wind, which allows it to move slowly past the ranks of murres, looking for an exposed egg or an inattentive parent. Extra-territorial gulls flying downwind across a territory are rarely attacked, even if they pass close to the cliff. However, any bird flying into the wind crossing the territorial boundary within about 50 m of the cliff will immediately be chased. It is remarkable how swift and agile the normally sluggish Glaucous Gull can become under these circumstances.

Occasionally, because of a limited availability of suitable breeding ledges, even Glaucous Gulls breeding within a murre colony may nest in colonial groups of up to 20 pairs. Other Glaucous Gulls, feeding as predators and scavengers among the large arctic Snow Goose colonies, nest in a much more dispersed fashion on small islets, often single erratic boulders, in lakes. However, in coastal areas where there are few other seabirds, Glaucous Gulls breed in colonies of up to 100 pairs and feed at sea. Similarly, Herring Gulls in Newfoundland that feed mainly at sea breed closer together than those that specialise in robbing fish from puffins, which defend feeding territories at the puffin colony (Pierotti, 1982). Clearly colonial breeding is a very flexible habit in these large gulls, and one that adapts quickly to differences in the type of diet and the distribution of breeding sites. A similar breeding distribution can be observed among South Polar Skuas breeding among penguin colonies in the Antarctic (Young, 1994).

THE *BRACHYRAMPHUS* MURRELETS

Perhaps the most dispersed nesters among birds that are marine foragers during the breeding season are the Marbled, Long-billed and Kittlitz's Murrelets. All feed in inshore waters of the North Pacific, especially in bays and sheltered inlets. Marbled Murrelets, which breed from California north, nest mainly on the large, horizontal branches of old trees, which in that part of the world may grow to more than 60 m in height. Some evidence suggests that nests may be somewhat clumped, but so few have been found that no one knows for sure. In any case, it is evident that they are not colonial in the sense of other auks.

Kittlitz's Murrelet occurs along the coast of Alaska and is particularly associated with bays and inlets where tidewater glaciers discharge. Only a dozen or so nests have ever been found (Day *et al.*, 1999), but all have been on open alpine tundra, above the treeline. As noted in Chapter 4, these two species exhibit the sort of plumage in summer that is cryptic in terrestrial habitats; cryptic plumage and dispersed nesting tend to go together as both are responses to predator pressure.

Why the *Brachyramphus* murrelets should have adopted a solitary, inland-nesting habit, rather than breeding in crevices and islets along the coast, as the guillemots do, is a matter for speculation. However, the deep, glaciated inlets and the calm waters within island archipelagos that are favoured by the murrelets are so sheltered that dense forest extends right to the high-tide mark. The murrelets are, in many areas, by far the most common marine birds to be found in these narrow waterways, accompanied only by Mew Gulls, which also nest solitarily on inland lakes. Colonial shoreline nesting in most areas would be susceptible to predation by mink, marten and others members of the weasel family. By shifting to a dispersed, cryptic nesting habitat, the murrelets have been able to make use of a portion of the saltwater environment denied to most other seabirds.

COLONIES AS INFORMATION CENTRES

Ward & Zahavi (1973) suggested that bird colonies function as 'information centres'—places where birds obtain information on the whereabouts of food—and that this has been an important factor in the evolution of coloniality. One of their lines of evidence was that many colonial-breeding birds feed together in flocks, suggesting that they exchange cues about where to go and feed while at the colony. In addition, many colonial birds leave the breeding colony in flocks that could include both leaders and followers.

The coincidence between colonial breeding and social feeding is certainly true of seabirds. However, not all seabirds feed in flocks. More importantly, even those seabirds that do feed in flocks often do not search in flocks. Albatrosses and large petrels frequently aggregate at food sources, especially behind fishing boats, but when they are travelling they are usually solitary. Moreover, many seabirds that do travel in flocks do so when flying towards the colony, as well as away from it, so the flight formations must have some value in themselves, other than following leaders to choice feeding areas.

The constraints on seabird breeding created by the separation between their feeding and nesting habitats, and by their difficulty in coping with various elements of the terrestrial environment (predators, trees) probably has been the main factor leading to coloniality in seabirds. However, that many birds set out to forage from a single spot clearly gives some scope for leaders and followers to develop (Clode, 1993). Given that fishermen have frequently used seabirds as clues to the whereabouts of fish, it would be very surprising if the birds themselves did not observe and benefit from the actions of others. I argued for Thick-billed Murres at Prince Leopold Island (Gaston & Nettleship, 1981) that the streams of birds constantly commuting between the colony and the feeding area, at that latitude unbroken throughout the 24 hours of daylight, might allow birds to efficiently track changes in the location of feeding areas caused by shifting patterns of ice cover. Such a benefit may arise for many species of seabirds as a secondary consequence of coloniality.

WHY NOT TERRITORIES?

The absence of feeding territories at sea hardly requires comment. Probably, it is impossible to defend an area that must be deserted for long periods in order to attend the nest. In addition, the prey aggregations on which many seabirds feed (fish shoals, swarms of krill), being large and ephemeral, are exactly the type of food sources for which territorial defence is uneconomical. However, examples of temporary territories, such as those maintained by gulls along a tideline, have been reported (Drury & Smith, 1968). Their existence at sea would be very hard to confirm and the possibility that inshore feeders, such as guillemots, dependent on sedentary, dispersed prey, sometimes do defend temporary feeding territories is one that might be worth investigating.

BREEDING SITES

Most seabirds nest on the ground in the open. They protect themselves by choosing remote, predator-free areas for breeding, and by mobbing predators. Of the remainder, a few nest in trees or on cliffs and the majority nest in concealed sites: either crevices in cliffs, under boulders, or among scree, or in burrows that they dig themselves or take-over from other creatures (Table 8.1).

Breeding sites do not vary much within seabird families: all albatrosses, cormorants and gulls and all but one tern nest in the open, while all storm-petrels, and most petrels and shearwaters nest in concealed sites. The majority of penguins breed on the surface, but about one-third breed in burrows. Among auks, most breed in burrows or crevices, but six species breed in the open. As in

Table 8.1 Nest sites of seabirds. Some species occupy different sites in different areas, or even in the same area (e.g. Razorbills and tropicbirds may nest on open cliff ledges or in crevices). Consequently, some assignments are somewhat arbitrary. Data from Williams (1995), Warham (1990), Johnsgard (1993), Burger & Gochfeld (1996), Gochfeld & Burger (1996) and Gaston & Jones (1998)

Group	Ground	Cliffs	Trees	Burrows	Crevices	Scree	Total
Penguins	12			4	1		17
Albatrosses	14						14
Fulmarines	2	5			1		8
Gadfly Petrels	1			31	2		34
Shearwaters	1			18	2		21
Diving-petrels				4			4
Other petrels	2			8	3		13
Storm-petrels				16	5		21
Pelicans	8						8
Boobies	5	2	2				9
Tropicbirds					3		3
Frigatebirds	2		3				5
Cormorants	18	11	9				38
Skuas	8						8
Gulls	46	3	1				50
Terns	35	3	5	1			44
Auks	1	3	2	6	7	4	23

considering coloniality, it is more enlightening to consider the species that form exceptions to their groups than to compare those that adopt typical sites.

Most individuals of the *Spheniscus* penguins breed in burrows, as does the Little Penguin, although the Galápagos Penguin frequently uses surface sites. These species are all at the lower end of the size distribution for penguins. In addition, most *Spheniscus* species breed on the coasts of the African and South American continents, where they may be subject to predation by a wide range of land-based predators. In contrast, the other penguins, all surface nesters, mainly breed in New Zealand, the subantarctic islands and on the Antarctic continent itself, where they are much less likely to be threatened by terrestrial predators.

The case of the cryptically coloured *Brachyramphus* murrelets has already been discussed. Although they are technically open nesters, the tree nests of the Marbled Murrelet are generally well concealed from above by overhanging branches, while the cryptic plumage of Kittlitz's Murrelet makes it equally well concealed in its alpine tundra nesting habitat. Apart from these murrelets, the only open nesters among auks are the murres, which breed on cliff ledges, as Razorbills sometimes do, or on open flat-topped islets. The murres are the largest auks and mostly breed out of reach of avian predators, although Common Murre colonies on the Pacific coast of North America are subject to predation by Bald Eagles which may partially explain their virtual absence between Washington state and the central Gulf of Alaska (see below).

Most open-nesting petrels and shearwaters are tropical species that breed only on islands where gulls, skuas and raptors are absent. Despite the absence of predators, most of the open nesters still seek some shelter among vegetation or rocks, although this may be to obtain shade, rather than to avoid predators. Some burrow- and crevice-nesting petrels breed on islands without predators. In some cases, a habit evolved in response to predation may have been maintained by advantages for thermoregulation.

The fulmars and their relatives, most of which breed at high latitudes, where burrow excavation is impossible, spit stomach oil at potential predators. Even relatively small nestlings are capable of projecting oil up to 0.5 m. This technique works well against gulls and eagles, which lose waterproofing if they are showered in oil, but is no defence against mammals. Northern Fulmars must breed on cliffs in order to avoid the attention of Arctic Foxes: the rest of the family are confined to the Antarctic or to islands without resident terrestrial predators.

ACTIVITY ON THE COLONY

For most gulls and cormorants, visiting land is hardly a novel experience. Cormorants and coastal gulls roost ashore at night, and often at certain states of the tide, while many gulls are as apt to forage along the shore as they are to do so at sea. Likewise, many coastal terns, boobies and frigatebirds rest ashore.

For other seabirds, coming ashore is a seasonal activity, associated with breeding and, for penguins, with moulting. Young petrels and albatrosses may not touch land for several years from the time they fledge. For some seabirds, perhaps most, the act of coming ashore exposes them to a much higher risk of predation than they run while at sea.

PREDATION OF BREEDERS ON LAND

Predation on seabirds at their breeding colonies has been well documented for many species and appears to be a major factor in choice of breeding sites and in the prevalence of nocturnal colony visitation. Large seabird colonies frequently support dependent predators: in the southern hemisphere, skuas and giant petrels, in the northern hemisphere, gulls, sea eagles (*Haliaeetus*), owls and falcons. There has been no general review of predation and its impact on breeding seabirds, and there are many complicating factors that would make this a very difficult subject upon which to generalise. However, there are many situations where seabirds are an important item in raptor diets and where the pressure from predators could be an important factor in seabird biology.

Peregrine Falcons are widespread in Eurasia and in Arctic North America. As they nest on cliffs, they often breed in coastal areas and in such places seabirds are usually an important, sometimes an exclusive, part of the diet. In northwest Scotland, coastal Peregrines prey on a wide variety of seabirds, with Northern Fulmars, Black-headed Gulls, Black-legged Kittiwakes, Black Guillemots and Atlantic Puffins prominent (Ratcliffe, 1980). In the equivalent situation on the northwest coast of North America, the coastal race, Peale's Peregrine takes large numbers of the smaller auks, especially Ancient Murrelets and Cassin's Auklets (Nelson & Myres, 1975). These falcons appear to specialise almost exclusively on seabirds and in British Columbia nest only in the Queen Charlotte Islands, where the bulk of the world population of Ancient Murrelet also nests. In northern Hudson Bay, the Black Guillemot forms an important element in the prey of the rather dense population of Peregrines.

The Peregrine's big brother, the Gyrfalcon, also sometimes breeds in coastal areas and may take significant numbers of seabirds. A Russian study (in Cramp & Simmons, 1980) mentioned a diet comprising mainly Black Guillemots, Atlantic Puffins, Black-legged Kittiwakes and Common Eiders. At Digges Island, where I worked in 1980–82, a single pair of Gyrfalcons nested annually and appeared to rear their brood exclusively on Thick-billed Murres (Gaston *et al.*, 1985).

The other group of raptors regularly taking significant numbers of seabirds are the sea eagles, especially the Bald Eagle, Steller's Sea Eagle and the White-tailed Eagle. Though all occur inland they tend to reach their highest densities in coastal areas and they frequently breed in close proximity to seabird colonies. Wilgohs (1961) reported that seabirds (Common Eider, auks, gulls, cormorants) comprised about half of the diet of Norwegian White-tailed Eagles. For Bald Eagles, which reach very high densities along the coasts of British Columbia and the Gulf of Alaska, seabirds may constitute up to 75% of the diet. In Alaska, two studies showed that Northern Fulmars, cormorants, eiders, murres, auklets, gulls and shearwaters all formed important prey (Murie, 1940; Sherrod *et al.*, 1976).

In Oregon and Washington, Bald Eagle overflights at Common Murre colonies frequently cause panic departures, enabling gulls and crows to snatch unattended eggs. It is striking that the murres are virtually absent as breeders between the southern tip of Vancouver Island and the central Gulf of Alaska. This coast has many suitable breeding cliffs, but supports a very high density of Bald Eagles, as a result of abundant salmon and a lack of historical persecution. It seems that the threat of predation by eagles may be sufficient to deter the murres from a large area of otherwise suitable breeding range.

PREDATION AT SEA

In addition to land-based predators, marine predators pose a potential threat to colonial seabirds, especially penguins. In the Antarctic, Leopard Seals *Hydrurga leptonyx* regularly patrol coasts occupied by Adélie Penguin colonies, with some individuals making the penguins a principal food item (Ainley & DeMaster, 1980). Killer Whales *Orcinus orca* have been observed killing cormorants in large numbers off South African colonies (Williams *et al.*, 1990), while at French Frigate Shoals, Hawaii, sharks take many juvenile Laysan Albatrosses which fail to clear away offshore on their first flight (Rauzon, 2001). Both the exposure to land-based raptors and the concentration of marine predators in the vicinity of colonies constitute part of the costs that must be born by individual seabirds in the process of reproducing.

NOCTURNALITY

One strategy to cope with day-hunting predators is to visit land only after dark. This habit has evolved in several seabird groups independently and finds few parallels among terrestrial birds, although it resembles the strategy of Oilbirds and small bats, which remain hidden during daylight.

Although the majority of seabirds are active at their colonies in daylight, nocturnal colony visits are characteristic of many smaller seabirds. All but one storm-petrel visits the colony only at night, as well as all diving-petrels, prions and most gadfly petrels and shearwaters (Table 8.2). Nocturnal colony visits are closely related to the habit of breeding in concealed nest sites, with 80% of seabirds having concealed nests being nocturnal visitors, compared with fewer than 5% of open nesters.

Some species, including the Little Auk, several auklets and puffins, and the smaller petrels breeding on the Antarctic continent (Snow Petrel and Antarctic Petrel) visit their colonies in daylight but have concealed nest sites. All of these species have ranges that extend into high latitudes, where there is 24-hour daylight during part of the summer. In the case of the auks, all breed in very large dense colonies where the sheer numbers of birds may swamp the ability of potential predators to pose a threat. Auklets adopt specific tactics to overwhelm potential predators by synchronising their colony visits so that they arrive over land in vast flocks that reduce the chance of any individual being killed.

Raymond McNeil and colleagues (1993) summarised the various selection pressures that determine the incidence of nocturnal colony visits in seabirds. There are two separate but related problems, the vulnerability of the adult and the vulnerability of the nestling, and both relate to the size of the bird, hence the vulnerability of the nestling changes as it grows. Where both adult and nestling are vulnerable to predation, we may anticipate concealed nest sites and nocturnal colony visits, as in the case of the precocial murrelets and most storm-petrels. If the adult is not threatened, but the nestling is, as is the case for *Spheniscus* penguins, concealed nest sites and diurnal colony visits are found.

Switching to night-time colony visits looks like a simple way to outwit diurnal predators, such as eagles and falcons, but it brings some other problems: how to find the nest site, how to land safely

Table 8.2 Seabird breeding sites and the proportion of species that visit their breeding site only at night, or at dawn and dusk (species totals differ from other tables, because information on breeding sites and visit timing is not available for all species, and because Warham's [1990] classification was used for tubenoses). Data from Williams (1995), Warham (1990), Johnsgard (1993), Burger & Gochfeld (1996), Gochfeld & Burger (1996) and Gaston & Jones (1998)

	Open		Concealed		Totals
	Daylight	*Nocturnal/ Crepuscular*	*Daylight*	*Nocturnal/ Crepuscular*	
Penguins	11		5	1	17
Albatrosses	14				14
Petrels and shearwaters	11	2	1	57	71
Storm-petrels			2	19	21
Tropicbirds, frigatebirds and boobies	14		3		17
Cormorants	26		1		27
Gulls and skuas	58	1			59
Terns	43		1		44
Auks	2	3	11	7	23
	179	6	24	84	293

and how to communicate with your mate when displays of plumage and posture are invisible. Diving birds may be to some extent pre-adapted to nocturnal colony visits, as their eyes need to be adapted to the low levels of light under which they hunt for their prey underwater. Having a sense of smell apparently helps storm-petrels to find their burrow (Grubb, 1974); shearwaters may do so as well, although they also use visual clues (Brooke, 1978).

GUARDING THE NESTLINGS

Another way to deal with the vulnerability of the nestling is for one parent to remain constantly guarding and brooding the chick. This is common in frigatebirds, boobies, cormorants, gulls, terns and skuas until the chicks approach adult size. Nestlings in open nest sites are deserted at a young age by both parents only in the fulmarine petrels which, as mentioned above, are capable of defending themselves by spitting stomach oil at potential predators and by albatrosses (the chick is soon too large to be worried by predators) and a few tropical tubenoses that inhabit islands where there are no potential predators of small chicks.

The main drawback to guarding the nestling is that only one parent can forage at a time, halving the potential rate at which the nestling can be fed. That the chick can be brooded by the parent at the nest reduces its energy expenditure, which must compensate to some extent for the slower rate of feeding. However, this effect is likely to be more important for seabirds breeding in cold climates. In the case of oceanic seabirds, which must make foraging trips of several days to provision their nestling, the option of one parent guarding the chick may reduce feeding rates to unacceptably low levels. This may account for why most petrels and shearwaters are burrow nesters that leave their chicks unattended within a week of hatching, while the coastal feeding gulls mainly nest on the surface and guard their nestlings for several weeks. Hence, we can add foraging range to body size as a factor determining nest site selection.

FAMILY ARRANGEMENTS

MONOGAMY RULES, OK?

Birds have developed all sorts of fascinating social arrangements, including polygamy, polyandry, harems and single-parent arrangements. However, most seabirds are monogamous, at least within a single breeding season. The interesting arrangement described for Razorbills, where males congregate atop a boulder (a 'lek') and females visit the lek briefly to obtain copulations (Wagner, 1992) has not been described for other species and appears to be only a slight extension of the more common case, typical of murres, where females may solicit periodic copulations with neighbouring non-mates, perhaps as insurance against infertility in their own mate.

The main reason for the prevalence of monogamy in seabirds is probably the need for two parents to cooperate in order to incubate the egg and rear the chick. For the male to make a significant contribution towards these activities, he must be fairly certain that he is the father. The first observers of penguin 'crèches' thought that parents fed chicks randomly, but we now know that parents only feed their own chick. Likewise, early observers of murre chicks leaving the colony thought that parents adopted any chick to rear at sea. In fact, the male parent stays very close to its chick throughout the departure process and at least the majority of murres are reared at sea only by their own male parent (Gilchrist & Gaston, 1997).

The involvement of both parents in incubation is necessitated for surface nesters by the prevalence of predators around the colony: the eggs, and also the chicks while small, must be defended at all times for them to have a chance of survival. Burrow nesters could potentially desert their eggs periodically, as is done by female eider ducks (which hide their eggs under down), which take all incubation duties. However, the eiders' very brief trips are made to drink close to the nest. For oceanic birds, the amount of time required to forage effectively probably precludes single-parent incubation. Periods of egg-neglect are seen in many tubenoses, especially burrow-nesting storm-petrels (Warham, 1990), and in murrelets, but these periods are usually short relative to the total incubation period. The neglect adds substantially to the overall length of incubation, delaying hatching, so is likely to be caused by stress rather than being a deliberate incubation strategy (Gaston & Powell, 1989). Hence, the fact that most seabirds cannot forage effectively without travelling a long way from the colony has been responsible for their monogamy, just as it has contributed to most of their other adaptations.

GENDER ROLES

Contributing further to their reputation as admirable parents, seabirds also are rather egalitarian in the division of work between the sexes. In the tubenoses, there is little difference in the amount of time contributed to incubation by the two sexes, though there is a tendency for males, which normally take the first incubation shift after the egg has been laid, to contribute slightly more time than the females. In penguins, some species share equally (Gentoo, Magellanic), while in others the male takes a preponderant share (Fjordland, Macaroni) and in the Emperor Penguin the male does it all in a single nine-week shift during the Antarctic winter.

Most Charadriiform seabirds divide incubation fairly equally between the sexes, if we except those shorebirds turned seabirds, the phalaropes, where the male performs the complete task. Among terns, gulls and skuas there is a tendency for the female to incubate for longer than the male, but the difference is not great. Auks divide the job very equitably. Among cormorants, frigatebirds and boobies the situation is similar, with sexes taking fairly equal turns, but females putting in a little more time.

The gender roles in chick rearing tend to be even more equally divided between the sexes, but there are a few prominent exceptions. In the Little Auk, the murres and the Razorbill, the chick is cared for entirely by the male after leaving the colony: this is a relatively brief period in the Little Auk, but can last six weeks in the murres. During that period the best evidence is that food for the growing chick is provided entirely by the parent, although it would be nice to know more concerning this. The apparently rather unequal distribution of effort in incubation by male Emperor Penguins, and in chick rearing by male murres and razorbills, seems anomalous and begs some special explanation: so far none is forthcoming.

PAIR FORMATION AND DISPLAYS

Display activities of birds are often very conspicuous, emphasising highly coloured or ornamental plumage, unusual vocalisations and other sounds and weird antics. However, in this respect, seabirds do not differ from landbirds, so I do not intend to discuss their breeding displays overly. Nonetheless, it must be stated that they constitute a great field for study, and social behaviour within colonies has been responsible for the evolution of the most striking and bizarre ornamentation, including the massive throat pouch of the male frigatebird, the long tail plumes of the tropicbirds and the extraordinary head ornaments of puffins and auklets.

One striking aspect of seabird breeding is the importance of vocal communication among species that visit their breeding sites by night. Calls are very important in all nocturnal birds, for the obvious reason that visual communication is very limited. The vocalisations of nocturnal seabirds are not necessarily more complex than those of seabirds that come to land by day, but they are uttered much more frequently. If you are sitting in a burrow waiting for a potential mate to drop in there is no way for them to detect your presence except by call. Hence, the likelihood of attracting a mate will expand in direct relationship to the amount of time spent calling. That is why Ancient Murrelets, Cassin's Auklets and Manx Shearwaters, while visiting the colony as pre-breeders, keep up a constant stream of calls throughout the night. Their performance is more akin to the nocturnal choruses of tree-frogs or nightjars than it is to any vocal displays found among terrestrial colonial breeders.

CLUTCH SIZE, INCUBATION PERIODS AND CHICK GROWTH RATES

The topic of clutch size is covered in Chapter 10. Most seabirds lay rather small clutches and all pelagic feeders lay a single egg, leaving little variation to discuss. Incubation periods are generally much longer than those of landbirds and include the longest among birds (79 days, Royal Albatross). Nestling periods also tend to be much longer than those of similarly sized landbirds. As David Lack (1968) pointed out, there is a strong correlation between the duration of incubation and the length of the developmental period. Hence it appears that most variation in incubation periods relates to the growth strategy of the chick and that this is determined by the provisioning abilities of the adults. Here, I intend to concentrate on chick development and the factors affecting it.

DEVELOPMENT IN SEABIRDS

Margaret Nice (1962), a pioneer in the field of birds' life histories, divided the state of nestling at hatching into *altricial*—young born blind, naked and helpless and fed to near adult size in the nest (e.g. cormorants); *semi-altricial*—downy and with eyes open at birth, but initially helpless (e.g. hawks, herons); *semi-precocial*—young born active but fed at the nest to near adult size (e.g. gulls); and *precocial*—young born active and leave the nest more or less immediately to forage for themselves, or to be fed elsewhere by their parents (e.g. ducks, shorebirds). Among seabirds, the Pelecaniform group are mainly altricial (boobies, cormorants, pelicans, frigatebirds), with the tropicbirds being considered semi-altricial. Penguins, albatrosses and petrels are semi-altricial or semi-precocial, while all the Charadriiform seabirds are semi-precocial, except for the *Synthliboramphus* murrelets, which are precocial. Nestling strategies are generally constant within families of birds. Auks represent the only family in which there is wide variation in the developmental strategy of the chicks (O'Connor, 1984) ranging from the semi-precocial development of puffins, auklets and guillemots, through the 'intermediate' strategy of the murres and Razorbill, to precocial nest departure in the *Synthliboramphus* murrelets (Sealy, 1973).

VARIATION AMONG AUKS

The lack of variation in nestling strategies within families of birds suggest that these tend to be very conservative characteristics, which is another way of saying that moving from one method to another is difficult. It is worth considering why the auks exhibit such diversity. To do this we need to consider what their ancestral development strategy may have been.

Among the Charadriiformes, some families comprise entirely precocial species (sandpipers, plovers) and others entirely semi-precocial species (gulls, terns, jaegers/skuas). The gulls are normally considered the closest relatives of the auks. Hence, the rearing of semi-precocial chicks probably is the ancestral condition; a hypothesis strengthened by the fact that all subfamilies of auks contain semi-precocial species, whereas intermediate and precocial species occur in only one subfamily each. In addition, the fact that all other seabirds have either semi-precocial or altricial chicks is suggestive. If auks and gulls, both basically marine families at present, were marine before they diverged, then it makes sense that their ancestor had already developed a strategy of rearing chicks at the nest site.

The following factors have been identified as potential contributors to the variation in brood size and departure strategies found among the auks (Gaston & Jones, 1998).

(1) Distance to the feeding area and the consequent expenditure of time and energy in travelling back and forth.
(2) The low load-carrying capacity of the auks, especially the larger, intermediate, species.
(3) The choice of nest site and the relative vulnerability of the chick to predation.
(4) The consequent need, at open sites, for one parent to guard the chick constantly, so that only one parent can forage at a time.
(5) The risk to adults of predation associated with coming ashore to breed.
(6) The effect on chick energy requirements of ambient temperature and parental brooding.

Like most questions in evolutionary ecology, there is probably no single factor that can explain all the diversity seen among auks. The largest auks (murres) carry relatively the smallest food loads to their chicks, because of their very high wing-loading (Chapter 3). This limitation must affect their ability to rear a chick to fully adult size and has been considered the main factor leading to the 'intermediate' departure strategy adopted by their chicks. Moreover, breeding Thick-billed Murres undergo an abrupt loss of mass at about the time of hatching, which has been considered an adaptation to facilitate transporting loads to the chick (Croll *et al.*, 1991). This adjustment suggests that losing a little weight helps when transporting loads. However, other factors may be involved. For instance, arctic breeding sites and poor landing/take-off ability on the ground lead to cliff nesting, but the presence of gulls means that only one parent can forage at a time; large colonies mean distant foraging. These factors lead to low provisioning rates and cause selection for a strategy where partial development occurs at the colony, followed by a departure at well below adult weight.

None of the features listed above as leading to the intermediate departure strategy apply to the *Synthliboramphus* murrelets. This genus includes the most southerly breeding auks, with three of the four species breeding in, or at the edge of, subtropical waters. They are fairly small, without a particularly high wing-loading, they nest in burrows, and before people began to travel in ships, they bred on islands where nest predators were absent. Clearly, the arguments that we have advanced to explain the intermediate strategy will not work for these birds.

Spencer Sealy (1976) considered that the precocial strategy was an adaptation to a peculiarly unpredictable food supply that precluded commuting from the breeding site. However, I have argued (Gaston, 1992) that if the food supply was unpredictable, taking the chicks to sea would be the worst strategy, because it would reduce searching mobility to the swimming speed of the chicks. Precocial departure seems to require that food be more, rather than less predictable because family parties have very poor mobility until the chicks can fly. Predictable food supplies within swimming distance of the colony may be necessary, but hardly seem to provide a compelling cause. It is possible that the food is indeed predictable, but that the only suitable feeding areas are far from the colony, making precocial departure a more efficient strategy than commuting to the nest site. However, the idea that shifting the chicks to the feeding area would reduce commuting time applies equally to all pelagic seabirds, so it does not explain why these murrelets and no other seabirds adopted this particular strategy. Cassin's Auklets take very similar prey to Ancient Murrelets living in the same area, but retain a semi-precocial chick that is fed at the nest for about six weeks. There is also the intriguing fact that the precocial murrelets rear two chicks, whereas all other pelagic seabirds that fly have adapted to the constraint on food delivery rates imposed by their lengthy foraging trips by reducing their brood size to one.

Why did the ancestor of *Synthliboramphus* not reduce its clutch to one before adopting the precocial departure strategy? The simplest explanation is that the ancestor was an inshore species which evolved a reduced nestling period, not because it was incapable of finding enough food to rear its chicks at the nest, but because the constant visits required by rearing chicks at the colony exposed the parents to a very high risk of predation (Gaston, 1992). Breeding adults of all *Synthliboramphus* species suffer heavy mortality at their colonies, despite being nocturnal, nesting in concealed sites and taking other precautions. Predation on adults is clearly a strong selection pressure. If the ancestral murrelet occupied breeding areas with a similar risk of predation, selection for a reduction in the length of the chick-rearing period could have come about without any constraints on the parent's ability to find food. It is also worth noting that, as Ron Ydenberg pointed out to me, the advantage that accrues in saved travelling time by taking two chicks to sea is double the advantage that would accrue to a bird rearing a single chick. In fact, it seems possible that the precocial murrelets might be capable of rearing more than two chicks. The main thing preventing them from doing so may be the difficulty of laying and incubating a clutch of three such enormous eggs. The evolution of the precocial strategy would surely have been easier if, as seems likely, the ancestral murrelet inhabited fairly warm seas, reducing the difficulty that precocial chicks might otherwise have encountered in maintaining their body temperature.

PRECOCIAL DEPARTURE IN SEABIRDS, OR LACK THEREOF

Having come up with a plausible explanation for precocial departure in the murrelets, it is worth considering why no other seabirds are precocial, a strategy adopted by many land and freshwater birds (gamebirds, ducks, shorebirds, sandgrouse). There are several possibilities.

(1)   The families and orders to which marine birds belong all derive from ancestors in which precocial chick rearing is absent.

(2)   Precocial young need to be fully mobile with complete sensory capabilities and able to thermoregulate in the environment of the feeding area: for marine species this is an exceptional physiological challenge.

(3)   Marine birds often forage at great distances from their breeding sites and it would be beyond the powers of hatchlings to reach suitable feeding areas. Moreover, for species that forage mainly on the wing, chicks would be incapable of foraging until their wings were fully developed.

(4)   If parents require to forage at sea over wide areas, they would need to relocate the family group after each foraging trip.

(5)   Many precocial young are highly cryptic in their typical habitat and avoid predation by a combination of cryptic appearance and remaining in heavy cover: such predator avoidance measures are difficult or impossible at sea.

Of these we can rule out (1) because the Charadriiformes include many precocial genera (most shorebirds, jacanas *Jacana*, thick-knees *Burhinus* and coursers *Cursorius*). Semi-precocial behavior is probably ancestral to the gull/auk lineage (Gaston, 1992), but the occurrence of precocial behaviour in *Synthliboramphus*, and the 'intermediate' behavior of nestling *Uria* and *Alca*, which leave the breeding site when less than one-third grown (Sealy, 1973) suggests that the potential to re-evolve precocial behaviour is present within this family. There is no obvious reason why this should not be true of other seabird families.

The existence of precocial murrelets and of high-latitude sea ducks (eiders, Long-tailed Duck), the ducklings of which are fully precocial in arctic waters, indicates that physiological constraints are not insuperable. Moreover, if thermoregulation was a significant problem, we might predict that precocial marine birds would be principally found in the tropics. The reverse is true: there are no precocial sea ducks or seabirds in the tropics, except for Craveri's Murrelet in the Gulf of California. The other murrelets are temperate or subarctic in their distribution, the seaducks largely arctic.

The *Synthliboramphus* murrelets lay exceptionally large eggs relative to female body mass (Sealy, 1975) and the eggs contain exceptionally large amounts of yolk (Birkhead & Gaston, 1988). Birkhead & Harris (1985) argued that inability to lay a sufficiently large egg, owing to allometric constraints on body size, has limited the precocial strategy to relatively small auks. However, larger seabirds lay eggs that, although smaller than those of *Synthliboramphus* in relation to body size, are absolutely larger. There is no evident reason why such eggs should not produce precocial chicks as capable of going to sea as those of *Synthliboramphus*. The Great Auk, largest of the recent auks, may have been precocial (Bengtson, 1984; Gaston & Jones, 1998).

The argument from foraging constraints is true for all petrels (possibly excepting some *Pelecanoides* populations; Warham, 1996), some penguins (Williams, 1995), some boobies, all tropicbirds (Lack, 1968) and auks (all except *Brachyramphus* and *Cepphus* spp.), but not true of many cormorants, gulls and terns that forage within a few kilometres of their breeding sites. It cannot provide a general explanation for the lack of precocial behaviour in seabirds.

In most species where the young are precocial, one or both parents remain with them for a substantial portion of the growth period. Usually, parents and chicks forage in the same area (e.g. ducks, gamebirds, shorebirds). However, in some cases the parents leave their young to find food (e.g. oystercatchers *Haematopus*). In those seabirds that exhibit parental care after the nestlings have departed from the breeding site (murres, Razorbill), parent and offspring stay very close together throughout the rearing period, the parents virtually giving up flight altogether. The option of remaining permanently with the brood is presumably not open to birds such as tropicbirds and petrels, which need to forage over large areas. Moreover, if the parents took turns to forage away from the brood, winds and currents would probably have shifted the rest of the family party far enough during their absence to make relocating them very difficult. The need to remain with their brood must limit precocial behaviour among seabird species that are forced to forage over large areas.

Precocial young, though fully mobile, are always more vulnerable to predators than older birds, through inexperience and flightlessness. Except for limited areas where kelp forms floating mats, there is no cover available at sea and all seabirds except penguins spend the majority of their time on or above the sea surface. Moreover, breeding colonies form a major attraction for avian predators. The vulnerability to sight-hunting predators of young seabirds dispersing from the colony is illustrated by the fact that many make their initial departure in the late evening or at night (puffins, auklets, murres). Ancient Murrelets depart only in the darkest hours. Given that departure from the nest site before being fully developed and prolonged parental care away from the nest site are found in the auks, the risk of predation by sharks or marine mammals seems the only obvious reason why a similar strategy should not be adopted by some penguins.

The occurrence of precocial behavior among young Charadriiformes suggests that no single cause serves to explain the paucity of this behaviour among seabirds. Phylogenetic and physiological factors must influence the likelihood of becoming precocial, but the existence of seaducks and precocial murrelets indicates that these problems are not insuperable. The transition from semi-precocial to nidifugous behaviour appears to be much more feasible than making the same leap from altricial rearing; this may explain the lack of precocial behaviour among some families. For colonial seabirds, predation may be a major factor preventing chicks from leaving the colony while still flightless. For seabirds dependent on widely dispersed prey, the need for the parents to leave the brood periodically imposes strong selection against precocial departure and may explain why it has evolved only among auks which, because of their deep diving, can provision their brood by feeding within a relatively small area.

FOOD CARRYING AND NESTLING FOOD

The majority of seabirds feed their nestling(s) at the breeding site until they are more or less of adult size. In fact, in many species, the chick becomes substantially heavier than its parents. To rear the chick, substantial quantities of food must be transported from the feeding area to the nest. Seabirds have several strategies for accomplishing this. Terns and some auks (murres, puffins, guillemots) carry food externally, holding it in the bill. This is an awkward arrangement that has several disadvantages: it hampers flying by reducing aerodynamic streamlining and shifting the centre of gravity, it makes it difficult to catch additional prey after the first has been grasped and it also offers a clear target to piratical kleptoparasites. It is not coincidence that terns are among the most common targets of kleptoparasites (Furness, 1987b).

Hence, it is unsurprising that the majority of seabirds carry food to the nestlings internally. This is usually done in the proventriculus, an expanded sack between the throat and the stomach. However, among the plankton-feeding auks, a special diverticulum (a little pouch) for storing food develops in the throat during the breeding season. As it disappears during the non-breeding season, it is clear that it functions only to carry food for the nestlings. These birds also possess a proventriculus, so it is not clear why they need the additional structure. However, we need to note that those birds that transport food in the normal alimentary canal require some mechanism that switches off, or slows, the normal progress of digestion, so that the food arrives at the nestlings more or less intact. This is unlikely to be a problem for Great Black-backed Gulls feeding within a few hundred metres of their nest, and bringing food directly after capture, but could be a problem for the oceanic Red-legged Kittiwake, which may be away from the nest for 12 hours on foraging trips.

Even if digestion of stored food can be prevented by switching off enzyme production, the temperature of the bird's body is something that cannot be adjusted and stored food will begin to decompose as soon as it is dead. The exceptionally noxious 'rotten shrimp' smell of Cassin's Auklet regurgitations, well known to all who have handled them, suggests that some fermentation may take place in the throat pouch. Seabirds can reduce this decomposition by feeding themselves first on their foraging trip and loading up for their nestlings just before returning. However, if the trip is long, or if feeding conditions are best in the early morning, but colony visits must be made at night, substantial decomposition may occur before the food is delivered.

The stomach oil produced by tubenoses may have a role in preserving food during transport. For instance, the regurgitations delivered by Fork-tailed Storm-petrels smell much less decomposed than deliveries of the same organisms by Cassin's Auklets. Yet storm-petrels may take several days between deliveries, whereas Cassin's Auklets normally deliver food nightly. The preservative quality of tubenose stomach oil has not been investigated, but seems a potentially useful area for research. More generally, it is possible that the problem of keeping food in edible condition may affect the length of foraging trips for nestlings, forcing birds to deliver smaller loads than they might be capable of carrying. This would be a difficult hypothesis to test, but has important implications for foraging-theory.

FAT CHICKS

Among the tubenoses and some other seabirds, such as the Northern Gannet and the Atlantic Puffin, parental provisioning of nestlings is sufficient to permit the nestlings to become extremely obese. Young shearwaters, albatrosses and petrels may weigh almost double the weight of their parents partway through the growth period. This phenomenon has stimulated considerable comment, because it appears that the parents are working much harder than they need to.

The initial explanation for the obesity of young tubenoses was that fat stores allowed the nestlings "to tide over temporary periods of [food] shortage, which in shearwaters, for instance, may last for several days and at times for one or two weeks" (Lack 1968). This seemed a simple enough idea, but was subsequently rejected by researchers who reasoned that the reserves were much too big to be accounted for by the variation in provisioning rates that they recorded at their study colonies.

An alternative explanation, proposed by Ricklefs (1984), suggested that the development of obesity was a by-product of the diet fed to young tubenoses, which contains a very fatty stomach oil, with very concentrated energy content, but low in other nutrients. The chick must eat large quantities of this diet in order to obtain sufficient amounts of certain critical nutrients. Under this theory, the large fat deposits laid down by the chick are an 'energy sink' with no purpose. They prolong the nestling period because chicks must burn off the excess weight before they can fledge. The problem with this idea is that it rests on the assumption that tubenoses evolved a way to concentrate fats, but not other nutrients. That so ancient an adaptation would not have been tuned to provide a balanced formula for the chick seems at odds with the abilities of natural selection to optimise most features of biology (but not all, as Stephen Gould would have insisted).

Moreover, the theory that the fat is an energy sink does not explain why, among shearwaters, nestling obesity increases with the mean length of inter-feed intervals, presumably reflecting foraging range. This was pointed out by Lack and seems to support the idea that the energy deposits are some kind of insurance against food shortages.

More recently, Ricklefs & Schew (1994) proposed another idea, championed by Keith Hamer and others, that "lipid reserves provide a buffer against the cumulative effects of stochastic variation in food delivery at the level of the individual chick. This avoids chance starvation, but results in obesity in most cases" (Hamer *et al.*, 2000) [translation: chance variation in the parents' success in finding food may lead to a run of bad luck sufficient that the unfortunate chick needs large fat reserves to tide itself over]. Though it does not sound as though this hypothesis differs much from Lack's, the results obtained by recent researchers apparently accord better with the idea of 'chronic stochastic variation' than with 'temporary periods of food shortage'.

Actually, all these ideas tend to concentrate on the needs of the nestling. However, the needs of the parents also may be involved. The energy needs of the nestling increase as it grows larger, generally peaking about two-thirds of the way to fledging, when tissue synthesis and maintenance needs are highest. In most landbirds, parental feeding efforts more or less track nestling needs. This also applies in seabird species where chicks do not become obese (guillemots and murres). In many of these species, though not in murres, the parents adjust their feeding directly to the needs of the chicks, which communicate with their parents by varying the insistence of their calls. Some tubenoses do not do this. They feed approximately the same load to their chick at each visit and they do not vary their feeding in response to communications from the chick. They may vary the rate of feeding over the course of the nestling period, but this variation does not respond to the energy demands of the chick.

Consider the incubation period. During this, each parent can spend only half its time travelling to and from the feeding area and actually foraging. The rest must be spent sitting on the egg. As soon as the chick is deserted, usually after *c.*20% of the nestling period has elapsed, both parents can spend all their time travelling and feeding. During incubation each parent must feed one bird (itself) on half time. After chick desertion each must feed a maximum of $1\frac{1}{2}$ birds (itself + half the chick's needs) while free to forage full time. This calculation suggests that it is the incubation period, rather than the chick-rearing period, that imposes the greatest demands on the parents, as Mike Brooke (1990) proposed for Manx Shearwaters.

If this argument is correct, we should expect tubenoses, and other seabirds that leave their nestlings unattended, to time their breeding so that the seasonal peak of food availability occurs while they are incubating. Hence, when chick desertion occurs, the availability of food may be declining. In that case, there would be a premium on stuffing the chick with as much food as possible during the early part of the nestling period, to avoid having to work hard when conditions are less favourable.

Whatever the explanation for chick obesity in tubenoses, it is a characteristic of the entire group, absent only in the inshore-feeding diving-petrels. The ubiquity of the phenomenon suggests that it relates to development patterns adopted by the order before the divergence of recent groups. The adaptive significance of such characters is often hard to determine, but it is easy to believe that it might be related to the fact that tubenoses provision their chicks with a diet that is especially high in lipids.

CONCLUSIONS

At first sight, breeding behaviour might appear to be an area little affected by foraging ecology. However, in considering coloniality and breeding behaviour in seabirds we find ourselves referring continually to constraints created by the distance to the foraging area. Coloniality leads to monogamy, forced on seabirds by the demands of incubation and chick rearing, and this determines the lack of distinction between the sexes in size and plumage (though there are exceptions, e.g. frigatebirds). Coloniality also creates the need for small seabirds to use protected nest sites and for some of the most vulnerable to become nocturnal in their colony visits. This is reinforced by the concentration of predators and pirates that colonies attract and which also create the need for offspring to be able to fly before departing the colony. Colony and breeding sites, social behaviour, nocturnality and nestling strategies are all ultimately elements of seabird biology determined by the inevitable separation between their breeding and feeding areas.

Polar bear (top) and Artic Fox (below): two reasons why breeding on flat ground, as penguins do in the Antartic, is a bad idea in the Arctic. (Tony Gaston)

CHAPTER NINE

Birth and death — theory

And nothing 'gainst Time's scythe can make defense
Save breed . . .

William Shakespeare, Sonnet 12

The Thick-billed Murres that breed on Coats Island are generally a rather phlegmatic bunch. Those who have worked with the species elsewhere agree with me that we found an exceptionally compliant group of subjects when we chose to work there. Still, even for Coats Island, the behaviour of certain individuals in 1997 was cause for comment. Most incubating birds will take an occasional nap, but that summer we had birds flopping down everywhere, lolling from side to side, resting their heads on the ground, leaning against their neighbours and generally 'nodding off'. It looked rather touching until we realised that some of the prostrate birds were not just resting—they were dead.

What had happened was that an exceptionally warm spell of weather had coincided with a major emergence of mosquitoes. Although mosquitoes cannot suck blood from murres through their feathers, they attack the feet and webs in large numbers. When the weather is hot, the murres tend to expose their feet and pump blood into their webs to increase the radiation of heat. This created a bonanza for the mosquitoes and they sometimes covered the feet and legs of the incubating murres so thickly that it looked as though the birds were wearing furry black boots. A combination of water loss through panting and blood loss through mosquito parasitism was enough to kill some birds nesting in especially exposed sites. With the general increase in summer temperatures that we have observed, such dehydration deaths have occurred in most years since then, presumably a symptom of 'global warming'.

What was striking about these deaths was that many more birds simply left their eggs and took the few seconds necessary to fly to the sea to cool off and drink. Some lost their eggs to gulls by doing so, but as far as we know it was only the birds that sat it out on the breeding ledges that died. Normally, we would not expect a murre to court death in order to save its egg, because the adult bird may reasonably expect to survive many more summers and rear many more chicks if it saves itself. That these birds failed to do so indicated that the population probably had not been exposed to this particular form of mortality in the past—further evidence that the events we saw were part of a new phenomenon. Some theories about how much risk we may expect an individual to accept in order to reproduce, along with other theories relating to population processes, are the subject of this chapter.

POPULATION DYNAMICS AND LIFE-HISTORY STRATEGY

The study of population dynamics is the study of population change and its causes. Life-history strategy, the field that considers why some birds lay many eggs and live short lives, while others lay a single egg and live a very long time, forms the theoretical basis for discussion of comparative population dynamics. Hence, population dynamics and life-history strategy can be thought of as opposite sides of the same coin. When we have accumulated sufficient information about the demographic characteristics of seabird species, we can speculate about the evolutionary causes of variation among them. Information for seabirds can then be related to general theories about the underlying causes of life-history variation among animals and plants.

POPULATION LIMITATION AND DENSITY DEPENDENCE

We would like to be able to identify the factors that limit seabird populations for a variety of reasons. On the practical side, we may wish to be able to manage populations and it helps to know which stage of the life cycle is most influential in determining population changes. From a theoretical standpoint, we may wish to know whether populations are limited by food supplies, whether competition or predation are most influential in limiting them, or what combination of factors causes the changes that we observe.

To determining the most important factor controlling population size we can subdivide the life history into stages (egg, chick, pre-breeder, breeder, etc.), measure mortality at each stage, and then compare population change from one year to the next with annual variation in the mortality occurring at each stage. The mortality rate most closely correlated with inter-annual population change should be the most important in determining the population trend. Though some analyses of seabird populations have considered the role of mortality at different life-history stages (e.g. Potts *et al.*, 1980, for the European Shag; and Harris & Wanless, 1991, for Atlantic Puffin), a complete analysis of mortality at different stages of the life cycle has not been published for a seabird population. Probably the main reason for this omission is that mortality during the first year of life, widely regarded as a critical period, is almost impossible to measure in species, including most seabirds, that do not visit breeding colonies until two years or older.

We may also be interested to know if the limiting factors operate in a density-dependent manner. Populations are said to be density dependent when their rate of population change declines as the size of the population, or the population density, increases. The prime promoter of density dependence as a mechanism in bird population regulation was David Lack (1954, 1966). He believed that the majority of bird populations were controlled by food availability during the worst season (generally winter) and that this regulation was usually density dependent.

Different opinions have been expressed about the role of density dependence in limiting seabird populations (Croxall & Rothery, 1991; Wooller *et al.*, 1992). Because some seabird populations have changed enormously since records began, without any apparent density dependence operating, and because catastrophic mortality resulting from extreme weather or oceanographic events (e.g. Schreiber & Schreiber, 1986), which is almost certainly not density dependent, is common in some seabird populations, many seabird researchers believe that the concept of density dependence either does not apply to seabirds or is relatively unimportant for them. This is part of a larger argument about whether density-dependent processes are important in population limitation for animals in general.

LIFE-HISTORY STRATEGY

If we have density-dependent processes operating at different stages of the life history, then an adaptation improving survival at one stage (say, increasing clutch size) will simply increase negative feedback in older age classes (higher mortality of nestlings or juveniles because there are more of them). Like a bypass, relieving a traffic bottleneck, the traffic jam simply moves to another spot. Hence, life-history evolution must be the product of a continual balancing of different life stages.

This central question of life-history evolution is often simplified into a dichotomy between reproduction and survival. R. A. Fisher, who managed to outline most of the important problems of evolutionary ecology before anyone else, summarised the approach rather nicely:

> *It would be instructive to know . . . what circumstances in the life-history and environment would render profitable the diversion of a greater or lesser share of the available resources towards reproduction.*

> R.A. Fisher, *The Genetical Theory of Natural Selection*, 1930

David Lack (1947–48, 1954) was the first person to seriously consider life-history variation in birds. He concentrated especially on variation in clutch size. In his presidential address to the 1966 International Ornithological Congress and in his subsequent book *Ecological Adaptations for Breeding in Birds* (Lack, 1968), he discussed the peculiarities of seabird life histories at some length. Lack pointed out that the major determinant of reproductive strategy in seabirds was *foraging range*. The basis for this generality was an inter-species comparison between pelagic and near-shore species. He observed that the former are nearly all long-lived and lay a single egg, while the latter have lower adult survival and lay multi-egg clutches (see below). This observation is indisputable, cuts across all phylogenies, and is the nearest thing to a biological 'law' you are likely to find in seabird biology.

There are a few exceptions to the inshore/offshore generalisation, but all form special cases that help to strengthen, rather than weaken, the general rule. The precocial murrelets (*Synthliboramphus*) are offshore feeders that lay two eggs, but they do not feed their young in the nest and hence are not subject to the usual constraint on foraging range. Conversely; the *Brachyramphus* murrelets, which are inshore feeders and lay only a single egg, breed far inland from the coast, giving them just as far to commute from the breeding site to the sea as puffins and murres. Whatever theory we use to explain the life-history attributes of marine birds, foraging range has to be an important element in it.

r- AND K-SELECTION

Interest in life-history evolution flowered into a sub-discipline of theoretical ecology in the 1970s. Like much ecological theory, it was given a boost by Robert MacArthur (MacArthur & Wilson, 1967), who coined the dichotomy of *r*-selection and *K*-selection. MacArthur's idea was that species could be placed along a continuum of life-history strategies, based on the degree to which their populations were constrained by resources. At one extreme, *r*-selected species were those involved in the colonisation of disturbed habitats, where resources were more or less unlimited, and those individuals that maximised reproduction at the expense of growth and survival were the most successful (e.g. fruit flies, mice). In contrast, *K*-selected populations were those that remain permanently close to the carrying capacity of their habitat. For these species, reproduction might be difficult and there was intense competition among recruiting organisms, placing a premium on producing high-quality offspring (e.g. elephants, Orangutans *Pongo pygmaeus*, large whales). Among birds, *r*- and *K*-selection provides an explanation for the differences in clutch size between passerine birds of tropical seasonal forests (fluctuating food supplies, larger clutches) and non-seasonal forests (stable food supplies, smaller clutches). The concept can also be applied among different populations, with greater investment in reproduction being adaptive where the population is expanding (presumably because food is abundant) and greater investment in survival where the population is declining.

The demographic characteristics of seabirds, with their high adult survival, deferred breeding and low reproductive rates, are a perfect fit with the predictions of life-history theory for animals evolving under *K*-selection (Goodman, 1974). This similarity, first elucidated by Cody (1966), has been very influential in causing seabird life histories to be thought the product of *K*-selection and hence assumed to have evolved under severe resource constraints. David Cairns (1992) exemplified this assumption:

> . . . *seabirds have low reproductive rates, delayed maturity and high longevity . . . Seabirds are therefore adapted to situations where resource availability rarely falls below the level required to sustain adult life.*

The jump from life-history traits to assumptions about resource constraints goes unnoticed because we have become so accustomed to the idea that, as Croxall & Rothery (1991) put it: "[seabirds] *are a convenient paradigm of extreme K-selected species*".

But if seabirds are strongly limited by resources, we might expect to find density dependence operating. The potential contradiction between rejecting density dependence while accepting the idea of *K*-selection does not seem to be widely recognised. Our theories need some modification if we are to uphold both these points of view.

Actually, the idea of *r*- and *K*-selection may not be very useful in understanding population dynamics, or life-history evolution, in seabirds. With their enormous mobility, it is always going to be difficult to demonstrate the relationship between populations and their food resources. Although some traits of seabirds are similar to those associated with *K*-selected species, the latter also are widely held to have stable populations. Fifty years ago it was probably legitimate to think that most seabird populations tended to be stable, because changes from one year to the next are often small. However, the length of time over which observations are made dramatically influences our perception of stability. Long-term studies show that seabird populations fluctuate much more than was originally thought. That stability seems to be the exception, rather than the rule, was the undisputed consensus of a seabird conference that I attended in Alaska in 1995.

The idea of *K*-selection has been further interpreted to include reduced 'reproductive investment' made by individuals of breeding age. Hence, Cody (1971) and Ricklefs (1977, 1990) suggested that reproductive effort should be inversely related to lifespan, and this might explain why long-lived birds lay small clutches. It is hard to argue with the theory, but we find some contradictory examples. For instance, an Atlantic Puffin with a life expectancy of more than ten years, takes 12 weeks to complete its reproduction; a Bridled Tern, probably with a similar life expectancy, takes 16 weeks and some begin again nine month later. Both use breeding habitat otherwise unfamiliar and supporting predators that they would not normally encounter during the rest of the year. All this could be interpreted as indicating a high reproductive investment.

In contrast, a British Blue Tit, which has a life expectancy of only two years, completes its annual reproductive cycle (builds a nest, incubates and rears its brood) in about six weeks, without leaving its accustomed habitat. For the rest of the year it is mainly concerned with staying alive (investing in survival, in life history-speak). Of course, the Blue Tit lays ten times as many eggs as the puffin, but the clutch represents only a small proportion of the reproductive investment, if we consider this in terms of fitness (which the theory does). I am not arguing here that the puffin is making a greater investment in reproduction than the tit, but simply that the observations to hand do not really support the opposite assumption.

One can imagine the conversation between Cody and Ricklefs on the one hand, and a grumpy male Emperor Penguin that has spent the last two months incubating its egg on an ice floe in the depths of the Antarctic winter:

C to R "*this bird is clearly making a reduced investment in reproduction.*"

R to C "*certainly, so that it can survive better in future.*"

Penguin to both: "*aarghh*".

(Bob Ricklefs assures me that he talks regularly to Martin Cody, but Emperor Penguins have never been present).

Relying on a correspondence between seabird life histories and the predictions of *K*-selection would be a perilous way to establish resource limitation as the driving force in seabird life-history evolution, as it depends on the validity of the theory, which is seldom a very reliable guide in ecology. Moreover, what we know about seabird food resources does not fit the classical model of *K*-selection very well. As David Cairns (1987a) pointed out, the small schooling fishes on which many seabirds feed tend to fluctuate from year to year to a much greater degree than do seabird populations. Though many populations have decreased following apparent reductions in their food supplies, it appears that for most populations in most years, there must be adequate food available, and in many years there must be considerable excess. Of course, when people describe seabirds as a paradigm for *K*-selection, they probably mean they have the demographic characteristics associated with *K*-selection. But if that is all they mean, the statement is clearly tautological.

Despite the reservations that I have expressed about *r*- and *K*-selection, there are some ideas in life-history theory that seem to fit seabirds rather well. One of the earlier writers on life-history theory, Hal Caswell (1981), pointed out that investment in survival at the expense of reproduction would be selected for where survival was predictable and reproduction unpredictable. This fits the case for many seabirds. Take the case again of our landbird and seabird paradigms, the Blue Tit and the Atlantic Puffin: some puffin colonies have gone years without producing a single fledgling, while others show high reproductive success; annual survival, although not unaffected by feeding conditions, is consistently much higher than that of Blue Tits. On the other hand, for Blue Tits, while survival from one year to the next is highly unpredictable, the chance of rearing multiple offspring occurs unfailingly every spring, as the spreading leaves of the oaks provide fodder for the caterpillars on which their nestlings are reared.

ASHMOLE'S HALO

Philip Ashmole, a student of David Lack's, described a conceptual model for population regulation in tropical seabirds (Ashmole, 1963, 1971). He began with Lack's (1954) assumption that bird populations must be subject to density-dependent regulation. Ashmole developed his ideas in the context of observations made at Ascension Island, in the tropical Atlantic, and he restricted them to the case of 'oceanic' (pelagic) species in the tropics. He based his theory on the following observations and deductions:

1. No evidence of regulation by predation (except where exotic predators have been introduced);
2. No evidence of regulation by disease;
3. Most colonies have additional breeding sites available (hence not limited by breeding sites);
4. Potential foraging area outside breeding season very extensive;
5. Food supply around colonies presumably restricted by competition.

Given the foregoing, he argued that regulation was most likely to occur during breeding, because adherence to the breeding site restricted the foraging area, and because the concentration of birds in large colonies must cause competition for local food supplies. Outside the breeding season, he reasoned that the birds could spread out to take advantage of the best feeding areas, irrespective of proximity to land and hence were less likely to be under competitive pressure. Though he did not make this point explicitly, he assumed that, given the choice between their own survival and that of their offspring, seabirds would choose the former. Hence, regulation in the size of a given colony was likely to occur through density-dependent reduction in clutch size and chick survival, rather than through an increase in adult mortality.

> *Competition for food around colonies will gradually become important as the population increases, so that the birds will . . . find difficulty in raising young. Eventually the food shortage will become so acute that the production of young will decrease to the level [at which the population balances].*
> Ashmole, 1963

He went on to point out that all the breeding-biology traits that characterise pelagic seabirds (single-egg clutch, prolonged incubation and chick growth period, deferred maturity) might be expected where intense competition for food occurs during breeding. Ashmole's hypothesis assumes that colony sites are limited, which is almost certainly true for the area of the tropical Atlantic where he worked, but might not be true for oceanic birds in other parts of the world.

Subsequently, Robert Ricklefs expressed the same idea, but in a more generalised form:

> *The direct relationship between fecundity and adult mortality [in birds] . . . reflects primarily the density dependent feedback of adult survival on resources for reproduction.* Ricklefs, 1977

There are several important elements to Ashmole's hypothesis, which were neatly summarised by Furness & Monaghan (1987), from whom Figure 9.1 is adapted. As colony size (N) increases, foraging range (r) must increase through reduction in the availability of food close to the colony. At

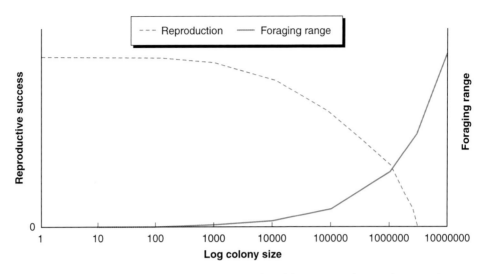

Figure 9.1   Ashmole's theory of seabird population regulation (adapted from Furness & Monaghan, 1987).

some point, the increased time spent in commuting to distant feeding areas, or the extra feeding time caused by reduced food availability close to the colony, will be reflected in reduced food delivery to the chicks. This will create selection for reduced brood size, slower growth rates and other energy-conserving adaptations. As potential foraging area increases with the square of foraging range, foraging range should be proportional to the square root of the population size.

Ashmole's hypothesis, as described above, predates *K*-selection theory and short-circuits the debate about whether typical seabird life histories require resource limitation. It does this because his hypothesis includes an obvious mechanism for creating competition (i.e. breeding in large colonies). The idea requires us to assume that large numbers of birds based at a single colony site create a local depletion of the food supply (Vicki Friesen coined the term 'Ashmole's halo' to describe this local food vacuum; Birt *et al.*, 1987). Indeed, an *ad absurdum* argument suggests that this must be true up to a certain point: a million birds clearly need more food than a thousand.

It is important to notice that Lack's (1968) ideas were completely different from Ashmole's, although Lack himself does not seem to have noticed the contradiction. He regarded foraging range as a fixed trait and considering that foraging range explained colony size, rather than vice-versa:

Offshore feeders have anyway to fly long distances from their nests to feed, so that it makes proportionately little difference to the distance flown whether they nest in a few large groups, or more smaller ones.   Lack, 1968

Lack's idea worked at the level of inter-group comparisons, because some seabirds are tied to feeding in areas very remote from land: albatrosses, gadfly petrels and storm-petrels are the most obvious examples. On the other hand, practically all auks will feed close to land if conditions are suitable, as will many shearwaters, fulmars, boobies, kittiwakes and terns. I am vividly reminded of dense flocks of Hutton's Shearwaters foraging almost in the surf zone off North Island, New Zealand. For these groups, pelagic feeding during the breeding season may be regarded as facultative, rather than obligate. In addition, for temperate-zone seabirds, at least, Lack considered that population regulation probably occurred in winter. Studies of the timing of mortality in temperate seabirds seem to support this view, as most appears to occur in winter.

Within species, comparisons have shown some evidence for the existence of 'Ashmole's halo' among temperate- and arctic-breeding seabirds. Both George Hunt and I observed independently that colony size may have an effect on reproductive success and chick growth, with larger colonies having lower success and growth rates than small ones (Figure 9.2). David Cairns (1992) called this 'the hungry horde effect'. Why birds at large colonies, presumably indicative of superior conditions, should do worse than those of small colonies is unknown, but the effect is suggestive of density dependence affecting reproduction (Gaston *et al.*, 1983a; Hunt *et al.*, 1986).

Similar circumstantial evidence for food competition around breeding colonies is provided by the distribution of colony size for certain British seabirds, suggesting that large colonies suppress the development of adjacent colonies (Furness & Birkhead, 1984). Again, the exact cause of the effect is enigmatic, although it seems to indicate competition for food during breeding. Of course, if populations are limited by the availability of nest sites, rather than by food, then none of this is likely to happen.

Antony Diamond (1978) provided a useful test of Ashmole's idea, when he compared population sizes among resident and migratory seabirds breeding on tropical oceanic islands. He demonstrated that the populations of migratory species were generally much larger than those of resident species and that populations of migratory inshore feeders were larger than those of pelagic residents. This seemed to indicate that migration, presumably conferring a much larger potential foraging area, was a more important determinant of population size than foraging range during breeding—apparent evidence for Lack's view. However, he did not consider any burrow nesters, cutting out the tubenoses: it would be interesting to know how their inclusion would have affected the outcome, which otherwise depended mainly on the difference between migratory and resident terns (they comprised more than half the species considered).

It seems likely that a full understanding of factors determining seabird populations will require elements of both Ashmole's and Lack's ideas. I will return to the ideas of Lack, Ashmole and Diamond and the concept of density dependence, once I have reviewed the different elements of seabird demography and life history.

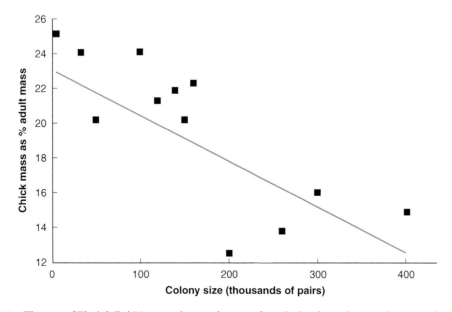

Figure 9.2   The mass of Thick-billed Murre nestlings at departure from the breeding colony in relation to colony size (data from Gaston et al., *1983a and unpubl.).*

CHANGES IN REPRODUCTIVE EFFORT WITH AGE

The allocation of resources to reproduction and survival not only varies among species, it may vary for the same individual as it gets older. In fact, age-related changes in fecundity are almost universal among birds, as well as many other organisms (fishes, trees). Because it is such a common phenomenon among birds, change in fecundity with age has attracted substantial comment and theory. As seabirds live a long time the effects on them are especially apparent.

Three hypotheses have been suggested to account for the pattern of increase, plateau and decline in reproductive performance with age observed for many birds (Forslund & Part, 1995). These hypotheses may not be mutually exclusive.

(1)   Reproductive success increases with age because older birds put more effort into reproduction as the opportunity for future reproduction declines. This 'optimization of reproductive effort hypothesis' assumes an increase in mortality with age. To my knowledge, no study has estimated what the future reproductive success is likely to be at different ages for a seabird population, though similar information is available for another relatively long-lived bird (Newton & Rothery, 1997). Among seabirds, this hypothesis has been supported mainly by studies on the California Gull breeding at inland sites (Pugesek, 1981; Pugesek & Diem, 1990).

(2)   Reproductive performance changes with age because of changes in the representation of different phenotypes in the breeding population. This could occur in three ways: (a) birds with low reproductive output suffer higher mortality or tend to disperse more frequently than those with high output, leaving a higher proportion of birds with a high reproductive output among older age classes; (b) high-quality individuals may begin to breed when older and thereby represent a greater proportion of the older age classes; (c) birds that have a high reproductive output die younger than those with a lower reproductive output, leaving a greater proportion of low-output birds among older age classes. The latter mechanism could explain the decline in reproductive performance and survival among the oldest birds that has otherwise been attributed to senescence. These ideas may collectively be referred to as 'the selection hypothesis'. One or other variant has been supported by some studies where individual variation in reproductive performance has been quantified (e.g., Coulson & Thomas, 1985a,b) or in cases where individuals within a population may be following different reproductive strategies (i.e. some birds put greater effort into reproduction than others; Pugesek & Wood, 1992). In the latter example, some individuals started breeding early and bred intensively for a relatively short period of time, whereas other individuals deferred breeding and reproduced intermittently. Less dramatic, but similar, trends have been detected in Short-tailed Shearwaters (Bradley *et al.*, 1989). The survival of the second group may have been enhanced because they put less effort into reproduction. Removing their eggs, so that they did not suffer the strain of rearing chicks, increased adult survival among Black-legged Kittiwakes in Prince William Sound, Alaska, an area where reproductive success, at the time, was generally rather low (Golet *et al.*, 1998).

(3)   Reproductive success increases with age because, as birds get older, they become more experienced at obtaining good-quality territories and mates and at caring for eggs, nestlings, etc.—the improvement in competence hypothesis (Reid, 1988; de Forest & Gaston, 1996). This hypothesis has been supported by many studies, although it has been rarely rigorously tested against alternatives. It may be invoked where there is little support for other explanations.

Overall, the most important difference among these hypotheses is the question of whether changes in reproduction with age are caused by unavoidable constraints (young birds cannot feed large broods) or by voluntary restraint (young birds choose to rear small broods to improve their survival). Unfortunately, this distinction is very hard to tease apart and the dichotomy itself is somewhat artificial. No bird is likely to drive itself to the brink of death in order to reproduce unless it is unable to realise its own danger (like the murres that permitted themselves to be sucked to death by mosquitoes). Hence, every bird must be practicing a certain degree of restraint in the amount of effort devoted to reproduction. That being so, the argument reduces to whether some birds are showing more restraint than others, and whether this relates to age. How important such differential restraint may be remains obscure for the majority of seabirds. We shall look at some of the evidence in the next chapter.

Two faces of research at Prince Leopold Island: (above) the fat 70s, heated Weatherhavens with support from the offshore oil industry and (below) the lean 80s, canvas tents after an ice storm. (Tony Gaston)

CHAPTER TEN

Birth and death—observations

May of 1985 was a very exceptional month for Sooty Shearwaters in Hecate Strait. Almost daily, we watched streams of birds moving south, their wings beating close over the surface of the sea, or held stiff as they made arcs high above the waves. Many others could be glimpsed bobbing on the water. However, this did not prepare us for the sight that greeted us on 14 May. That morning, when we set up our telescopes at the usual watchpoint, the northeast horizon appeared clouded with a dark haze that resolved itself, on closer inspection, into a wheeling mob of shearwaters that stretched as far as we could see. The flying birds were only a fraction of those that formed an almost solid raft on the sea surface. In the parlance of Newfoundland (said formerly, but no longer, of cod), 'you could have walked on their backs'.

Estimating these sorts of numbers through a telescope from more than a kilometre distant is clearly a very uncertain task. We made independent counts, estimating numbers of birds in a telescope field and then calculating the number of fields required to cover the entire horizon. We concluded that there could not be less than a quarter of a million birds, and there might be as many as half a million. Given that our field of view was truncated by Reef Island, about halfway across the potential view of Hecate Strait, there is little doubt that there were half-a-million or more Sooty Shearwaters within sight of Reef Island that morning. Many of the birds were moulting and in subsequent days the tideline became strewn with a thick layer of moulted feathers.

That aggregation of Sooty Shearwaters is the most birds that I have ever seen at once. However, seabirds are celebrated for their dense aggregations, both while breeding and at sea. There are many other accounts of enormous concentrations, especially of shearwaters. On aerial surveys of Baffin Bay in 1978, observers estimated 14 million Little Auks (Renaud *et al.*, 1982). How is it that seabirds can achieve and maintain such enormous numbers? How are their populations regulated and how does population size relate to the seabird syndrome? This chapter deals with population size and other demographic factors.

POPULATION SIZE

Many seabirds are very numerous. Among those that breed in the southern hemisphere, Macaroni and Chinstrap Penguins, Wilson's Storm-petrels, Great, Sooty and Short-tailed Shearwaters, Antarctic and Salvin's (Medium-billed) Prions and Common and South Georgia Diving Petrels all number in the tens of millions. Four other penguins, four species of fulmarine petrels, four shear-waters, two other prions, the Black-browed Albatross, the White-chinned Petrel and the Blue Petrel all number over a million. In the northern hemisphere, Leach's Storm-petrel, the two murres, the Atlantic and Tufted Puffins, the Least Auklet and the Little Auk have populations exceeding ten mil-lion birds: perhaps also the Black-legged Kittiwake. At least six other auks number more than one million breeders, as do four species of gulls, though all these have substantial inland-breeding popu-lations and three (Herring, Ring-billed and Black-headed Gulls) have recently increased by taking advantage of human activities. In the tropics, Sooty Terns occur in tens of millions, as did the Guanay Cormorant before declines in the 1980s.

At the other end of the scale, most very small populations can be explained in terms of some kind of recent human intervention. However, some species do appear to be naturally uncommon. Several of the New Zealand cormorants (Rough-faced, Stewart [Bronze], Campbell Island and Auckland Island Shags) all have populations of fewer than 10,000 pairs, though apparently not affected by human-induced changes. Apart from the Guanay Cormorant, among the more than 30 species of cormorant worldwide, only the Great and Double-crested Cormorants approach one million birds, but both these species have substantial populations living inland. None of the frigatebirds or tropic-birds exceeds 100,000 pairs. Apart from the Sooty Tern, none of the more than 40 species of tern numbers more than a million. The Black-legged Kittiwake is the only wholly marine gull to reach six figures. Even some widespread species are quite uncommon. Roseate and Caspian Terns, though found almost throughout tropical and temperate waters, are nowhere numerous. The Roseate usu-ally nests alongside much more abundant congeners. Kittlitz's Murrelet, found along much of the extensive coastline of Alaska, numbers only a few tens of thousands.

We should note also that seabird populations in areas where they have been monitored intensively (Europe and North America) have been grossly affected by human activities over the past few cen-turies. Many of them may exist at levels far below those characteristic of conditions under which their species evolved. Hence large populations may have been characteristic of many more seabird species in the past.

What are the ecological factors influencing population size? Mike Brooke (2001) noted that underwater pursuit divers constitute a much higher proportion of the hyper-abundant species than their overall representation among seabirds would predict and suggested that this was the result of having a greater volume of foraging space available to them than surface feeders. This argument would account for why more than half the auks and six species of penguins have populations of over a million, while only one tern and only one marine gull reach this level. It also explains why half the diving-petrels and seven species of shearwater exceed one million, while only one gadfly petrel does so (though many populations of gadfly petrels are severely depleted at present). On the other hand, the very small size of many marine cormorant populations indicates that other factors are involved.

The relatively small size of most cormorant populations apparently stems from two causes: the very small ranges occupied by many species, and the need to return to land to roost, which constrains the area over which they can forage. Only in the extremely productive waters of the coastal upwelling zones can cormorants form large populations. In contrast, the auks, which roost at sea and tend to steer away from land when not breeding, have the whole ocean, or at least the entire continental shelf, in which to forage. The same argument applies to the fairly modest populations of most terns and gulls, which feed in the coastal zone and often roost ashore, whereas the highly mobile and pelagic-foraging Sooty Tern can maintain large populations in the relatively low-productivity waters of the tropics. Likewise, the productive waters of the southern ocean, combined with the extensive foraging ranges of the southern petrels, has created conditions where a high proportion of highly abundant species can occur.

A combination of oceanic productivity, foraging range and diving ability appears to explain much of the variation among seabirds in population size. As all these factors determine the total amount of food available to a given species, it is difficult not to feel that, as Lack suggested, many seabird populations are limited by the availability of food. Although breeding range would seem important, there are many cases of very abundant species that have restricted breeding sites (Great Shearwater, Buller's Shearwater, Juan Fernández Petrel, South Georgia Diving-petrel).

POPULATION CHANGE

Seabird population change can occur rapidly or slowly depending upon species and location. In variable environments, such as upwelling-dominated coastal marine ecosystems of Peru and California, populations may respond catastrophically to massive changes in food availability associated with El Niño events (Tovar *et al.*, 1987; Schreiber, 2001). However, even in ecosystems that appear more stable, seabird populations can vary considerably. Perceptions of stability or relatively slow change in seabird numbers may have more to do with when observations are made, than with actual lack of population variability. For example, Nur & Sydeman (1999a) demonstrated that, over a quarter-century of surveys, Brandt's Cormorant numbers on southeast Farallon Island, California, changed in a 'staircase' fashion, showing periods of relative stability interspersed with years of major decline. The upward trend in Thick-billed Murre populations in the eastern Canadian Arctic over the past two decades has been more ratchet-like, with a few years of increases followed by one or two years of decline.

POPULATION PROCESSES

Population dynamics are described in terms of three processes: mortality, reproduction and dispersal (emigration and immigration). I shall try to characterise each of these processes for seabirds and place them in the context of birds in general.

Because most seabirds breed in large colonies to which they return annually, it is relatively easy to obtain information on breeding population size, reproductive success and, to a lesser extent, survival and age at first breeding. There is a substantial literature relating to these aspects of seabird biology.

However, because seabirds are so long-lived, studies of their demography are the work of lifetimes, not the stuff of three-year grants. If we can now claim to have a good overview of seabird survival rates and other population measurements, it is due to the farsightedness and persistence of a small number of individuals who laboured for years with relatively small reward. Long-term demographic studies on seabirds have been conducted since the 1930s, usually as integrated population studies, aiming to measure breeding and pre-breeding survival, age at first breeding and reproductive success. Some examples of pioneer long-term seabird studies are shown in Table 10.1.

Seabirds were among the first birds subjected to long-term population studies. Lack's (1966) landmark *Population studies on birds* included four seabirds among 15 species of birds for which useful data were available at that time. The dominance of Antipodeans in early seabird population studies is striking. If we had to name the father of demographic studies on seabirds, it would have to be L. E. Richdale, who not only initiated one of the earliest banding studies, on the Yellow-eyed Penguin (Richdale, 1957), but also provided information on the survival rates of several other New Zealand seabirds including Sooty Shearwater, White-faced Storm-petrel and Common Diving-petrel (Richdale, 1963, 1965). His penguin and shearwater studies involved making his own bands, experimenting with both celluloid and aluminum: the latter each took 15 minutes to make!

MORTALITY

The principle characteristics of the 'seabird syndrome' that I have described are low reproductive rates, due to small clutch size and deferred breeding, and high adult survival. These characteristics are especially well developed in the King and Emperor Penguins, tubenoses, boobies, tropicbirds and frigatebirds, the tropical terns and the larger auks. All these lay a single egg and most begin to breed at four years or older. Most adults have a better than 90% chance of surviving from one year to the next, so that any given breeding population will consist largely of birds with several years of previous breeding experience and a maximum longevity of more than 25 years. Even a bird as small as a Manx Shearwater is capable of living more than 50 years.

Some estimates of mortality rates for seabirds have been based on the recovery of birds found dead (the typical practice for most birds), but much of our information on seabird mortality derives from observations at selected breeding colonies in successive years, assuming that adult seabirds, once they begin to breed, nest annually (or biannually, in the case of King Penguins, frigatebirds and some albatrosses) and rarely shift between colonies.

Table 10.1   Pioneering studies on seabird populations

Species	Initiated	Location	Reference
Manx Shearwater	1929	Skokholm, Wales	Lockley, 1942
Yellow-eyed Penguin	1936	Otago, New Zealand	Richdale, 1957
Laysan Albatross	1944	Midway Island	Fisher, 1975
Short-tailed Shearwater	1947	Fisher Island, Australia	Serventy & Curry, 1984
Black-legged Kittiwake	1952	Newcastle, UK	Coulson & Thomas, 1985b
Royal Penguin	1956	Macquarie Island, subantarctic waters	Carrick, 1972
Red-billed Gull	1958	Kaikoura, New Zealand	Mills, 1989
Adélie Penguin	1961	Ross Island, Antarctica	Sladen (in Ainley *et al.*, 1983)

Mean annual mortality among seabirds of breeding age has now been estimated for at least 60 species. Recent reviews and handbooks reveal the following numbers (including only estimates based on samples of >30 birds): petrels and albatrosses, 27 spp.; cormorants, three spp.; pelicans, boobies and tropicbirds, four spp; gulls, 11 spp.; terns, six spp.; jaegers and skuas, three spp.; auks 11 spp (Cramp, 1985; Jouventin & Weimerskirch, 1991; Poole & Gill, 1992–98; Williams, 1995; Warham, 1996; Gaston & Jones, 1998). As in most other aspects of their biology, knowledge of cormorants seems to lag behind that for other groups. Auks, with estimates available for half of the extant species, are the best known.

The lowest estimates of adult mean annual survival for seabirds are 75% for the Common Diving-petrel (Richdale, 1965) and 77% for Least Auklet and Ancient Murrelet (Gaston & Jones, 1998). An estimate of 62% for Cassin's Auklets in British Columbia involves a population probably in rapid decline at the time (Bertram *et al.*, 2000). The highest are 97% for Wandering Albatrosses at South Georgia before longline mortality became prevalent (Croxall *et al.*, 1990) and Atlantic Puffins at the Isle of May, Scotland, when the population was increasing during the 1980s (Harris *et al.*, 1997). Northern Fulmars in Orkney are close behind, with adult survival of 96% in the 1960s and 1970s (Dunnet & Ollason, 1978). As with most organisms, there is a tendency for larger seabirds to have a higher survival rate than small ones (Figure 10.1).

There is a widespread idea that mortality rates among seabirds are much lower than those for land or freshwater birds. As Wynne-Edwards (1939) put it (specifically of pelagic seabirds):

Their reproductive rate would appear to be slower than that of any other birds, or indeed, of any animals at all, with the exception, perhaps of elephants and whales.

This statement is broadly true, although probably it was founded mainly on comparisons with temperate and cold-climate landbirds. However, with the exception of the tubenoses, seabirds do not suffer markedly less mortality than passerines, once the allometric relationship with size is taken into account (Figure 10.2). The highest survival rates among passerines tend to be associated with

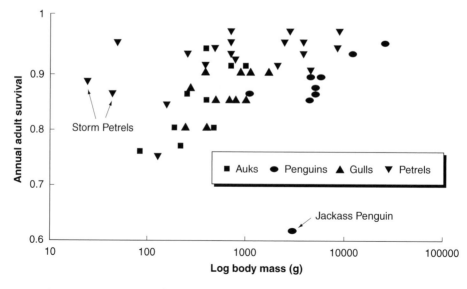

Figure 10.1   Adult survival in relation to body mass for seabirds (data from Cramp, 1985; Croxall & Gaston, 1988; Poole & Gill, 1992–98; Williams, 1995; Warham, 1996; Gaston & Jones, 1998).

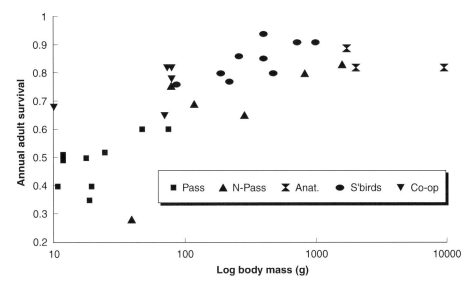

Figure 10.2   Adult survival in relation to body mass for selected bird species (data from Newton, 1989; Perrins et al., 1991, Stacey & Koenig, 1991): Pass = passerines; N-pass = non-passerine landbirds; Anat = Anatidae; S'birds = seabirds; Co-op = Co-operative breeders.

cooperative breeding. However, this may be a consequence, rather than a cause, of high survival rate: many of these birds are resident in tropical or warm-temperate climates (Stacey & Koenig, 1990). As a group, only the storm-petrels can be stated to have adult survival well outside of the range of passerines of a similar size. All birds have the capacity to live a long time compared to mammals of similar size.

Among seabirds, penguins have lower survival rates than might be predicted from their size (Figure 10.1): overall their adult survival rates tend to be lower than those of their smaller northern counterparts, the auks. There is no obvious explanation for this difference, except that their inability to fly may make them susceptible to predators that flying seabirds can avoid (Pomeroy, 1990). For instance, penguins form an important component of the diet of Leopard Seals *Hydrurga leptonyx* (Kooyman, 1981; Riedman, 1990) and may also suffer significantly from the attacks of Killer Whales *Orcinus orca* and sea lions (Boswall, 1972). The possibility that vulnerability to predation might partially explain their absence (along with other underwater diving birds) from tropical waters, where large, fast-swimming predatory fish, such as sharks, are common, was discussed in Chapter 5.

Jared Diamond, in a brief aside in his magisterial account of how our animal heritage affects human behaviour (*The Rise and Fall of the Third Chimpanzee*; Diamond, 1991) suggested that birds tend to live longer than mammals because the ability to fly allows them to escape many predators. He further suggested that the longevity of seabirds is a result of the lack of predators at sea, a point already touched on (Chapter 6). The lower than expected survival rates of penguins certainly seem to support this view, though other explanations are possible. What is certainly true is another point made by Diamond, that the longevity of seabirds is not just a matter of less-frequent chance of predation or accidental death, but depends on the evolution of repair mechanisms that keep the organism functioning in top condition for far longer than would be true for a similarly sized grouse or other gamebird.

Survival rates seem to be determined partially by species ecology, with offshore feeders generally exhibiting higher survival rates than inshore feeders, as noted by Lack (1968). However, survival rates vary substantially both among populations, and in the same population between years. Scott Hatch and others (Hatch *et al.*, 1993b) demonstrated that adult annual mortality of Black-legged Kittiwakes at a colony in the Gulf of Alaska was less than half that observed for the same species in northeast England over many years (Aebischer & Coulson, 1990). At the Farallon Islands, several species exhibited significant annual variability in adult survival including Common Murre (Sydeman, 1993), Brandt's Cormorant (Nur & Sydeman, 1999b), Western Gull and Cassin's Auklet (both Point Reyes Bird Observatory, unpubl. data). Interannual variability in survival of European Shags and Atlantic Puffins also has been demonstrated in the North Atlantic (Harris *et al.*, 1994, 1997).

A decrease in survival among older birds in a population (i.e., evidence of senescence) occurs in a number of seabirds (Black-legged Kittiwake, Coulson & Wooller, 1976; Northern Fulmar, Ollason & Dunnet, 1983; Short-tailed Shearwater, Wooller *et al.*, 1989; California Gull, Pugesek & Diem, 1990; European Shag, Harris *et al.*, 1994; Atlantic Puffin, Harris *et al.*, 1997). A particularly interesting case was described by Harris *et al.* (1998): in a winter of very high overall mortality for Shags at the Isle of May, Scotland, mortality of young and old birds was higher than that of 'middle-aged' birds (7–16 years). Moreover, those middle-aged birds that had bred the previous summer survived less well than those that had not.

An increase in mortality after reaching the age to which less than 10% of the population would normally survive is probably a normal feature of seabird life histories (and other birds, for that matter), but information on this trait is rare. It has strong implications for life-history strategies as, according to theory, a decline in future life expectancy may lead to an increase in current reproductive effort (see below). However, reproductive success sometimes declines with age, as well, so the effect of future life expectancy on reproductive investment may be fairly small.

REPRODUCTION

This aspect of seabird population dynamics has been the subject of much investigation. Studies of clutch size, hatching success and overall reproductive success have been undertaken for most northern hemisphere seabirds, often at many sites and over many years (for North Pacific seabirds, see reviews in Vermeer *et al.*, 1993).

AGE AT FIRST BREEDING

No seabird breeds regularly at one year of age. A few begin at two years (e.g. some cormorants, some small gulls, Cassin's Auklets and Ancient Murrelets), but most do not breed until at least three years, and the large albatrosses and frigatebirds defer breeding until at least seven years (Figure 10.3). Within vertebrate classes, age at first breeding appears to be determined partially by allometric relationships with body size (Stearns, 1980) and this also applies within orders of birds. However, compared to other birds, seabirds appear to be older when they begin breeding, though they may not be very different from cooperatively breeding passerines (Figure 10.4). The relationship of age at first breeding to adult size also differs among different seabird orders: petrels start to breed when much older than penguins of the same size, with auks, gulls and terns intermediate. The slope of the regressions of mean age at first breeding on body mass are similar for the three groups. The differences among the intercepts of the regressions seem to be largely explained by differences in survival rates. When mean ages at first breeding are plotted against adult annual survival rate, there are no

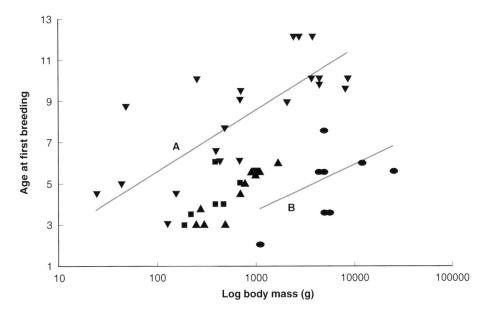

Figure 10.3   Age at first breeding in relation to body mass for seabirds (sources and symbols as for 10.1). Regression A, petrels; regression B, penguins

differences among the groups, or between marine and terrestrial birds (Figure 10.5). Hence, age at first breeding appears to be determined by adult survival. This is well demonstrated by the Wandering Albatross, where an increase in adult mortality caused by longline fishing, has wrought a dramatic reduction in the age at first breeding (Weimerskirch & Jouventin, 1987; Croxall *et al.*, 1990).

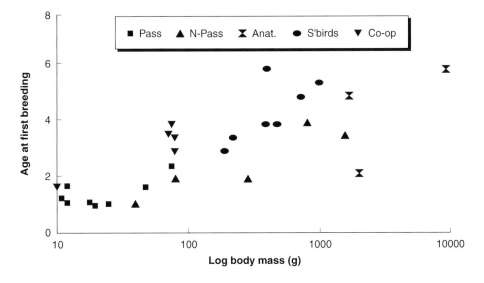

Figure 10.4   Age at first breeding in relation to body mass for selected bird species (sources and abbreviations as for 10.2).

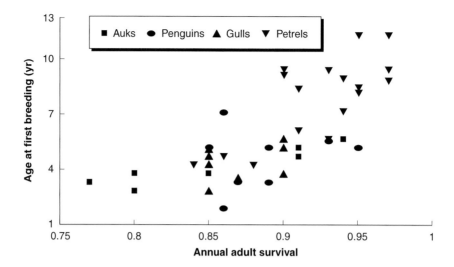

Figure 10.5   Age at first breeding in relation to mean annual survival (sources as for 10.1).

Why should seabirds take so long to make up their minds to breed? Is it peculiarly difficult to develop the skills necessary to forage in the marine environment? Certainly first-year seabirds of several species have been proved to have lower foraging success than older birds (Ryder, 1980). However, if feeding was more difficult to learn in the marine environment than on land, we might predict prolonged post-fledging parental care or, in the absence of such care, exceptionally high post-fledging mortality, among seabirds. Post-fledging care is prolonged in the frigatebirds, boobies and some terns, which is perhaps accounted for by their feeding techniques: plunge-diving is both difficult (the bird needs to learn to allow for parallax) and potentially hazardous—Gannets that cannot distinguish deep and shallow waters may end up with a broken neck (Nelson, 1978), while frigatebirds require exceptional flight skills for their aerial piracy (Diamond, 1975). Otherwise, post-fledging care is variable, being absent in penguins and most tubenoses, absent or rather brief in most Charadriiform seabirds, and otherwise prolonged only in some cormorants. There is no evidence for exceptionally high post-fledging mortality among seabirds, though evidence on comparative post-fledging mortality across groups is rather thin. Even fewer seabirds feed their young away from the breeding colony, perhaps because it is too difficult for far-ranging birds to keep in touch with their offspring once they have quit the nest.

An alternative explanation for deferred maturity in seabirds is that breeding confers risks not attendant on daily existence at sea. This must be true for all birds, because breeding requires repeated visits to the nest and increased foraging both of which confer some risk of predation. However, most landbirds breed in similar habitat to that which they occupy year-round, so no special adjustments in behaviour are needed, whereas seabirds, normally at home on the broad expanses of the ocean, must cope with the complexities of terrestrial environments and predators. The additional risks inherent in breeding may be greater for seabirds than for landbirds, hence the time needed to learn how to cope with them may be greater. In the South Polar Skua, which begins to breed at about eight years, birds that began to breed at older ages lived longer than those that began to breed young, suggesting that the stress imposed by breeding prematurely may also have a cost in terms of subsequent survival (Ainley *et al.*, 1990).

CLUTCH SIZE

Among birds in general, those that live a long time generally lay small clutches (Lack, 1966, 1968). However, notwithstanding this relationship, the proportion of seabirds that lay one-egg clutches is very high (all tubenoses, frigatebirds and tropicbirds, most auks, some penguins and terns) and this seems to be their most outstanding demographic trait. Among thousands of species of landbirds, only a few large eagles, vultures and bustards, a few frugivorous tropical passerines, large parrots, swifts, and frogmouths, the Crab Plover, the flamingos *Phoenicopterus* spp. and the kiwis *Apteryx* spp., lay single-egg clutches. Part of this difference may be due to the fact that almost all seabirds rear their young to full size in the nest: precocial species tend to lay larger clutches than non-precocial species (Lack, 1968). However, this explanation is not complete because, even when precocial species are excluded, a much greater proportion of seabirds than landbirds lay one-egg clutches.

When we examine seabirds, there is relatively little variation in mean clutch size within families (Table 10.2). Only the terns, and to a lesser extent the gulls, show any substantial inter-specific variation in clutch size (1–3). For penguins and auks, there appears to be a correspondence between clutch size and adult survival (Figure 10.6). This may be true of the terns as well, but there is little information on survival in the tropical terns that lay one egg.

As Lack pointed out, clutch size among seabirds is closely related to their foraging range during the chick-rearing period. He made this point by comparing 'inshore/offshore' species pairs (e.g. Black-legged Kittiwake [offshore] versus Black-headed Gull [inshore]). We can now make the same point with more general information. For instance, among penguins, *Aptenodytes* spp., which lay a single egg, have much longer foraging trips (i.e. they spend much longer away from the colony on provisioning trips) than the smaller *Pygoscelis* spp., which lay two eggs (Williams, 1995). *Eudyptes* spp., which lay two eggs, but never rear more than one chick, are intermediate (Figure 10.7). Similarly, among auks, the only genera that lay two eggs are the inshore guillemots, and the precocial murrelets. Among terns, clutch size decreases from fresh water to inshore marine to offshore marine species, presumably relating to foraging range (Figure 10.8; Langham, 1984).

Table 10.2 Clutch size and adult annual survival among seabird families and subfamilies (marine species, experienced breeders only)

Order/family	Clutch	Survival
Sphenisciformes	1–2	0.85–0.95
Procellariiformes		
All genera	1	0.75–0.97
Pelecaniformes		
Fregatidae	1	
Sulidae	1–2	0.94
Pelecanidae	2	
Phalacrocoracidae	2–5	0.73–0.89
Phaethontidae	1	
Charadriiformes		
Laridae	1–3	0.8–0.9
Sternidae	1–3	0.83–0.93
Stercorariidae	2	0.9–0.96
Alcidae	1–2	0.76–0.94

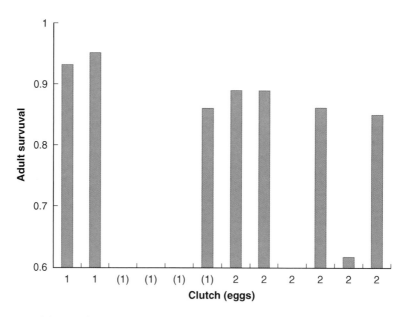

Figure 10.6   Mean adult annual survival in relation to clutch size for 12 species of penguins (data from Williams, 1995). (1) = lays 2 eggs but rears only one chick.

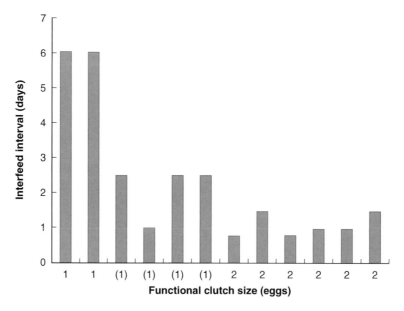

Figure 10.7   Mean interval between feeds (a measure of feeding frequency) in relation to clutch size in 12 species of penguins (data from Williams, 1995). (1) = lays 2 eggs but rears only one chick.

For the majority of seabird species, clutch size is relatively constant, although first-time breeders often lay smaller clutches than more experienced birds. Among auks, species of *Cepphus* and *Synthliboramphus* that normally lay two-egg clutches, show little variation in the small proportion of one-egg clutches laid (Gaston, 1992; Ewins *et al.*, 1993), though at the Farallon Islands, where there

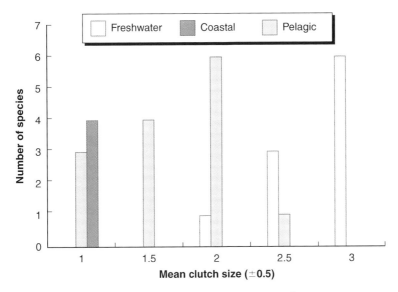

Figure 10.8 Clutch size in terns in relation to breeding habitat (data from Ali & Ripley, 1981; Cramp, 1985; Poole & Gill, 1992–98).

is an exceptionally large concentration of Pigeon Guillemots, the proportion of one-egg clutches increased in years when less food was available (Ainley & Boekelheide, 1990). Similarly, large gulls appear to be limited to a clutch of three and show no variation between inland and coastal-nesting populations (Vermeer, 1970). Despite three-egg clutches being the most successful in terms of young fledged in many studies, four-egg clutches are very rare. Although clutches of more than three eggs are difficult for gulls to incubate, having only three brood patches, this explanation merely begs the question of why they do not have more brood patches. So far, there has been no convincing explanation for the truncation of clutch size in large gulls (Reid, 1987).

Cormorants, which lay up to five eggs, are the seabirds that stand out most obviously when number of eggs is considered. In terms of their diet, their breeding sites, their clutch size, their nests and their nestlings (born helpless and confined to the nest throughout development), they closely resemble herons and egrets. The two groups often intermingle nests at inland colonies. Recent classifications suggest that these families may be closer to one another than outward appearances suggest, so these traits may have been characteristic of a common ancestor. However, they also share the common ecological characteristics of foraging on small, scattered waterbodies (or inshore in the case of cormorants) and being colonial because of a limited supply of nest sites.

Because cormorants must return to land to roost, their populations are just as constrained by foraging range while breeding as they are when not breeding. Hence, the intense breeding-season competition envisaged by Ashmole's model does not operate for them. The fact that cormorants never evolved small clutches definitely supports the idea that breeding-season competition may be an ultimate cause for reduced clutch size.

ANNUAL REPRODUCTIVE SUCCESS

In contrast to clutch size, reproductive success appears to be subject to great variability, both within and between populations. This is probably because, as Cairns (1992) pointed out, the food supplies on which most seabirds rely during the breeding season are subject to fluctuations orders of magnitude larger than typical inter-annual changes in seabird populations. Examples of variation in reproductive success are too numerous to detail, but the contrast between Black-legged Kittiwakes in the North Pacific and in the eastern Atlantic is especially striking: many Atlantic populations fledge more than one offspring/pair annually, while among 22 kittiwake colonies in the Bering Sea and Gulf of Alaska, none averaged more than 0.5 fledglings/pair (Hatch *et al.*, 1993a).

Within regions, some species show great inter-year variation in reproduction: e.g. the Humboldt and California Current upwelling zones, where reproduction is curtailed for most species by periodic El Niño events (Duffy, 1983; Ainley *et al.*, 1995). However, seabirds breeding together at the same site may show great differences in the extent of variation in reproductive success. At the Farallon Islands, over 27 years, Pelagic Cormorants and Cassin's Auklets did not differ significantly in mean numbers of young fledged annually, but inter-year variation was significantly higher for the cormorant (variance .697 and .033, respectively). Overall, the two cormorants at the Farallons show hugely greater inter-year variation in success than the Common Murres and Cassin's Auklets breeding alongside them (Figure 10.9). In contrast with Common Murres in the California Current ecosystem (Ainley *et al.*, 1995), Thick-billed Murres in the eastern Canadian Arctic, where oceanographic conditions vary little between years, show variation among colonies, but little inter-year variation at a single colony (e.g. success during 15 years at Coats Island never fell below 55% and never rose above 70%).

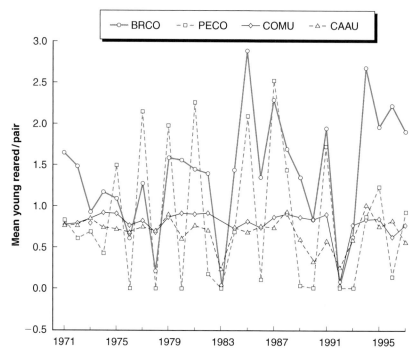

Figure 10.9   Variation in the breeding success of four species (Brandt's Cormorant [BRCO], Pelagic Cormorant [PECO], Common Murre [COMU] and Cassin's Auklet [CAAU]) nesting at the Farallon Islands, California, in 1971–1998. These results demonstrate the strong effects of certain ENSO events (1978, 1983, 1992). The success of Pelagic Cormorants fluctuated greatly even outside ENSO years, whereas that of Common Murres was otherwise stable (data courtesy of Bill Sydeman, Point Reyes Bird Observatory).

Quite dramatic differences in reproductive success can persist even among colonies spread over relatively small geographical areas. This is illustrated by Black-legged Kittiwakes in Britain where, between 1986 and 1996, birds in Shetland showed a sharp decline in chick production in the late 1980s that was scarcely detected in adjacent Orkney and the Outer Hebrides. Because of the great, environmentally induced, variation in reproductive success, it cannot be characterised for individual species, except to the extent that (virtually all seabirds being single-brooded) maximum annual reproduction is equivalent to maximum clutch size.

LIFETIME REPRODUCTIVE SUCCESS

We should recognise that birds as a group have very low reproductive rates relative to other vertebrates, including mammals (Blueweiss *et al.*, 1978). The maximum recorded lifetime reproductive success (LRS, in young fledged) is 60 (Blue Tit); an Arabian Babbler comes close, with 53. Data on seabirds are insufficient to be worth very much: they live for so long that collecting LRS information is a work of human generations, but the maximum LRS for Red-billed Gulls was nine and for Short-tailed Shearwaters, 12 (all LRS from Newton, 1989). A few Thick-billed Murres at Coats Island have managed double figures, and we anticipate that maximum LRS may be in the region of 15. For Western Gulls at the Farallon Islands, cumulative (almost lifetime) reproductive success has been measured for the 1979 and 1980 cohorts. Up to 1996, maximum fledgling production was in the range of 20–25 chicks, spanning breeding lifetimes of 11–13 years (W. J. Sydeman, pers. comm.). Such extreme results are clearly highly dependent on sample sizes. Evidence to date suggests that seabirds tend to have a lower maximum LRS than small passerines (Figure 10.10): to produce 60 young a Wandering Albatross that begins breeding at ten and breeds every other year would have to live at least 130 years and be successful at every attempt!

When we examine mean lifetime reproductive success, the difference between landbirds and seabirds disappears and there is no evidence, either that body size affects mean LRS, or that seabirds have any lower LRS than other birds (Figure 10.11). This result suggests a relatively constant LRS across birds, with breeding birds producing up to 5–6 times the number of young that would be needed to replace themselves. This observation accords with the fact that the relationships of annual

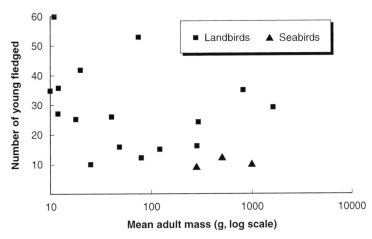

Figure 10.10   Maximum lifetime reproductive success in relation to adult body mass for selected bird species (data from Newton, 1989).

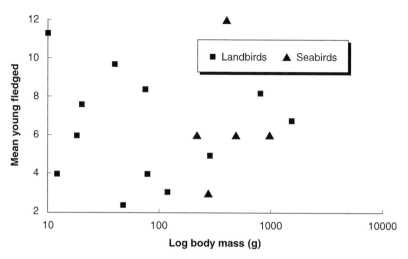

Figure 10.11   Mean lifetime reproductive success in relation to adult body mass for selected bird species (data from Newton 1989).

birth rate and mean life expectancy with adult body mass, cancel each other (Calder, 1984). The semblance of a universal law here is not only found in seabirds (Charnov, 1993) — it is something that deserves some serious empirical investigation.

EMIGRATION AND IMMIGRATION

We know much less about dispersal of seabirds, and how it affects population dynamics, than we know about mortality and reproduction. On the other hand, we may know more than we think we know, because there has been no systematic review of this topic (but see Kharitonov & Siegel-Causey, 1988).

The majority of seabirds appear to be amazingly good at finding their way back to the breeding colony where they were reared. Not only do they return to the same island or headland, but also they often return very close to the exact site. At Coats Island, Uli Steiner and I found that half of all the Thick-billed Murres that returned to breed at the colony did so within 3 m of where they were reared. Similar results have been obtained for other species (e.g. Bradley *et al.*, 1999). It is easy to see why a homing tendency might develop in a migratory species where colonies are widely dispersed. However, the value of returning so precisely to the natal site is not obvious when suitable breeding areas are clearly defined by the overall spread of the colony.

Clearly, emigration from somewhere must occur when a new colony is founded. For certain species and populations this has been frequently observed: e.g. Northern Gannet in Britain (Nelson, 1978) and Black-legged Kittiwake in Britain and eastern North America (Coulson & Nève de Mévergnies, 1992; Chapdelaine & Brousseau, 1989), and Northern Fulmar in the eastern North Atlantic (Fisher, 1952). For all these species the foundation of new colonies occurred during periods of rapid population expansion. During the expansion of the Northern Fulmar in Britain, some new colonies were founded at the periphery of the range, while others were established among existing colonies. The number of colonies roughly kept pace with the expansion of the population, though mean colony size crept up slightly, from *c.*100 breeding pairs in the early-20th century to nearly 500 pairs in 1986 (Figure 10.12). For seabirds as a whole, especially where populations are not expanding, the

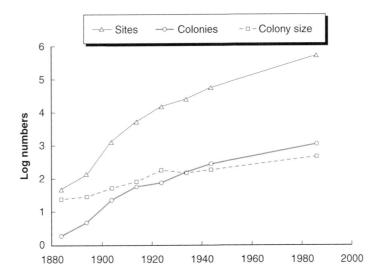

Figure 10.12   The expansion of Northern Fulmar colonies and breeding sites in Britain between 1880 and 1986 (from Fisher, 1952; Lloyd et al.*, 1991).*

foundation of new colonies is a relatively rare event, at least measured on the scale of human lifetimes.

Recently founded colonies may expand at a much faster rate than appears possible on the basis of the number of young they rear (Nelson, 1978). Apparently, new colonies sometimes attract a disproportionate share of emigrants from established colonies. The causes of differential recruitment could relate to the success of resident breeders, as may have been the case for Black-legged Kittiwakes at colonies in Brittany (Danchin & Monnat, 1992). In that study, adults of breeding age shifted colonies, as well as those recruiting for the first time, but this appears to be a relatively rare phenomenon. The distance involved was only a few kilometres.

Movement between well-established colonies is poorly known. Some of the best information comes from Mike Harris and co-workers at the Isle of May, Scotland. They obtained evidence that as many as 50% of young Atlantic Puffins may settle away from their natal colony (Harris & Wanless, 1991). Substantial emigration from the natal colony has been reported in several gulls and shearwaters (e.g. Coulson & Nève de Mévergnies 1992; Bradley *et al.*, 1999). However, although substantial inter-colony movement of pre-breeding Common Murres also has been observed (Halley & Harris, 1993), it appears that the majority settle on their natal colony. Conversely, three weeks of intensive searching for ringed birds at the Thick-billed Murre colony at Digges Island failed to reveal any of the 20,000 chicks banded at the closest other colony, Coats Island, suggesting a low rate of emigration from Coats. However, although we inspected thousands of legs for rings, our sample constituted less than 3% of those present among the 180,000 breeding pairs at Digges Island. Moreover, one of our Coats Island chicks was found breeding at a colony in Thule, northwest Greenland (Kampp & Falk, 1999). Measuring low rates of dispersal among these very abundant birds is a real problem.

The amount of inter-colony movement may vary considerably within species. Northern Fulmar colonies in the eastern Canadian Arctic show striking variation in the proportion of different colour morphs (Hatch & Nettleship, 1999). Assuming colour morphs to be genetically determined, this suggests that most birds return to breed in the colony where they were reared. Conversely, in Britain, fulmars appear to show little philopatry, with only 6% of chicks reared at an Orkney colony returning there to breed (Ollason & Dunnett, 1983). It may be significant that the Orkney colony formed part of a population that has been expanding for several centuries, while the population of the eastern Canadian Arctic currently appears to be stable.

DENSITY DEPENDENCE

BREEDING SEASON

There has been no rigorous analysis of density dependence for any seabird population. However, there is some evidence to suggest that density-dependent adjustments in demographic processes occur, especially during breeding. A very striking, albeit unnatural, example involves changes in the age at first breeding for large albatrosses resulting from increased mortality from longline fisheries (Weimerskirch & Jouventin, 1987; Croxall *et al.*, 1990; Jouventin & Weimerskirch, 1991): there has been a progressive decrease in mean age at first breeding among Wandering Albatrosses at the Crozet Islands and at South Georgia (Figure 10.13). Notice that this effect is probably not caused by a relaxation of competition for food, as the change in population size has been small (–1% annually). Rather, it is likely to reflect increased availability of experienced mates for first-time breeders.

Among seabirds where breeding-site quality is an important determinant of breeding success, density-dependent reductions in breeding success in an expanding population may be caused by a decline in mean breeding site quality as the population runs out of good-quality sites. A strong effect of nest-site quality was observed for European Shags in Northumberland, where a population crash brought about by 'red tide' poisoning, led to an improvement in the reproductive success of young breeders, which were able to gain access to good-quality breeding sites (Potts *et al.*, 1980). Breeding density can also have a negative relationship with reproductive success through an increase in the frequency of intra-specific predation and kleptoparasitism with increased nest density: this has been observed for large gulls in situations of decreasing (Coulson *et al.*, 1982) and increasing (Spaans *et al.*, 1987) populations. Although these observations accord with Ashmole's (1963) contention that seabird populations could be controlled by density-dependent effects on reproduction, they lend it no support because the ecological mechanism is different from the one that he envisioned.

For Thick-billed Murres, where breeding success is strongly affected by prior breeding experience, birds breeding at a declining colony are likely to have a higher mean reproductive success than those at an expanding colony, because at a declining colony a higher proportion of first-time breeders can

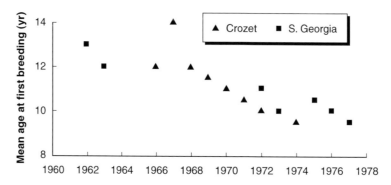

Figure 10.13   Changes in age at first breeding in Wandering Albatross (from Weimerskirch & Jouventin, 1987, Croxall et al., *1990).*

obtain experienced mates. On the other hand, a drastic reduction in numbers of breeding murres caused by oiling and hunting, may lead to reduced breeding success in the whole population by making the surviving birds more vulnerable to nest predation by gulls (Gilchrist, 1999).

The 'hungry horde' effect, referred to in Chapter 9, is suggestive of density-dependent prey deple-tion around colonies. Additional information, including data on foraging range and food availabil-ity, for Black-legged Kittiwakes in Alaska (Ainley *et al.*, 2003) and Magellanic Penguins in Argentina (Forero *et al.*, 2002), as well as data on colony size and foraging range in Northern Gannets in Britain (Lewis *et al.*, 2001), has confirmed that, at least in some places, larger colonies have to forage further afield and tend to deplete local food supplies more than is the case for small colonies. In one case, the foraging range varied between years, with birds traveling further when the colony was large than when it was small. Moreover, in Alaska, the kittiwake population remained stable while some colonies increased and others decreased, again suggesting a limitation on the total breeding population of the area considered.

That chicks at small colonies are better nourished and their parents work less hard to achieve this result than those at large colonies could be because competition with conspecifics is greater at large colonies: a major prediction of Ashmole's theory. However, these observations mostly beg the ques-tion of why birds from large colonies do not recruit to small colonies up to a point where competi-tion balances out. The tendency for most seabirds to return to breed at their natal colony has no proven explanation at present.

There are some examples of density-independent relationships among seabird population density and reproductive success. The reproductive success and adult survival of Brandt's Cormorants on the Farallon Islands were higher in years when the population size also was larger (Nur & Sydeman, 1999a). This was thought to be because more birds attempted to breed under favourable conditions.

NON-BREEDING SEASON

Evidence for density-dependent regulation outside the breeding season is generally lacking and would, in any case, be very hard to obtain. However, a possible example is provided by the incidence of Thick-billed Murre 'wrecks' in eastern North America. Until 1952, large numbers of first-year Thick-billed Murres appeared every few years inland in the northeastern USA and eastern Canada, especially around the Great Lakes. These visitations normally occurred in early winter and involved almost exclusively young of the year: there has been none since 1952 (see Chapter 6). Since the 1950s, mortality from hunting and gillnet drowning in the wintering areas is believed to have increased substantially (Elliot, 1991), perhaps reducing competition for food resources. The cessation of Thick-billed Murre irruptions to the Great Lakes could be a density-dependent response to a decline in the wintering population off eastern Canada.

LIFE-HISTORY STRATEGY

The effects of age on reproduction and survival have been relatively well studied in a number of seabirds, though the sample of species is biased towards gulls and in most cases information on the oldest age classes is poor. Generally, reproductive success increases with age for the first few years of breeding and the effect may continue for as many as six breeding attempts (Saether, 1990). At Coats Island, Thick-billed Murres begin breeding at five years, but do not reach maximum reproductive success until ten, and breeding success in Short-tailed Shearwaters continues to increase for the first eight years of breeding (Wooller *et al.*, 1990), while Wandering Albatrosses at South Georgia, which begin breeding at 10–12 and, if successful, nest only every other year, may not attain maximum reproductive success until 25 years old (Croxall *et al.*, 1992). A decline in reproductive success for birds that survive after the age at which most of the population is already dead has been observed for all populations studied long enough: Adélie Penguin, Black-legged Kittiwake, Northern Fulmar, Short-tailed Shearwater and Wandering Albatross.

Adult survival, likewise, has been found to decline in old birds, although the available information is rather scanty. There is no evidence for an increase in survival with age among birds that are already breeding. Whether such an increase occurs among pre-breeders is difficult to ascertain, as the survival of these birds cannot be accurately determined by commonly used methods. Practically all species show evidence of much higher mortality among first-year birds than older age classes. It seems probable that in long-lived species, experience permits a progressive improvement in survival over several years. Quite small differences in mortality can have big effects on life expectancy, and the fact that we cannot detect a difference among age classes does not mean that important differences are not present.

In general, while the effect of age on reproductive performance has been examined in detail, there is much less information concerning its effect on survival. Moreover, as survivorship has a major effect on population growth (compared to reproductive success), assessing survival is critical to understanding population change and to conservation planning. In particular, patterns of survival in relation to age and reproduction in the oldest age classes remain, for the most part, unknown. Obtaining sufficient sample sizes to investigate this stage of life history is a challenge. Nonetheless, some aspects of life-history strategies can only be understood by estimating reproduction and survival for the oldest members of a population.

SO . . .

A huge amount of empirical data concerning the population dynamics of seabirds has been amassed since Lockley and Richdale began their pioneer work more than half a century ago. Despite such an abundance of observations, we seem to have moved only slowly towards understanding the mechanisms controlling seabird populations. One of the greatest difficulties is posed by the fact that many seabird populations appear to fluctuate over periods of decades: a very long time in the life of a researcher. Single-colony studies, which comprise the bulk of long-term population research, seldom outlive their instigator. The work of the Point Reyes Bird Observatory at the Farallon Islands, Landcare Research of New Zealand in the Antarctic, the Edward Grey Institute at Skomer Island, Wales, and the British and French Antarctic Surveys at South Georgia and Crozet, respectively, form important exceptions that demonstrate the benefits of institutional involvement. The value of these long-term datasets in detecting gradual but significant changes in marine environments, whether from natural or human causes, cannot be over-emphasised. Their maintenance is an important task for future seabird scientists. In addition, the establishment of further long-term studies, especially in the northern North Pacific, where they have not been pursued until recently, is a future challenge.

If theory has been more prominent in the last two chapters of this book than earlier, it is because, (a) we have some theories that are specific to seabirds and (b) I regard demographics as the core of the 'seabird syndrome'. In Chapter 9, I suggested that the classical idea of *r*- and *K*-selection, is probably not a good model for the evolution of the 'seabird syndrome'. On the other hand, the dichotomy between relatively predictable survival and relatively unpredictable reproduction for seabirds seems to fit the case nicely. In addition, this pattern is consistent with Ashmole's argument that non-breeding survival should be high because seabirds are not tied to a breeding site. It may be significant that many species shift from the marine to freshwater or terrestrial environments to breed (skuas, phalaropes and many gulls), but none move in the opposite direction: the sea is a good place to survive, but a poor place to reproduce.

Ashmole's ideas concerning population regulation in seabirds remain potentially the single most unifying theory in seabird biology, providing explanations for evolutionary strategies and current behavioural tactics. Considering the significance of his ideas, it is remarkable that only one *a priori* test of whether breeding seabirds actually deplete prey around their colonies has been attempted (Birt *et al.*, 1987). Otherwise, there have been only a few, largely opportunistic, attempts to test predictions of the theory retrospectively. We must try much harder to test this and other theories relating to population regulation in seabirds. The following comment was made by David Ainley and co-authors 20 years ago:

> *An exciting opportunity is before us to learn about the mechanisms of population regulation in penguins and perhaps other seabirds. All we need now is some additional long-term research.*
>
> Ainley, LeResche & Sladen, 1983

Well, their advice was followed, probably to a greater extent than they could have imagined. As a result, today we can turn the comment around: an exciting opportunity is before us to learn about the mechanisms of population regulation in seabirds. All we need now is some additional synthesis.

AFTERWORD

My first real encounter with seabirds was at Cape Clear Island, off the southwestern tip of Ireland. On the worst days, when the wind roared out of the southwest and drenched the observatory windows with a mixture of rain and spray, and the clouds scarcely cleared the top of the chimney stack, we would don our heaviest raingear and force our way into the teeth of the wind. Our object was Blannanaragaun, a barren rocky ridge projecting from the southwest corner of the island. We staggered and crawled as close to the point as we could get without being totally overcome by spray. For all the discomfort of watching from 'the tip' ("It may be madness to go to such a place at such a time", as Tim Sharrock put it), this was not an enforced penance, but a celebratory pilgrimage, because it was in weather like this that we would be privileged with the appearance of those deep-ocean birds which would not grace us with their presence in fine weather.

Though I spent many years watching birds in deserts, forests and mountains of Asia, I never forgot my Cape Clear days: the flash of the underwing as the shearwater reached the top of its arc, the stiff flapping of the fulmars, the trembling flutter of storm-petrels. The lines of the waves formed a kind of stave on which the seabirds wrote their music, creating the refrain that ran through the immense symphony being performed upon the ocean by Conrad's 'Great Westerly Wind'. The music will remain with me always. As my partner likes to remind me, nothing in life is really worthwhile unless it sings.

> *For a further union, a deeper communion*
> *Through the dark, cold and empty desolation,*
> *The wave cry, the wind cry, the vast waters*
> *Of the petrel and the porpoise. In the end is my beginning.*
>
> Four Quartets: *East Coker*, T. S. Elliot, 1943

A De Havilland Twin-otter after landing on sea-ice covered in wet snow, Coats Island, May 1995. At this time of year we always had a problem deciding whether to take wheels or skis. (Tony Gaston)

Bibliography

ADAMS, N. J. & BROWN, C. R. 1990. Energetics of moult in penguins. In: Davis, L. S. & Darby, J. T. (eds.) *Penguin Biology*. Academic Press, San Diego.

AEBISCHER, N. J. & COULSON, J. C. 1990. Survival of the kittiwake in relation to sex, year, breeding experience and position in the colony. *J. Anim. Ecol.* 59, 1063–71.

AINLEY, D. G. 1980. Geographic variation in Leach's Storm-Petrel. *Auk* 97, 837–53.

AINLEY, D. G. 1984. Storm-Petrels. In: Haley, D. (ed.) *Seabirds of Eastern North Pacific and Arctic Waters*. Pacific Search Press, Seattle.

AINLEY, D. G. & BOEKELHEIDE, R. J. (eds.) 1990. *Seabirds of the Farallon Islands*. Stanford University Press, Palo Alto, CA.

AINLEY, D. G. & DEMASTER, D. P. 1980. survival and mortality in a population of Adélie Penguins. *Ecol.* 61, 522–30.

AINLEY, D. G., CARTER, H. R., ANDERSON, D. W., RIGGS, K. T. B., COULTER, M. C., CRUZ, F., CRUZ, J. B., VALLE, C. A., FEFER, S. I., HATCH, S. A., SCHREIBER, E. A., SCHREIBER R. W. & SMITH, N. G. 1988. Effects of the 1982–83 El Niño Southern Oscillation on Pacific Ocean bird populations. *Proc. Intern. Orn. Congr.* 19, 1747–58.

AINLEY, D. G., FORD, R. G., BROWN, E. D., SURYAN, R. M. & IRONS, D. B. 2003. Prey resources, competition and geographic structure of kittiwake colonies in Prince William Sound. *Ecol.* 84, 709–23.

AINLEY, D. G., LERESCHE, R. E. & SLADEN, W. J. L. 1983. *Breeding biology of the Adélie Penguin*. University of California Press, Berkeley.

AINLEY, D. G., RIBIC, C. A. & WOOD, R. C. 1990. A demographic study of the South Polar Skua *Catharacta maccormicki* at Cape Crozier. *J. Anim. Ecol.* 59, 1–20.

AINLEY, D. G., SYDEMAN, W. J. & NORTON, J. 1995. Upper trophic level predators indicate interannual negative and positive anomalies in the California Current food web. *Marine Ecol. Progress Ser.* 118, 69–79.

ALCOVER, J. A., FLORIT, F., MOURER-CHAUVIRI, C. & WEESIE, P. D. M. 1992. The avifaunas of isolated Mediterranean islands during the middle and late Pleistocene. In: Campbell, K. E. (ed.) *Papers in Avian Palaeontology Honoring Piece Brodkorb*. Natural History Museum of Los Angeles County, Los Angeles.

ALEXANDER, W. B. 1928. *Birds of the Ocean*. Putnam's Sons, New York.

ALI, S. & RIPLEY, S. D. 1981. *Handbook of the Birds of India and Pakistan*, vol. 3, second edn. Oxford University Press, New Delhi.

ANDERSON, D. J., SCHWANDT, A. J. & DOUGLAS, H. D. 1997. Foraging ranges of Waved Albatross in the eastern tropical Pacific Ocean. In: Robertson, G. & Gales, R. (eds.) *Albatross Status and Conservation*. Surrey Beatty & Sons, Chipping Norton, Australia.

ANDERSON, J. G. T. 1991. American White Pelicans coordinate drives for fish in a freshwater lake. *Colonial Waterbirds* 14, 166–72.

ANDERSSON, M. 1971. Breeding behaviour of the Long-tailed Skua (*Stercorarius longicaudus* Vieillot). *Ornis Scand.* 2, 35–54.

ANDERSSON, M. 1973. Behaviour of the Pomarine Skua *Stercorarius pomarinus* Temm. with comparative remarks on the Stercorariinae. *Ornis Scand.* 4, 1–16.

ASHMOLE, N. P. 1963. The regulation of numbers of tropical oceanic birds. *Ibis* 103, 458–73.

ASHMOLE, N. P. 1971. Seabird ecology and the marine environment. In: Farner, D. S., King, J. S. & Parkes, K. C. (eds.) *Avian Biology*, vol. 1. Academic Press, New York.

ASHMOLE, N. P. & ASHMOLE, M. J. 1967. Comparative feeding ecology of sea birds of a tropical oceanic island. *Yale Univ. Bull.* 24: 1–131.

AU, D. W. & PITMAN, R. L. 1986. Seabird interactions with dolphins and tuna in the eastern tropical Pacific. *Condor* 88, 304–17.

AU, D. W. & PITMAN, R. L. 1988. Seabird relationships with tropical tuna and dolphins. In: Burger, J. (ed.) *Seabirds and other Marine Vertebrates: Competition, Predation and Other Interactions*. Plenum Press, New York.

BAILEY, E. P. & KAISER, G. 1993. Impacts of introduced predators on nesting seabirds in the northeast Pacific. In: Vermeer, K., Briggs, K. T., Morgan, K. H. & Siegel-Causey, D. (eds.) *The Status, Ecology and Conservation of Marine Birds of the North Pacific*. Canadian Wildlife Service, Ottawa.

BAILEY, R. S. 1966. The seabirds of the southeast coast of Arabia. *Ibis* 108, 224–64.

BALLANCE, L. T. 1995. Flight energetics of free-ranging Red-footed Boobies (*Sula sula*). *Physiol. Zool.* 68, 887–914.

BALLANCE, L. T. & PITMAN, R. L. 1999. Foraging ecology of tropical seabirds. *Proc. Intern. Orn. Congr.* 22, 2057–71.

BALLANCE, L. T., PITMAN, R. L. & REILLY, S. B. 1997. Seabird community structure along a productivity gradient: importance of competition and energetic constraint. *Ecol.* 78, 1502–18.

BANG, B. G. & COBB, S. 1968. The size of the olfactory bulb in 108 species of birds. *Auk* 85, 55–61.

BANG, B. G. & WENZEL, B. M. 1985. Nasal cavity and olfactory system. In: King, A. S. & McClelland, J. (eds.) *Form and Function in Birds*. Academic Press, London.

BATCHELOR, A. L. 1981. The August 1981 seabird (*Pachyptila* and *Halobaena* spp.) wreck off Port Elizabeth, South Africa. *Cormorant* 9, 105–12.

BELLAIRS, A. D'A. & JENKIN, C. R. 1960. The skeleton of birds. In: Marshall, A. J. (ed.) *Biology and Comparative Physiology of Birds*. Academic Press, New York.

BENGTSON, S. A. 1984. Breeding ecology and extinction of the Great Auk (*Pinguinus impennis*): anecdotal evidence and conjectures. *Auk* 101, 1–12.

BENVENUTI, S., BONADONNA, F., DALL'ANTONIA, L. & GUDMUNDSSON, G. A. 1998. Foraging flights of breeding Thick-billed Murres (*Uria lomvia*) as revealed by bird-borne direction recorders. *Auk* 115, 66–75.

BERGMANN, G. 1982. Why are the wings of *Larus f. fuscus* so dark? *Ornis Fenn.* 59, 77–83.

BERTHOLD, P. 1993. *Bird Migration: A General Survey*, 2nd edn. Oxford University Press, Oxford.

BERTRAM, D. F., JONES, I. L., COOCH, E. G., KNECHTEL, H. A. & COOKE, F. 2000. Survival rates of Cassin's and Rhinoceros Auklets at Triangle Island, British Columbia. *Condor* 102, 155–62.

Birdlife International 2000. *Threatened Birds of the World*. Lynx Edicions, Barcelona & BirdLife International, Cambridge.

BIRKHEAD, T. R. & GASTON, A. J. 1988. The composition of Ancient Murrelet eggs. *Condor* 90, 965–6.

BIRKHEAD, T. R. & HARRIS, M. P. 1985. Ecological adaptations for breeding in the Atlantic Alcidae. In: Nettleship, D. N. & Birkhead, T. R. (eds.) *The Atlantic Alcidae*. Academic Press, London.

BIRKHEAD, T. R. & NETTLESHIP, D. N. 1987. Ecological relationships between Common Murres, *Uria aalge*, and Thick-billed Murres, *Uria lomvia*, at the Gannet Islands, Labrador III: feeding ecology of the young. *Can. J. Zool.* 65, 1638–49.

BIRT, V. L., BIRT, T. P., GOULET, D., CAIRNS, D. K. & MONTEVECCHI, W. A. 1987. Ashmole's halo: direct evidence for prey depletion by a seabird. *Marine Ecol. Progress Ser.* 40, 205–8.

BLOMQVIST, S. & PETERZ, M. 1984. Cyclones and pelagic seabird movements. *Marine Ecol. Progress Ser.* 20, 85–92.

BLUEWEISS, L., FOX, H., KUDZMA, V., NAKASHIMA, D., PETERS, R. & SAMS, S. 1978. Relationships between body size and some life history parameters. *Oecologia* 37, 257–72.

BOGAN, J. A., BOURNE, W. R. P., DAWSON, P. & PARSLOW, J. L. F. 1974. Seabird mortality in the north Irish Sea and Firth of Clyde early in 1974.

BOSWALL, J. 1972. The South American Sea Lion *Otaria byronia* as a predator on penguins. *Bull. Brit. Orn. Club* 92, 129–32.

BOURNE, W. R. P. 1963. A review of oceanic studies of the biology of seabirds. *Proc. Intern. Orn. Congr.* 13, 831–54.

BOWMAKER, J. K. & MARTIN, G. R. 1985. Visual pigments and oil droplets in the penguin *Spheniscus humboldti*. *J. Comp. Physiol.* A 156, 71–7.

BOYD, H. 1954. The "wreck" of Leach's Petrels in the autumn of 1952. *Brit. Birds* 47, 137–63.

BOYD, I. & CROXALL, J. P. 1996. Dive durations in pinnipeds and seabirds. *Can. J. Zool.* 74, 1696–1705.

BRADLEY, J. S., WOOLLER, R. D., SKIRA, I. J. & SERVENTY, D. L. 1989. Age-dependent survival of breeding Short-tailed Shearwaters *Puffinus tenuirostris*. *J. Anim. Ecol.* 58, 175–88.

BRADLEY, J. S., GUNN, B. M., SKIRA, I. J., MEATHREL, C. E. & WOOLLER, R. D. 1999. Age-dependent prospecting and recruitment to a breeding colony of Short-tailed Shearwaters *Puffinus tenuirostris*. *Ibis* 141, 277–85.

BRETAGNOLLE, V. 1993. Adaptive significance of seabird coloration: the case of the Procellariiforms. *Amer. Nat.* 142, 141–73.

BRIGGS, K. T., TYLER, W. B., LEWIS, D. B. & CARLSON, D. R. 1987. Seabird communities at sea off California: 1975–1983. *Stud. Avian Biol.* 11, 1–74.

BROOKE, M. DE L. 1978. A test for the visual location of burrows by Manx Shearwaters *Puffinus puffinus*. *Ibis* 120, 347–9.

BROOKE, M. DE L. 1990. *The Manx Shearwater*. Poyser, London.

BROOKE, M. DE L. 2001. Seabird systematics and distribution: a review of current knowledge. In Schreiber, E. A. & Burger, J. (eds.) *Biology of Marine Birds*. CRC Press, New York.

BROOKE, M. DE L. & PRINCE, P. A. 1991. Nocturnality in seabirds. *Proc. Intern. Orn. Congr.* 20: 1113–21.

BROTHERS, N., GALES, R., HEDD, A. & ROBERTSON, G. 1998. Foraging movements of the shy albatross *Diomedea cauta* breeding in Australia: implications for interactions with longline fisheries. *Ibis* 140, 446–57.

BROWN, R. G. B. 1980. Seabirds as marine animals. In: Burger, J., Olla, B. L. & Winn, H. E. (eds.) *Behaviour of Marine Animals*, vol. 4. Plenum Press, New York.

BROWN, R. G. B. 1985. The Atlantic Alcidae at Sea. In: Nettleship, D. N. & Birkhead, T. R. (eds.) *The Atlantic Alcidae*. Academic Press, London.

BROWN, R. G. B. 1986. *Atlas of Eastern Canadian Seabirds*. Canadian Wildlife Service, Ottawa.

BROWN, R. G. B., BOURNE, W. R. P. & WAHL, T. R. 1978. Diving by shearwaters. *Condor* 80, 123–5.

BROWN, R. G. B. & NETTLESHIP, D. N. 1984. Capelin and seabirds in the northwest Atlantic. In: Nettleship, D. N., Sanger, G. A. & Springer, P. F. (eds.) *Marine Birds: Their Feeding Ecology and Commercial Fisheries Relationships*. Canadian Wildlife Service, Ottawa.

BROWN, R. G. B., NETTLESHIP, D. N., GERMAIN, P., TULL, E. & DAVIS, T. 1975. *Atlas of Eastern Canadian seabirds*. Canadian Wildlife Service, Ottawa.

BROWN, R. S., NORMAN, F. I. & EADES, D. W. 1986. Notes on blue and Kerguelen petrels found beach-washed in Victoria, 1984. *Emu* 86, 228–38.

BURGER, A. E. 1991. Sneak thief of the sub-Antarctic. *Afr. Wildl.* 45, 188–92.

BURGER, A. E. & POWELL, D. W. 1990. Diving depths and diet of Cassin's Auklet at Reef Island, British Columbia. *Can. J. Zool.* 68, 1572–7.

BURGER, A. E. & SIMPSON, M. 1986. Diving depths of Atlantic Puffin and Common Murre. *Auk* 103, 828–30.

BURGER, A. E., WILSON, R. P., GARNIER, D. & WILSON, M. P. T. 1993. Diving depths, diet and underwater foraging of Rhinoceros Auklets in British Columbia. *Can. J. Zool.* 71, 2528–40.

BURGER, J. & GOCHFELD, M. 1996. Laridae (gulls). In: del Hoyo, J., Elliott, A. & Sargatal, J. (eds.) *Handbook of the Birds of the World*, vol. 3. Lynx Edicions, Barcelona.

BYRD, G. V. & DAY, R. H. 1986. The avifauna of Buldir Island, Aleutian Islands, Alaska. *Arctic* 39, 109–18.

CAIRNS, D. K. 1986. Plumage colour in pursuit-diving seabirds: why do penguins wear tuxedos? *Bird Behav.* 6, 58–65.

CAIRNS, D. K. 1987a. Seabirds as indicators of marine food supplies. *Biol. Oceanography* 5, 261–71.

CAIRNS, D. K. 1987b. Diet and foraging ecology of Black Guillemots in northeastern Hudson Bay. *Can. J. Zool.* 65, 1257–63.

CAIRNS, D. K. 1992. Population regulation of seabird colonies. *Current Orn.* 9, 37–61.

CAIRNS, D. K., BREDIN, K. A. & MONTEVECCHI, W. A. 1987. Activity budgets and foraging ranges of breeding common murres. *Auk* 104, 218–24.

CAIRNS, D. K. & SCHNEIDER, D. C. 1990. Hot spots in cold water: feeding habitat selection by Thick-billed Murres. *Stud. Avian Biol.* 14, 52–60.

CALDER, W. A. 1984. *Size, Function and Life History*. Oxford University Press, Oxford.

CAMPHUYSEN, C. J., CALVO, B., DURINCK, J., ENSOR, K., FOLLESTAD, A., FURNESS, R. W., GARTHE, S., LEAPER, G., SKOV, H., TASKER, M. L. & WINTER, C. J. N. 1995. *Consumption of Discards by Seabirds in the North Sea*. Final Rep. EC DG XIV research contract BIOECO/93/10, NIOZ Rapport 1995–5. Netherlands Institute for Sea Research, Texel.

CANNELL, B. L. & CULLEN, J. M. 1998. The foraging behaviour of Little Penguins *Eudyptula minor* at different light levels. *Ibis* 140, 467–71.

CARRICK, R. 1972. Population ecology of the Australian Black-backed Magpie, royal penguin and silver gull. In: *Population Ecology of Migratory Birds: A Symposium*. US Department of Interior Research Rep. 2, Washington DC.

CARTER, M. 1984. A petrel strike. *Roy. Australian Orn. Union Newsl.* 61, 1.

CASWELL, H. 1981. Life history theory and the equilibrium status of populations. *Amer. Nat.* 120, 317–39.

CHAPDELAINE, G. & BROUSSEAU, P. 1989. Size and trends of Black-legged Kittiwake (*Rissa tridactyla*) populations in the Gulf of St. Lawrence (Quebec) 1974–1985. *Amer. Birds* 43, 21–4.

CHARNOV, E. L. 1993. *Life History Invariants*. Oxford University Press, Oxford.

CHEREL, Y. & KLAGES, N. 1998. A review of the food of albatrosses. In: Robertson, G. & Gales, R. (eds.) *Albatross Biology and Conservation*. Surrey Beatty, Chipping Norton, Australia.

CLODE, D. 1993. Colonially breeding seabirds: predators or prey? *Trends Ecol. & Evol.* 8, 336–8.

CODY, M. L. 1966. A general theory of clutch size. *Evol.* 20, 174–84.

CODY, M. L. 1971. Ecological aspects of reproduction. In: Farner, D. S. & King, J. S. (eds.) *Avian Biology*, vol. 1. Academic Press, New York.

COOPER, J. 1986. Diving patterns of cormorants (Phalacrocoracidae). *Ibis* 128, 562–9.

COOPER, J., WILSON, R. P. & ADAMS, N. J. 1993. Timing of foraging by the Wandering Albatross *Diomedea exulans*. *Proc. NIPR Symp. Polar Biol.* 6, 55–61.

COULSON, J. C., DUNCAN, N. & THOMAS, C. 1982. Changes in the breeding biology of the Herring Gull (*Larus argentatus*) induced by reduction in the size and density of the colony. *J. Anim. Ecol.* 51, 739–56.

COULSON, J. C. & NÈVE DE MÉVERGNIES, G. 1992. Where do young Kittiwakes *Rissa tridactyla* breed? *Ardea* 80, 187–97.

COULSON, J. C. & THOMAS, C. S. 1985a. Differences in the breeding performance of individual kittiwake gulls, *Rissa tridactyla*. In: Sibley, R. M. & Smith, R. J. (eds.) *Behavioural Ecology*. British Ecological Society, London.

COULSON, J. C. & THOMAS, C. S. 1985b. Changes in the biology of the kittiwake *Rissa tridactyla*: a 31–year study of a breeding colony. *J. Anim. Ecol.* 54, 9–26.

COULSON, J. C. & WOOLLER, R. D. 1976. Differential survival rates among breeding Kittiwake Gulls *Rissa tridactyla* (L.). *J. Anim. Ecol.* 45, 205–13.

COWAN, P. J. 1972. The contrast and colouration of seabirds: an experimental approach. *Ibis* 114, 390–3.

CRAMP, S. and SIMMONS, K. E. L. (eds.) 1980. *The Birds of the Western Palearctic*, vol. 2. Oxford University Press, Oxford.

CRAMP, S. (ed.) 1985. *The Birds of the Western Palearctic*, vol. 4. Oxford University Press, Oxford.

CROLL, D. A., GASTON, A. J., BURGER, A. E. & KONNOFF, D. 1992. Foraging behavior and physiological adaptation for diving in Thick-billed Murres. *Ecol.* 73, 344–56.

CROLL, D. A., GASTON, A. J. & NOBLE, D. G. 1991. Adaptive loss of mass in Thick-billed Murres. *Condor* 93, 496–502.

CROLL, D. A., JANSEN, J. K., GOEBEL, M. E., BOVENG, P. L. & BENGTSON, J. L. 1996. Foraging behavior and reproductive success in Chinstrap Penguins: the effects of transmitter attachment. *J. Field Orn.* 67, 1–9.

CROXALL, J. P., DAVIS, R. W. & CONNELL, M. J. 1988. Diving patterns in relation to diet of Gentoo and Macaroni Penguins at South Georgia. *Condor* 90, 157–67.

CROXALL, J. P. & GASTON, A. J. 1988. Patterns of reproduction in high-latitude northern- and southern-hemisphere seabirds. *Proc. Intern. Orn. Congr.* 19, 1176–94.

CROXALL, J. P., McINNES, S. J. & PRINCE, P. A. 1984. The status and conservation of seabirds at the Falkland Islands. In: Croxall, J.P., Evans, P. G. H. & Schreiber, R. W. (eds.) *Status and Conservation of the World's Seabirds*. International Council for Bird Preservation Tech. Rep. 2, Cambridge.

CROXALL, J. P., PRINCE, P. A., HUNTER, I., McINNES, S. J. & COPESTAKE, P. G. 1984. The seabirds of the Antarctic Peninsula, islands of the Scotia Sea, and the Antarctic coast between 80°W and 20°W: their status and conservation. In: Croxall, J.P., Evans, P. G. H. & Schreiber, R. W. (eds.) *Status and Conservation of the World's Seabirds*. International Council for Bird Preservation Tech. Rep. 2, Cambridge.

CROXALL, J. P., NAITO, Y., KATO, A., ROTHERY, P. & BRIGGS, D. R. 1991. Diving patterns and performance in the Antarctic Blue-eyed Shag *Phalacrocorax atriceps*. *J. Zool., Lond.* 225, 177–99.

CROXALL, J. P. & ROTHERY, P. 1991. Population regulation of seabirds: implications of their demography for conservation. In: Perrins, C. M, Lebreton, J.-D. & Hirons, G. M. (eds.) *Bird Population Studies*. Oxford University Press, Oxford.

CROXALL, J. P., ROTHERY, P. & CRISP, A. 1992. The effect of maternal age and experience on egg size and hatching success in Wandering Albatross *Diomedea exulans*. *Ibis* 134, 219–28.

CROXALL, J. P., ROTHERY, P., PICKERING, S. P. C. & PRINCE, P. A. 1990. Reproductive performance, recruitment and survival of Wandering Albatross, *Diomedea exulans*, at Bird Island, South Georgia. *J. Anim. Ecol.* 59, 775–96.

DANCHIN, É. & MONNAT, J.-Y. 1992. Population dynamics modelling of two neighbouring Kittiwake *Rissa tridactyla* colonies. *Ardea* 80, 171–80.

DAY, R. H., KULETZ, D. J. & NIGRO, D. A. 1999. Kittlitz's Murrelet (*Brachyramphus brevirostris*). In: Poole, A. & Gill, F. (eds.) *The Birds of North America*, 435. Birds of North America Inc., Philadelphia, PA & American Ornithologists' Union, Washington DC.

DAVID, R. 1981. *Hakluyt's voyages: A Selection*. Chatto & Windus, London.

DEAN, F. C., VALKENBURG, P. & MAGOUN, A. 1976. Inland migration of jaegers in northeast Alaska. *Condor* 76, 271–3.

DEWAR, J. M. 1924. *The Bird as a Diver*. Witherby, London.

DIAMOND, A. W. 1972. Sexual dimorphism in breeding cycles and unequal sex ratio in Magnificent Frigatebirds. *Ibis* 114, 395–398.

DIAMOND, A. W. 1975. Biology and behaviour of frigatebirds *Fregata* spp. on Aldabra Atoll. *Ibis* 117, 302–23.

DIAMOND, A. W. 1976. Subannual breeding and moult cycles in the Bridled Tern *Sterna anaethetus* in the Seychelles. *Ibis* 118, 414–19.

DIAMOND, A. W. 1978. Feeding strategies and population size in tropical seabirds. *Amer. Nat.* 112, 215–21.

DIAMOND, A. W. 1983. Feeding overlap in some tropical and temperate seabird communities. *Stud. Avian Biol.* 8, 24–46.

DIAMOND, J. 1991. *The Rise and Fall of the Third Chimpanzee*. Vintage, London.

DICKINSON, E. C., KENNEDY, R. S. & PARKES, K. C. 1991. *The Birds of the Philippines*. British Ornithologist's Union, London.

DRURY, W. H., & SMITH, W. J. 1968. Defence of feeding areas by adult Herring Gulls and intrusion by young. *Evol.* 22, 193–201.

DUFFY, D. C. 1980. Patterns of piracy by Peruvian seabirds: a depth hypothesis. *Ibis* 122, 521–5.

DUFFY, D. C. 1983. Environmental uncertainty and commercial fishing: effects on Peruvian guano birds. *Biol. Conserv.* 26, 227–38.

DUFFY, D. C., ARNTZ, W. A., SERPA, H. T., BOERSMA, P. D. & NORTON, R. L. 1988. Effects of the 1982–83 El Niño Southern Oscillation on Pacific Ocean bird populations. *Proc. Intern. Orn. Congr.* 19, 1747–58.

DUNN, E. K. 1973a. Changes in fishing ability of terns associated with wind speed and sea surface conditions. *Nature* 244, 520–1.

DUNN, E. K. 1973b. Robbing behaviour of Roseate Terns. *Auk* 90, 641–51.

DUNNET, G. M. & OLLASON, J. C. 1978. The estimation of survival rate in the Fulmar *Fulmarus glacialis*. *J. Anim. Ecol.* 47, 507–20.

ELKINS, N. & YÉSOU, P. 1998. Sabine's Gulls in western France and southern Britain. *Brit. Birds* 91, 386–97.

ELKINS, N. 1988. *Weather and Bird Behaviour*, 2nd edn. Poyser, Calton.

ELIOT, S. A. 1939. Hurricane aftermath: Connecticut Valley records. *Auk* 56, 177–9.

ELLIOT, R. D. 1991. The management of the Newfoundland turr hunt. In: Gaston, A. J. & Elliot, R. D. (eds.) *Studies of High Latitude Seabirds*, vol. 2. Canadian Wildlife Service, Ottawa.

ELLIS, H. I. 1984. Energetics of free-ranging seabirds. In: Whittow, G. C. & Rahn, H. (eds.) *Seabird Energetics*. Plenum Press, New York.

EMSLIE, S. D. & MORGAN, G. S. 1994. A catastrophic death assemblage and palaeoclimatic implications of Pliocene seabirds of Florida. *Science* 264, 684–5.

EVANS, P. G. H. 1987. *The Natural History of Whales and Dolphins*. Christopher Helm, London.

EWINS, P. J., CARTER, H. R. & SHIBAEV, Y. B. 1993. The status, distribution and ecology of inshore fish-feeding alcids (*Cepphus* guillemots and *Brachyramphus* murrelets) in the North Pacific. In: Vermeer, K., Briggs, K. T., Morgan, K. H. & Siegel-Causey, D. (eds.) *The Status, Ecology and Conservation of Marine Birds of the North Pacific*. Canadian Wildlife Service, Ottawa.

FALK, K., BENVENUTI, S., DALL'ANTONIA, L., KAMPP, K. & RIBOLINI, A. 2000. Time allocation and foraging behaviour of chick-rearing Brunnich's Guillemots *Uria lomvia* in high-arctic Greenland. *Ibis* 142, 82–92.

FISHER, J. 1952. *The Fulmar*. Collins, London.

FISHER, J. & LOCKLEY, R. M. 1954. *Seabirds*. Collins, London.

FISHER, H. I. 1975. The relationship between deferred breeding and mortality in the Laysan Albatross. *Auk* 92, 433–41.

FISHER, R. A. 1930. *The Genetical Theory of Natural Selection*. Oxford University Press, Oxford.

FORERO, M. G., TELLA, J. L., HOBSON, K. A., BERTELLOTTI, M. & BLANCO, G. 2002. Conspecific food competition explains variability in colony size: a test in Magellanic Penguins. *Ecol.* 83, 3466–75.

DE FOREST, L. N. & GASTON, A. J. 1996. The effect of age on timing of breeding and reproductive success in the Thick-billed Murre. *Ecol.* 77, 1501–11.

FORSLUND, P. & PART, T. 1995. Age and reproduction in birds—hypotheses and tests. *Trends Ecol. & Evol.* 10, 374–8.

FÜRBRINGER, M. 1902. Beitrag zur Geneologie und Systematik der Vögel. *Zeitschrift Naturw.* 36, 587–736.

FURNESS, B. L. 1983. The feeding behaviour of Arctic Skuas *Stercorarius parasiticus* wintering off South Africa. *Ibis* 125, 245–51.

FURNESS, R. W. 1978. Movements and mortality rates of skuas ringed in Scotland. *Bird Study* 25, 229–238.

FURNESS, R. W. 1987a. *The Skuas*. Poyser, Calton.

FURNESS, R. W. 1987b. Kleptoparasitism in seabirds. In: Croxall, J. P. (ed.) *Seabirds: Feeding Ecology and Role in Marine Ecosystems*. Academic Press, London.

FURNESS, R. W. & BIRKHEAD, T. R. 1984. Seabird colony distributions suggest competition for food supplies during the breeding season. *Nature* 311, 655–6.

FURNESS, R. W. & MONAGHAN, P. 1987. *Seabird Ecology*. Blackie, Glasgow.

GABRIELSON, G. W. 1994. Energy expenditure in Arctic seabirds. Ph.D. thesis, University of Tromsø.

GADOW, H. 1892. On the classification of birds. *Proc. Zool. Soc. Lond.* 1892, 229–56.

GARTHE, S., BENVENUTI, S. & MONTEVECCHI, W. A. 2000. Pursuit plunging by northern gannets (*Sula bassana*) feeding on capelin (*Mallotus villosus*) *Proc. Roy. Soc. Lond.* B 267, 1717–22.

GASTON, A. J. 1985. Development of the young in the Atlantic Alcidae. In: Nettleship, D. N. & Birkhead, T. R. (eds.) *The Atlantic Alcidae*. Academic Press, London.

GASTON, A. J. 1988. The mystery of the murres: Thick-billed Murres, *Uria lomvia*, in the Great Lakes region, 1890–1986. *Can. Field Nat.* 102, 705–11.

GASTON, A. J. 1991. Seabirds of Hudson Strait, Hudson Bay and Foxe Basin. In: Croxall, J. P. (ed.) *Seabird Status and Conservation: A Supplement*. International Council for Bird Preservation, Cambridge.

GASTON, A. J. 1992. *The Ancient Murrelet*. Poyser, London.

GASTON, A. J. & BROWN, R. G. B. 1991. Dynamics of seabird distributions in relation to variations in the availability of food on a landscape scale. *Proc. Intern. Orn. Conf.* 20, 2306–12.

GASTON, A. J., CARTER, H. & SEALY, S. G. 1993. Winter ecology and diet of Ancient Murrelets off Victoria, British Columbia. *Can. J. Zool.* 71, 64–70.

GASTON, A. J., CHAPDELAINE, G. & NOBLE, D. G. 1983a. The growth of Thick-billed Murre chicks at colonies in Hudson Strait: inter- and intra-colony variation. *Can. J. Zool.* 61, 2465–75.

GASTON, A. J., DE FOREST, L. N., DONALDSON, G. D. & NOBLE, D. G. 1994. Population parameters of Thick-billed Murres at Coats Island, Northwest Territories, Canada. *Condor* 96, 935–48.

GASTON, A. J., GOUDIE, R. I., NOBLE, D. G. & MACFARLANE, A. 1983b. Observations on turr hunting in Newfoundland: age, body composition and diet of Thick-billed Murres (*Uria lomvia*) and proportions of other birds killed off Newfoundland in winter. *Can. Wildl. Service Progress Notes* 141, 1–7.

GASTON, A. J., HIPFNER, J. M. & CAMPBELL, D. 2002. Heat and mosquitoes cause breeding failures and adult mortality in an arctic-nesting seabird. *Ibis* 144, 185–91.

GASTON, A. J. & JONES, I. L. 1998. *The Auks*. Oxford University Press, Oxford.

GASTON, A. J. & NETTLESHIP, D. N. 1981. *The Thick-billed Murres of Prince Leopold Island*. Canadian Wildlife Service, Ottawa.

GASTON, A. J. & NOBLE, D. G. 1986. The possible effect of food availability on incubation and brooding shifts of Brunnich's Guillemot *Uria lomvia* at Digges Island, Northwest Territories. *Seabird* 9, 47–51.

GASTON, A. J., NOBLE, D. G., CAIRNS, D. K. & ELLIOT, R. D 1985. *A Natural History of Digges Sound*. Canadian Wildlife Service Rep. 46, Ottawa.

GASTON, A. J. & POWELL, D. W. 1989. Natural incubation, egg neglect and hatchability in the Ancient Murrelet. *Auk* 106, 433–8.

GASTON, A. J. & SCOFIELD, P. 1994. Birds and tuataras on North Brother Island, Cook Strait, New Zealand. *Notornis* 42, 27–41.

GILCHRIST, H. G. 1999. Declining thick-billed murre *Uria lomvia* colonies experience higher gull predation rates: an inter-colony comparison. *Biol. Conserv.* 87, 21–9.

GILCHRIST, H. G. & GASTON, A. J. 1997. Factors affecting the success of colony departure by Thick-billed Murre chicks. *Condor* 99, 345–352.

GILCHRIST, G., GASTON, A. J. & SMITH, J. N. M. 1998. Wind and prey nest sites as foraging constraints on an avian predator, the Glaucous Gull. *Ecol.* 79, 2403–14.

GOCHFELD, M. & BURGER, J. 1996. Sternidae (terns). In: del Hoyo, J., Elliott, A. & Sargatal, J. (eds.) *Handbook of the Birds of the World*, vol. 3. Lynx Edicions, Barcelona.

GOLET, G. H., IRONS, D. B. & ESTES, J. A. 1998. Survival costs of chick rearing in Black-legged Kittiwakes. *J. Anim. Ecol.* 67, 827–41.

GOODMAN, D. 1974. Natural selection and a cost ceiling on reproductive effort. *Amer. Nat.* 108, 247–68.

GROVER, J. J. & OLLA, B. L. 1983. The role of the Rhinoceros Auklet (*Cerorhinca monocerata*) in mixed-species feeding assemblages of seabirds in the Strait of Juan de Fuca, Washington. *Auk* 100, 979–82.

GRUBB, T. C. 1974. Olfactory navigation to the nesting burrow in Leach's Petrel (*Oceanodroma leucorrhoa*). *Anim. Behav.* 22, 192–202.

HALLE, L. J. 1971. Pelagic birds and marine predators. *Brit. Birds* 64, 510.

HALLE, L. J. 1973. *The Sea and the Ice*. Cornell University Press, Ithaca, NY.

HALLEY, D. J. & HARRIS, M. P. 1993. Intercolony movement and behaviour of immature guillemots *Uria aalge*. *Ibis* 135, 264–70.

HAMER, K. C., HILL, J. K., BRADLEY, J. S. & WOOLLER, R. D. 2000. Contrasting patterns of nestling obesity and food provisioning in three species of *Puffinus* shearwaters: the role of predictability. *Ibis* 142, 146–50.

HANEY, J. C. & SOLOW, A. R. 1992. Analysing quantitative relationships between seabirds and marine resource patches. *Current Orn.* 9, 105–61.

HARDY, F. P. 1888. Testimony of early voyagers on the Great Auk. *Auk* 5, 380–4.

HARRIS, M. P., BUCKLAND, S. T., RUSSELL, S. M. & WANLESS, S. 1994. Year- and age-related variation in the survival of adult European Shags over a 24-year period. *Condor* 96, 600–5.

HARRIS, M. P., FREEMAN, S. N., WANLESS, S., MORGAN, B. J. T. & WERNHAM, C. V. 1997. Factors influencing the survival of Puffins *Fratercula arctica* at a North Sea colony over a 20-year period. *J. Avian Biol.* 28, 287–95.

HARRIS, M. P. & WANLESS, S. 1991. Population studies and conservation of Puffins *Fratercula arctica*. In: Perrins, C. M., Lebreton, J.-D. & Hirons, G. M. (eds.) *Bird Population Studies*. Oxford University Press, Oxford.

HARRIS, M. P., WANLESS, S. & ELSTON, D.A. 1998. Age-related effects of a non-breeding event and a winter wreck on the survival of Shags *Phalacrocorax aristotelis*. *Ibis* 140, 310–4.

HARRISON, C. S., HIDA, T. S. & SEKI, M. P. 1983. Hawaiian seabird feeding ecology. *Wildl. Monogr.* 85, 1–71.

HARRISON, P. 1983. *Seabirds: An Identification Guide*. Houghton Mifflin, Boston.

HARRISON, P. 1987. *Seabirds of the World: A Photographic Guide*. Christopher Helm, London.

HATCH, S. A. 1991. Evidence for colour phase effects on the breeding and life history of Northern Fulmars. *Condor* 93, 409–17.

HATCH, S. A., BYRD, G. V., IRONS, D. B. & HUNT, G. L. 1993a. Status and ecology of kittiwakes (*Rissa tridactyla* and *R. brevirostris*) in the North Pacific. In: Vermeer, K., Briggs, K. T., Morgan, K. H. & Siegel-Causey, D. (eds.) *The Status, Ecology and Conservation of Marine Birds of the North Pacific*. Canadian Wildlife Service, Ottawa.

HATCH, S. A. & NETTLESHIP, D. N. 1999. The Northern Fulmar. In: Poole, A. & Gill, F. (eds.) *Birds of North America*, no. 361. Academy of Natural Sciences of Philadelphia, PA & American Ornithologists' Union, Washington DC.

HATCH, S. A., ROBERTS, B. D. & FADELEY, B. S. 1993b. Adult survival of Black-legged Kittiwakes *Rissa tridactyla* in a Pacific colony. *Ibis* 135, 247–54.

HAURY, L. R., MCGOWAN, J. A. & WEIBE, P. H. 1978. Patterns and processes in the time-space scales of plankton distributions. In: Steele, J. H. (ed.) *Spatial Pattern in Plankton Communities*. Plenum Press, New York.

HOFFMAN, W., HEINEMANN, D. & WIENS, J. A. 1981. The ecology of seabird feeding flocks in Alaska. *Auk* 98, 437–56.

DEL HOYO, J., ELLIOTT, A. & SARGATAL, J. 1992. *Handbook of the Birds of the World*, vol. 1. Edicions Lynx, Barcelona.

DEL HOYO, J., ELLIOTT, A. & SARGATAL, J. 1996. *Handbook of the Birds of the World*, vol. 3. Edicions Lynx, Barcelona.

HULL, C. L. 2000. Comparative diving behaviour and segregation of the marine habitat by breeding Royal Penguins, *Eudyptes schlegeli*, and eastern Rockhopper Penguins, *Eudyptes chrysocome filholi*, at Macquarie Island. *Can. J. Zool.* 78, 333–45.

HULL, C. L., HINDELL, M. A. & MICHAEL, K. 1997. Foraging zones of royal penguins during the breeding season, and their associations with oceanographic features. *Marine Ecol. Progress Ser.* 153, 217–28.

HUNT, G. L. 1990. The pelagic distribution of marine birds in a heterogeneous environment. *Polar Res.* 8, 43–54.

HUNT, G. L., EPPLEY, Z. A. & SCHNEIDER, D. C. 1986. Reproductive performance of seabirds; the importance of population and colony size. *Auk* 103, 306–17.

HUNT, G. L., HARRISON, N. M., HAMNER, W. M. & OBST, B. S. 1988. Observations of a mixed species flock of birds foraging on euphausiids near St Mathews Island. *Auk* 105, 345–9.

HUNT, G. L., RUSSELL, R. W., COYLE, K. O. & WEINGARTNER, T. 1995. Foraging ecology of planktivorous auklets in an Aleutian Islands pass. *Colonial Waterbird Soc. Bull.* 19, 48.

HUNT, G. L. & SCHNEIDER, D.C. 1987. Scale-dependent processes in the physical and biological environment of marine birds. In: Croxall, J. P. (ed.) *Seabirds: Feeding Ecology and Role in Marine Ecosystems*. Cambridge University Press, Cambridge.

HUSTLER, K. 1992. Buoyancy and its constraints to underwater foraging behaviour of Reed Cormorants *Phalacrocorax africanus* and Darters *Anhinga melanogaster*. *Ibis* 134, 229–36.

HUTCHINSON, L. V. & WENZEL, B. M. 1980. Olfactory guidance in foraging by Procellariiformes. *Condor* 82, 314–9.

IMBER, M. J. 1984. The age of Kerguelen Petrels found in New Zealand. *Notornis* 31, 89–91.

JACKSON, K. H. 1951. *A Celtic Miscellany*. Penguin, London.

JENKINS, J. A. F. & GREENWOOD, E. 1984. Southern seabirds in New Zealand coastal waters, July 1984. *Notornis* 31, 325–30.

JOHNSGARD, P. A. 1993. *Cormorants, Darters and Pelicans of the World*. Smithsonian Institute Press, Washington DC.

JOHNSON, S. R. & HERTER, A. 1989. *Birds of the Beaufort Sea*. British Petroleum, Anchorage, AK.

JONES, I. L. 1993. The Crested Auklet (*Aethia cristatella*). In: Poole, A. & Gill, F. (eds.) *The Birds of North America*, no. 70. Academy of Natural Sciences of Philadelphia, PA & American Ornithologists' Union, Washington DC.

JONES, I. L. & HUNTER, F. M. 1993. Mutual sexual selection in a monogamous seabird. *Nature* 362, 238–9.

JONES, I. L., ROWE, S., CARR, S. M., FRASER, G. & TAYLOR, P. 2002. Different patterns of parental effort during chick rearing by female and male Thick-billed Murres (*Uria lomvia*) at a low-arctic colony. *Auk* 119, 1064–74.

JOUVENTIN, P., CAPDEVILLE, D., CUENOT-CHAILLET, F. & BOITEAU, C. 1994. Exploitation of pelagic resources by a non-flying seabird: satellite tracking of the king penguin throughout the breeding cycle. *Marine Ecol. Progress Ser.* 106, 11–19.

JOUVENTIN, P., STAHL, J. C., WEIMERSKIRCH, H. & MOUGIN, J. L. 1984. The seabirds of the French subantarctic islands and Adelie Land, their status and conservation. In: Croxall, J.P., Evans, P. G. H. & Schreiber, R. W. (eds.) *Status and Conservation of the World's Seabirds*. International Council for Bird Preservation Tech. Rep. 2, Cambridge.

JOUVENTIN, P. & WEIMERSKIRCH, H. 1990. Satellite tracking of wandering albatrosses. *Nature* 343, 746–8.

JOUVENTIN, P. & WEIMERSKIRCH, H. 1991. Changes in the population size and demography of southern seabirds: management implications. In: Perrins, C. M., Lebreton, J.-D. & Hirons, G. M. (eds.) *Bird Population Studies*. Oxford University Press, Oxford.

JURY, M. R. 1991. Anomalous winter weather in 1984 and a seabird irruption along the coast of South Africa. *Marine Orn.* 19, 85–9.

KAMPP, K. & FALK, K. 1999. A long distance colony shift by a Thick-billed Murre. *Colonial Waterbirds* 21, 91–3.

KATO, A., CROXALL, J. P., WATANUKI, Y. & NAITO, Y. 1992. Diving patterns and performance in male and female Blue-eyed Cormorants *Phalacrocorax atriceps* at South Georgia. *Marine Orn.* 19, 117–29.

KHARITONOV, S. P. & SIEGEL-CAUSEY, D. 1988. Colony formation in seabirds. *Current Orn.* 5, 223–72.

KING, W. B. 1967. *Seabirds of the Tropical Pacific Ocean*. Smithsonian Institute Press, Washington.

KING, W. B. 1970. The trade-wind zone oceanography pilot study. Part VII. Observations of seabirds, March 1964 to June 1965. *US Fish & Wildlife Service Special Rep.—Fisheries* no. 586. US Department of Interior, Washington DC.

KING, W. B. 1974. *Pelagic Studies of Seabirds in the Central and Eastern Pacific Ocean*. Smithsonian Institute Press, Washington DC.

KINSKY, F. C. 1968. An unusual seabird mortality in the southern North Island, New Zealand, April 1968. *Notornis* 14, 143–55.

KOOYMAN, G. L. 1981. Leopard Seal. In: Ridgway, S. H. & Harrison, R.J. (eds.) *Handbook of Marine Mammals*. Academic Press, New York.

KOOYMAN, G. L., CHEREL, Y., Le MAHO, Y., CROXALL, J. P., THORSON, P. H., RIDOUX, V. & KOOYMAN, C. A. 1992. Diving behavior and energetics during foraging cycles in King Penguins. *Ecol. Monogr.* 62, 143–63.

KREBS, J. R. 1970. Regulation in numbers in the Great Tit. *J. Zool., Lond.* 162, 317–33.

LA COCK, G. D. 1986. The southern oscillation, environmental anomalies and mortality of two southern African seabirds. *Climatic Change* 8, 173–84.

LACK, D. 1947–8.The significance of clutch size. *Ibis* 89, 302–52; 90, 25–45.

LACK, D. 1954. *The Natural Regulation of Animal Numbers*. Clarendon Press, Oxford.

LACK, D. 1966. Interrelationships in breeding adaptations, as shown by marine birds. *Proc. Intern. Orn. Congr.* 14, 3–42.

LACK, D. 1968. *Ecological Adaptations for Breeding in Birds*. Methuen, London.

LANGHAM, N. P. 1984. Growth strategies in marine terns. *Stud. Avian Biol.* 8, 73–83.

LE GRAND, H. E. 1990. Bird sightings in the Carolinas associated with Hurricane Hugo. *Chat* 54, 73–8.

LEQUETTE, B., VERHEYDEN, C. & JOUVENTIN, P. 1989. Olfaction in subantarctic seabirds: its phylogenetic and ecological significance. *Condor* 91, 732–5.

LEWIS, S., SHERRATT, T. N., HAMER, K. C. & WANLESS, S. 2001. Evidence of intra-specific competition for food in a pelagic seabird. *Nature* 412, 816–8.

LIPINSKI, M. R. & JACKSON, S. 1989. Surface-feeding on cephalopods by procellariiform seabirds in the southern Benguela region, South Africa. *J. Zool., Lond.* 218, 549–63.

LLOYD, C. S., TASKER, M. L. & PARTRIDGE, K. 1991. *The Status of Seabirds in Britain and Ireland*. Poyser, London.

LOBKOV, E. G. & NEUFELDT, I. A. 1986. Distribution and biology of the Steller's Sea Eagle *Haliaeetus pelagicus pelagicus* (Pallas). In: Neufeldt, I. A. (ed.) *The distribution and Biology of Birds of the Altai and Far East*. Proc. Zool. Inst., vol. 150, USSR Academy of Sciences, Leningrad.

LOCKLEY, R. M. 1942. *Shearwaters*. Dent, London.

LÖFGREN, L. 1984. *Ocean Birds*. Johnston & Co., Gothenburg.

LOOMIS, L. M. 1918. Expedition of the California Academy of Sciences to the Galapagos Islands, 1905–1906, XII A review of the albatrosses, petrels and diving petrels. *Proc. California Acad. Sci.* (IV Ser.) 2, 1–187.

MACARTHUR, R. H. & WILSON, E. O. 1967. *The Theory of Island Biogeography*. Princeton University Press, Princeton.

MAHON, T. E., KAISER, G. W. & BURGER, A. E. 1992. The role of Marbled Murrelets in mixed-species feeding flocks in British Columbia. *Wilson Bull.* 104, 738–43.

MAHONEY, S. A. 1984. Plumage wetability in aquatic birds. *Auk* 101, 181–5.

MARTIN, G. R. 1985. Eye. In: King, A. S. & McClelland, J. (eds.) *Form and Function in Birds*. Academic Press, London.

MARTIN, G. R. 1999. Eye structure and foraging in King Penguins *Aptenodytes patagonicus*. *Ibis* 141, 444–50.

MARTIN, L. D. 1980. Foot-propelled diving birds in the Mesozoic. *Proc. Intern. Orn. Conf.* 17, 1237–42.

MACGILLIVRAY, W. 1852. *A History of British Birds: Indigenous and Migratory*. William S. Orr & Co., London.

MAXSON, S. J. & BERNSTEIN, N. P. 1982. Kleptoparasitism by South Polar Skuas on Blue-eyed Shags in Antarctica. *Wilson Bull.* 94, 269–81.

MAY, R. M., LAWTON, J. H. & STORK, N. E. 1995. Assessing extinction rates. In: Lawton, J. H. & May, R. M. (eds.) *Extinction Rates*. Oxford University Press, Oxford.

McCLELLAND, J. 1989. Anatomy of the lungs and air sacs. In: King, A. S. & McClelland, J. (eds.) *Form and Function in Birds*, vol. 4. Academic Press, London.

McNEIL, R., DRAPEAU, P. & PIEROTTI, R. 1993. Nocturnality in colonial waterbirds: occurrence, special adaptations and suspected benefits. *Current Orn.* 10, 187–246.

MILLS, J. A. 1989. Red-billed Gull. In: Newton, I. (ed.) *Lifetime Reproduction in Birds*. Academic Press, London.

MONROE, B. L. & SIBLEY, C. G. 1993. *A World Checklist of Birds*. Yale University Press, New Haven & London.

MONTEIRO, L. R., RAMOS, J. A. & FURNESS, R. W. 1996. Past and present status and conservation of the seabirds breeding in the Azores archipelago. *Biol. Conserv.* 78, 319–28.

MURIE, O. J. 1940. Food habits of the Northern Bald Eagle in the Aleutian Islands, Alaska. *Condor* 42, 198–202.

MURPHY, R. C. 1915. The bird life of Trinidad Islet. *Auk* 32, 332–48.

MURPHY, R. C. 1936. *The Oceanic Birds of South America*. MacMillan & American Museum of Natural History, New York.

Natural Environments Research Council (NERC) 1971. *The Seabird Wreck in the Irish Sea, Autumn 1969*. NERC, Ser. C, no. 4.

NELSON, J. B. 1975. The breeding biology of frigatebirds—a comparative review. *Living Bird* 14, 113–54.

NELSON, J. B. 1978a. *The Sulidae: Gannets and Boobies*. Oxford University Press, Oxford.

NELSON, J. B. 1978b. *The Gannet*. Poyser, Berkhamsted.

NELSON, J. B. 1988. Abbott's Booby and Christmas Island. *Sea Swallow* 37, 22–8.

NELSON, R. W. & MYRES, M. T. 1975. Changes in the peregrine population and its seabird prey at Langara Island, British Columbia. *Raptor Res.* 3, 13–31.

NELSON, S. K. 1997. The Marbled Murrelet *Brachyramphus marmoratus*. In: Poole, A. & Gill, F. (eds.) *The Birds of North America*, no. 276. Academy of Natural Sciences of Philadelphia, Philadelphia & American Ornithologist's Union, Washington DC.

NEWTON, I. (ed.) 1989. *Lifetime Reproductive Success in Birds*. Academic Press, London.

NEWTON, I. & ROTHERY, P. 1997. Senescence and reproductive value in Sparrowhawks. *Ecol.* 78, 1000–8.

NICE, M. M. 1962. Development of behaviour in precocial birds. *Trans. Linn. Soc. New York* 8, 1–211.

NOL, E. & GASKIN, D. E. 1987. Distribution and movements of Black Guillemots (*Cepphus grylle*) in coastal waters of the southwestern Bay of Fundy, Canada. *Can. J. Zool.* 65, 2682–9.

NORDERHAUG, M. 1980. Breeding biology of the Little Auk (*Plautus alle*) in Svalbard. *Norsk Polarinstitutt Skrifter* 173, 1–45.

NORMAN, F. I. & BROWN, R. S. 1987. Notes on the Common Diving-Petrels *Pelecanoides urinatrix* found beach-washed in Victoria. *Emu* 87, 179–85.

NUNN, G. B., COOPER, J., JOUVENTIN, P., ROBERTSON, C. J. R. & ROBERTSON, G. G. 1996. Evolutionary relationships among extant albatrosses (Procellariiformes: Diomedeidae) established from complete cytochrome-*b* gene sequences. *Auk* 113, 784–801.

NUR, N. & SYDEMAN, W. J. 1999a. Survival, breeding probability and reproductive success in relation to population dynamics of Brandt's Cormorants *Phalacrocorax penicillatus*. *Bird Study* 46 Suppl: 92–103.

NUR, N. & SYDEMAN, W. J. 1999b. Demographic process and population dynamic models of seabirds: implications for conservation and restoration. *Current Orn.* 15, 149–88.

O'CONNOR, R. J. 1984. *The Growth and Development of Birds*. Wiley, New York.

OKA, N. 1994. Underwater feeding of three shearwaters: Pale-footed (*Puffinus carneipes*), Sooty (*Puffinus griseus*) and Streaked (*Calonectris leucomelas*). *J. Yamashina Inst. Orn.* 26, 81–4.

OLLASON, J. C & DUNNET, G. M. 1983. Modelling annual changes in numbers of breeding Fulmars *Fulmarus glacialis* at a colony in Orkney. *J. Anim. Ecol.* 52, 185–98.

OLSON, S. L. 1985. The fossil record of birds. In: Farner, D. S., King, J. R. & Parkes, K. C. (eds.) *Avian Biology*, vol. 8. Academic Press, New York.

OLSON, S. L. & JAMES, H. F. 1991. Descriptions of thirty-two new species of birds from the Hawaiian Islands: Part 1, Non-passeriformes. *Orn. Monogr.* 46, 1–88.

OLSON, S. L. & RASMUSSEN, P. C. 2001. Miocene and Pleiocene birds from the Lea Creek Mine, North Carolina. In: Ray, C. E. & Bohaska, D. J. (eds.) *Geology and Palaeontology of the Lee Creek Mine, North Carolina, III*. Smithsonian Institute Press, Washington DC.

PAINE, R. T., WOOTTON, J. T. & BOERSMA, P. D. 1990. Direct and indirect effects of Peregrine Falcon predation on seabird abundance. *Auk* 107, 1–9.

PASHBY, B. S. & CUDWORTH, J. 1968. The fulmar 'wreck' of 1962. *Brit. Birds* 62, 97–109.

PAYNE, R. 1995. *Among Whales*. Charles Scribner's Sons, New York.

PEAKER, M. & LINZELL, J. L. 1975. *Salt Glands in Birds and Reptiles*. Cambridge University Press, Cambridge.

PENNYCUICK, C. J. 1983. Thermal soaring compared in three dissimilar tropical bird species, *Fregata magnificens*, *Pelecanus occidentalis* and *Coragyps atratus*. *J. Experimental Biol.* 102, 307–25.

PENNYCUICK, C. J. 1987. Flight of seabirds. In: Croxall, J. P. (ed.) *Seabirds: Feeding Ecology and Role in Marine Ecosystems*. Cambridge University Press, Cambridge.

PERRINS, C. M., LEBRETON, J-D. & HIRONS, G. M. (eds.) 1991. *Bird Population Studies*. Oxford University Press, Oxford.

PHILLIPS, G. C. 1972. Survival value of the white coloration of gulls and other seabirds. D.Phil. thesis, University of Oxford.

PHILLIPS, J. G., BUTLER, P. J. & SHARP, P. J. 1985. *Physiological Strategies in Avian Biology*. Blackie, Glasgow.

PIANKA, E. 1970. On "r" and "K" selection. *Amer. Nat.* 104, 592–7.

PIATT, J. F. 1990. The aggregative response of Common Murres and Atlantic Puffins to schools of Capelin. *Stud. Avian Biol.* 14, 35–51.

PIEROTTI, R. 1982. Habitat selection and its effect on reproductive output in the Herring Gull in Newfoundland. *Ecol.* 63, 854–68.

PINKER, S. 1997. *How the Mind Works*. Norton & Co., New York.

POCKLINGTON, R. 1979. An oceanographic interpretation of seabird distributions in the Indian Ocean. *Marine Biol.* 51, 9–21.

POMEROY, D. 1990. Why fly? The possible benefits for lower mortality. *Biol. J. Linn. Soc.* 40, 53–65.

POOLE, A. & GILL, F. (eds.) 1992–8. *The Birds of North America*. Academy of Natural Sciences of Philadelphia, Philadelphia & American Ornithologist's Union, Washington DC.

PORTER, J. M. & SEALY, S. G. 1981. Dynamics of seabird multi species feeding flocks: chronology of flocking in Barkley Sound, British Columbia, in 1979. *Colonial Waterbirds* 4, 104–13.

PORTER, J. M. & SEALY, S. G. 1982. Dynamics of seabird multispecies feeding flocks: age-related feeding behaviour. *Behav.* 81, 91–109.

POTTS, G. R., COULSON, J. C. & DEANS, I. R. 1980. Population dynamics and the breeding success of the Shag *Phalacrocorax aristotelis* on the Farne Islands, Northumberland. *J. Anim. Ecol.* 49, 465–84.

POWLESLAND, R. G. 1986. Seabirds found dead on New Zealand beaches in 1984 and a review of fulmar recoveries since 1960. *Notornis* 33, 171–84.

PRINCE, P. A. & MORGAN, R. A. 1987. Diet and feeding ecology of Procellariiformes. In: Croxall, J. P. (ed.) *Seabirds: Feeding Ecology and Role in Marine Ecosystems*. Academic Press, London.

PRINCE, P. A., WOOD, A. G., BARTON, T. & CROXALL, J. P. 1992. Satellite tracking of Wandering Albatrosses *Diomedea exulans* in the South Atlantic. *Antarctic Sci.* 4, 31–6.

PUGESEK, B. H. 1981. Increased reproductive effort with age in the California Gull (*Larus californicus*). *Science* 212, 822–3.

PUGESEK, B. H. 1983. The relationship between parental age and reproductive effort in the California Gull (*Larus californicus*). *Behav. Ecol. & Sociobiol.* 13, 161–71.

PUGESEK, B. H. & DIEM, K. L. 1990. The relationship between reproduction and survival in known-aged California Gulls. *Ecol.* 71, 811–7.

PUGESEK, B. H. & WOOD, P. 1992. Alternative reproductive strategies in the California Gull. *Evol. Ecol.* 6, 279–95.

RAIKOW, R. J. 1985. Locomotor system. In: King, A. S. & McClelland, J. (eds.) *Form and Function of Birds*, vol. 3. Academic Press, London.

RANDALL, R. M. & RANDALL, B. M. 1990. Cetaceans as predators of Jackass Penguins *Spheniscus demersus*: deductions based on behaviour. *Marine Orn.* 18, 9–12.

RATCLIFFE, D. 1980. *The Peregrine Falcon*. Poyser, Calton.

RAUZON, M. 2001. *Isles of Refuge: Wildlife and History of the Northwest Hawaiian Islands*. University of Hawaii Press, Honolulu.

REED, S. 1981. Wreck of Kerguelen and Blue Petrels. *Notornis* 28, 239–40.

REID, W. V. 1987. Constraints on clutch size in the Glaucous-winged Gull. *Stud. Avian Biol.* 10, 8–25.

REID, W. V. 1988. Age-specific patterns of reproduction in the Glaucous-winged Gull: increased effort with age? *Ecol.* 69, 1454–65.

RENAUD, W. E. & BRADSTREET, M. S. W. 1980. Late winter distribution of Black Guillemots in northern Baffin Bay and the Canadian high arctic. *Can. Field-Nat.* 94, 421–5.

RENAUD, W. E., McLAREN, P. L. & JOHNSON, S. R. 1982. The dovekie, *Alle alle*, as a spring migrant in eastern Lancaster Sound and western Baffin Bay. *Arctic* 35, 118–25.

RICHDALE, L. E. 1957. *A Population Study of Penguins*. Oxford University Press, Oxford.

RICHDALE, L. E. 1963. Biology of the Sooty Shearwater *Puffinus griseus*. *Proc. Zool. Soc., Lond.* 141, 1–117.

RICHDALE, L. E. 1965. Biology of the birds of Whero Island, New Zealand, with special reference to the diving petrel and the White-faced Storm-Petrel. *Trans. Zool. Soc., Lond.* 31, 1–86.

RICKLEFS, R. E. 1977. On the evolution of reproductive strategies in birds: reproductive effort. *Amer. Nat.* 111, 453–78.

RICKLEFS, R. E. 1984. Some considerations of the reproductive energetics of pelagic seabirds. *Stud. Avian Biol.* 8, 84–94.

RICKLEFS, R. E. 1990. Seabird life histories and the marine environment: some speculations. *Colonial Waterbirds* 13, 1–6.

RICKLEFS, R. E. & SCHEW, W. A. 1994. Foraging stochasticity and lipid accumulation by nestling petrels. *Functional Ecol.* 8, 159–70.

RIEDMAN, M. 1990. *The Pinnipeds*. University of California Press, Berkeley.

RIJKE, A. M. 1971. The phylogenetic development of water repellency in water bird feathers. *Ostrich*, Suppl. 8, 67–76.

ROBERTSON, C. J. R. & BELL, B. D. 1984. Seabird status and conservation in the New Zealand region. In: Croxall, J. P., Evans, P. G. H. & Schreiber, R. W. (eds.) *Status and Conservation of the World's Seabirds*. International Council for Bird Preservation Tech. Rep. 2. Cambridge.

ROWLANDS, B. W., TRUEMAN, T., OLSON, S. L., McCULLOCH, M. N. & BROOKE, R. K. 1998. *The Birds of St. Helena*. British Ornithologists' Union, Tring.

RUSSELL, R. W., HUNT, G. L., COYLE, K. O. & COONEY, R. T. 1992. Foraging in a fractal environment: Spatial patterns in a marine predator-prey system. *Landscape Ecol.* 7, 195–209.

RYAN, P. G. 1987. Wreck of juvenile Black-browed Albatross on the west coast of South Africa during storm weather. *Ostrich* 58, 139–40.

RYAN, P. G., AVERY, G., ROSE, B., ROSS, G. J. B., SINCLAIR, J. C. & VERNON, C. J. 1989. The southern ocean seabird irruption to South African waters during winter 1984. *Cormorant* 17, 41–55.

RYDER, J. 1980. The influence of age on the breeding biology of colonial nesting seabirds. In: Burger, J., Olla, B. L. & Winn, H. E. (eds.) *Behaviour of Marine Animals*, vol. 4. Plenum Press, New York.

SAFINA, C. & BURGER, J. 1988. Ecological dynamics among preyfish, bluefish and foraging Common Terns in an Atlantic coastal system. In: Burger, J. (ed.) *Seabirds and Other Marine Vertebrates, Competition, Predation and Other Interactions*. Columbia University Press, New York.

SANGER, G. A. 1987. Trophic levels and trophic relationships of seabirds in the Gulf of Alaska. In: Croxall, J. P. (ed.) *Seabirds: Feeding Ecology and Role in Marine Ecosystems.* Academic Press, London.

SAETHER, B.-E. 1990. Age-specific variation in reproductive performance of birds. *Current Orn.* 7, 251–84.

SCHNEIDER, D. C., HARRISON, N. M. & HUNT, G. L. 1990. Seabird diet at a front near the Pribilof Islands, Alaska. *Stud. Avian Biol.* 14, 60–6.

SCHREIBER, E. A. 2001. Climate and weather effects on seabirds. In: Schreiber, E. A. & Burger, J. (eds.) *Biology of Marine Birds.* CRC Press, Boca Raton, FL.

SCHREIBER, R. W. & SCHREIBER, E. A. 1984. Central Pacific seabirds and the El Niño Southern Oscillation: 1982 and 1983 perspectives. *Science* 225, 713–6.

SCHREIBER, R. W. & SCHREIBER, E. A. 1986. Christmas Island (Pacific Ocean) seabirds and the El Niño Southern Oscillation (ENSO): 1984 perspectives. *Nato ASI Ser.* 612, 397–408.

SEALY, S. G. 1973. The adaptive significance of post-hatching developmental patterns and growth rates in the Alcidae. *Ornis Scand.* 4, 113–121.

SEALY, S. G. 1975. Egg size of murrelets. *Condor* 77, 500–1.

SEALY, S. G. 1976. Biology of nesting Ancient Murrelets. *Condor* 78, 294–306.

SERTILANGES, A.D. 1992. *The Thoughts of Leonardo da Vinci.* Le Clos-Lucé, Amboise.

SERVENTY, D. L. & CURRY, P. J. 1984. Observations on colony size, breeding success, recruitment, and inter-colony dispersal in a Tasmanian colony of short-tailed shearwaters *Puffinus tenuirostris* over a 30-year period. *Emu* 84, 71–9.

SHACKLETON, E. 1919. *South.* Heinemann, London.

SHARROCK, J. T. R. 1973. *The Natural History of Cape Clear Island.* Poyser, Berkhamsted.

SHERROD, S. K., WHITE, C. M. & WILLIAMSON, F. S. L. 1976. Biology of the Bald Eagle on Amchitka Island, Alaska. *Living Bird* 15, 143–82.

SIBLEY, C. G. & AHLQUIST, J. 1990. *Phylogeny and Classification of Birds.* Yale University Press, New Haven & London.

SIEGEL-CAUSEY, D. 1988. Phylogeny of the Phalacrocoracidae. *Condor* 90, 885–905.

SIEGFRIED, W. R., WILLIAMS, A. J., FROST, P. G. H. & KINAHAN, J. B. 1975. Plumage and ecology of cormorants. *Zool. Afr.* 10, 183–92.

SIMMONS, K. E. L. 1972. Some adaptive features of seabird plumage types. *Brit. Birds* 65, 465–79, 510–21.

SIMPSON, G. G. 1976. *Penguins, Past and Present, Here and Now.* Yale University Press, New Haven.

SPAANS, A. L., DE WIT, A. A. N. & VAN VLAARDINGEN, M. A. 1987. Effects of increased population size in Herring Gulls on breeding success and other parameters. *Stud. Avian Biol.* 10, 57–65.

SPEAR, L. B. & AINLEY, D. G. 1997. Flight speed of seabirds in relation to wind direction and wing morphology. *Ibis* 139, 221–33.

STACEY, P. B. & KOENIG, W. D. 1990. *Cooperative Breeding in Birds.* Cambridge University Press, Cambridge.

STALLCUP, R. 1990. *Ocean birds of the Nearshore Pacific.* Point Reyes Bird Observatory, Stinson Beach, CA.

STEARNS, S. C. 1980. A new view of life-history evolution. *Oikos* 35, 266–81.

STEARNS, S. C. 1992. *The Evolution of Life Histories.* Oxford University Press; New York.

STEMPNIEWICZ, L. 1993. The polar bear *Ursus maritimus* feeding in a seabird colony in Franz Josef Land. *Polar Res.* 12, 33–6.

STENHOUSE, I. J., GILCHRIST, H. G. & MONTEVECCHI, W. A. 2001. Reproductive biology of Sabine's Gull in the Canadian arctic. *Condor* 103, 98–107.

STODDART, D. R. (1984). Breeding seabirds of the Seychelles and adjacent islands. In: Stoddart, D. R. (ed.) *Biogeography and Ecology of the Seychelles Islands.* Junk, The Hague.

STONEHOUSE, B. 1962. Ascension Island and the British Ornithologists' Union Centenary Expedition 1957–59. *Ibis* 103, 107–23.

SYDEMAN, W. J. 1993. Survivorship of Common Murres on Southeast Farallon Island, California. *Ornis Scand.* 24, 1–7.

TAYLOR, I. R. 1979. The kleptoparasitic behaviour of the Arctic Skua *Stercorarius parasiticus* with three species of tern. *Ibis* 121, 274–83.

TEIXEIRA, A. M. 1987. The wreck of Leach's Storm-Petrels on the Portuguese coast in the autumn of 1983. *Ring. & Migr.* 8, 27–8.

TENNEKES, H. 1996. *The Simple Science of Flight: From Insects to Jumbo Jets.* MIT Press, Cambridge, MA.

THOMSON, A. L. 1966. An analysis of recoveries of Great Skuas ringed in Shetland. *Brit. Birds* 59, 1–15.

THOMSON, A. L. 1984. *A New Dictionary of Birds.* Witherby, London.

TICKELL, W. L. N. 2000. *Albatrosses.* Pica Press, Robertsbridge.

TOVAR, H., GUILLEN, V. & NAKAMA, M. E. 1987. Monthly population size of three guano birds off Peru, 1953 to 1982. In: Pauly, D. & Tsukayama, I. (eds.) *The Peruvian Anchoveta and its Upwelling Ecosystem: Three Decades of Change*. ICLARM Studies and Reviews 15. Instituto del Mar del Peru, Callao.

TUCK, L. M. 1961. *The Murres*. Canadian Wildlife Service Monogr. No. 1, Canadian Wildlife Service, Ottawa.

TUCK, L. M. 1968. Laughing Gulls (*Larus atricilla*) and Black Skimmers (*Rynchops nigra*) brought to Newfoundland by hurricane. *Bird-Banding* 29, 200–8.

VALIELA, I. 1995. *Marine Ecological Processes*. Springer, New York.

VAN FRANEKER, J. A. & WATTEL, J. 1982. Geographical variation of the fulmar *Fulmarus glacialis* in the North Atlantic. *Ardea* 70, 31–44.

VERHEYDEN, C. & JOUVENTIN, P. 1994. Olfactory behavior of foraging Procellariiforms. *Auk* 111, 285–91.

VERMEER, K. 1970. Breeding biology of California and Ring-billed Gulls. *Can. Wildl. Service Occ. Pap.* 12, 1–51.

VERMEER, K., BRIGGS, K. T., MORGAN, K. H. & SIEGEL-CAUSEY, D. 1993. *The Status, Ecology and Conservation of Marine Birds of the North Pacific*. Canadian Wildlife Service, Ottawa.

VOGEL, S. 1998. *Cat's Paws and Catapults*. Norton and Co., New York.

WACE, N. M. & HOLDGATE, M. W. 1976. *Man and Nature in the Tristan da Cunha Islands*. IUCN Nature Research, Morges.

WAGNER, R. H. 1992. Extra-pair copulations in a lek: the secondary mating system of monogamous razorbills. *Behav. Ecol. & Sociobiol.* 31, 63–71.

WALKER, C. A., WRAGG, G. M. & HARRISON, C. J. O. 1990. A new shearwater from the Pleistocene of the Canary Islands and its bearing on the evolution of certain *Puffinus* shearwaters. *Hist. Biol.* 3, 203–24.

WANLESS, S., HARRIS, M. P., BURGER, A. E. & BUCKLAND, S. T. 1997. Use of time-depth recorders for estimating depth and diving performance of European Shags. *J. Field Orn.* 68, 547–61.

WANLESS, S., HARRIS, M. P. & MORRIS, J. A. 1992. Diving behaviour and diet of the blue-eyed shag at South Georgia. *Polar Biol.* 12, 713–9.

WANLESS, S., MORRIS, J. A. & HARRIS, M. P. 1988. Diving behaviour of guillemot *Uria aalge*, puffin *Fratercula arctica* and razorbill *Alca torda*, as shown by radio-telemetry. *J. Zool., Lond.* 216, 73–81.

WARD, P. & ZAHAVI, A. 1973. The importance of certain assemblages of birds as "Information Centres" for food-finding. *Ibis* 115, 517–34.

WARHAM, J. 1977. Wing-loadings, wing-shapes and flight capabilities of Procellariiformes. *New Zealand J. Zool.* 4, 73–83.

WARHAM, J. 1990. *The Petrels: their Ecology and Breeding Systems*. Academic Press, London.

WARHAM, J. 1996. *The Behaviour, Population Biology and Physiology of the Petrels*. Academic Press, London.

WARHEIT, K. I. & LINDBERG, D. R. 1988. Interaction between seabirds and marine mammals through time: interference competition at breeding sites. In: Burger, J. (ed.) *Seabirds and Other Marine Vertebrates: Competition, Predation and Other Interactions*. Columbia University Press, New York.

WATANUKI, Y., KATO, A., MORI, Y. & NAITO, Y. 1993. Diving performance of Adélie penguins in relation to food availability in fast sea-ice areas: comparison between years. *J. Anim. Ecol.* 62, 634–46.

WATANUKI, Y., KATO, A. & NAITO, Y. 1996. Diving performance of male and female Japanese Cormorants. *Can. J. Zool.* 74, 1098–1109.

WEIMERSKIRCH, H. 1992. Reproductive effort in long-lived birds: age-specific patterns of condition, reproduction, and survival in the wandering albatross. *Oikos* 64, 464–73.

WEIMERSKIRCH, H. 2002. Seabird demography and its relationship with the marine environment. In: Schreiber, E. A. & Burger, J. (eds.) *Biology of Marine Birds*. CRC Press, Boca Raton, FL.

WEIMERSKIRCH, H., CHASTEL, O., ACKERMAN, L., CHAURAND, T., CUENOT-CHAILLET, F., HINDERMEYER, X. & JUDAS, J. 1994a. Alternate long and short foraging trips in pelagic seabird parents. *Anim. Behav.* 47, 472–6.

WEIMERSKIRCH, H., CHASTEL, O., CHEREL, Y., HENDON, J.-A. & TVERAA, T. 2001. Nest attendance and foraging movements of northern fulmars rearing chicks at Bjørnøya, Barents Sea. *Polar Biol.* 24, 83–8.

WEIMERSKIRCH, H., DONCASTER, C. P. & CUENOT-CHAILLET, F. 1994b. Pelagic seabirds and the marine environment: foraging patterns of wandering albatrosses in relation to prey availability and distribution. *Proc. Roy. Soc. Lond.* B 255, 91–7.

WEIMERSKIRCH, H. & GUIONNET, T. 2002. Comparative activity pattern during foraging of four albatross species. *Ibis* 144, 40–50.

WEIMERSKIRCH, H. & JOUVENTIN, P. 1987. Population dynamics of the Wandering Albatross (*Diomedea exulans*) of the Crozet Islands: causes and consequences of the population decline. *Oikos* 49, 315–22.

WEIMERSKIRCH, H., SALAMOLARD, M., SARRAZIN, F. & JOUVENTIN, P. 1993. Foraging strategy of Wandering Albatrosses through the breeding season: a study using satellite telemetry. *Auk* 110, 325–42.

WEIR, D. N., KITCHENER, A. C. & McGOWAN, R. Y. 2000. Hybridization and changes in the distribution of Iceland gulls (*Larus glaucoides/kumlieni/thayeri*). *J. Zool., Lond.* 252, 517–30.

WELCH, H. E., CRAWFORD, R. E. & HOP, H. 1993. Occurrence of Arctic Cod (*Boreogadus saida*) schools and their vulnerability to predation in the Canadian high arctic. *Arctic* 46, 331–8.

WHITE, C. M. N. & BRUCE, M. D. 1986. *The Birds of Wallacea*. British Ornithologists' Union, London.

WILGOHS, J. F. 1961. *The White-tailed Eagle Haliaeetus albicilla albicilla (Linné) in Norway*. Norwegian Universities Press, Bergen.

WILLIAMS, A. J. 1984. The status and conservation of seabirds on some islands in the South African sector of the southern ocean. In: Croxall, J. P., Evans, P. G. H. & Schreiber, R. W. (eds.) *Status and Conservation of the World's Seabirds*. International Council for Bird Preservation Tech. Rep. 2. Cambridge.

WILLIAMS, A. J., DYER, B. M., RANDALL, R. M. & KOMEN, J. 1990. Killer Whales *Orcinus orca* and seabirds: "play", predation and association. *Marine Orn.* 18, 37–41.

WILLIAMS, T. D. 1995. *The Penguins*. Oxford University Press, Oxford.

WILSON, J. A. 1975. Sweeping flight and soaring by albatrosses. *Nature* 257, 307–8.

WILSON, R. P. 1991. The behaviour of diving birds. *Proc. Intern. Orn. Congr.* 20, 1853–67.

WILSON, R. P. 1995. Foraging ecology. In: Williams, T. D. *The Penguins*. Oxford University Press, Oxford.

WILSON, R. P., BURGER, A. E., WILSON, B. L. H., WILSON, M. P. T. & NÖLDEKE, C. 1989. An inexpensive depth gauge for marine animals. *Marine Biol.* 103, 275–83.

WILSON, R. P., GRANT, W. S. & DUFFY, D. C. 1986. Recording devices on free-ranging marine animals: does measurement affect foraging performance. *Ecol.* 67, 1091–3.

WILSON, R. P., WILSON, M. P. & NÖLDEKE, E. C. 1992. Pre-dive leaps in diving birds: why do kickers sometimes jump? *Marine Orn.* 20, 7–16.

WINTERBOTTOM, J. M. 1971. The position of Marion Island in the sub-antarctic avifauna. In: van Zinderen Bakker, E. M., Winterbottom, J. M. & Dyer, R. A. (eds.) *Marion and Prince Edward Islands*. Balkema: Cape Town.

WOAKES, A. J. & BUTLER, P. J. 1983. Swimming and diving in Tufted Ducks *Aythya fuligula* with particular reference to heart rate and gas exchange. *J. Experimental Biol.* 107, 311–29.

WOODBY, D. A. 1984. The April distribution of murres and prey patches in the southeastern Bering Sea. *Limnological Oceanography* 29, 181–8.

WOOLLER, R. D., BRADLEY, J. S., SKIRA, I. J. & SERVENTY, D. L. 1989. Short-tailed Shearwater. In: Newton, I. (ed.) *Lifetime Reproduction in Birds*. Academic Press, London.

WOOLLER, R. D., BRADLEY, J. S., SKIRA, I. J. & SERVENTY, D. L. 1990. Reproductive success of Short-tailed Shearwaters *Puffinus tenuirostris* in relation to their age and breeding experience. *J. Anim. Ecol.* 59, 161–70.

WOOLLER, R. D., BRADLEY, J. S. & CROXALL, J. P. 1992. Long-term population studies of seabirds. *Trends Ecol. & Evol.* 7, 111–4.

WORTHY, T. H. & JOUVENTIN, P. 1999. The fossil avifauna of Amsterdam Island, Indian Ocean. In: Olson, S. L. (ed.) Avian Palaeontology at the close of the 20th century: *Proc. 4th Intern. Meeting Soc. Avian Palaeontology & Evol*. Smithsonian Institute, Washington DC.

WRAGG, G. M. 1995. The fossil birds of Henderson Island, Pitcairn group: natural turnover and human impact. *Biol. J. Linn. Soc.* 56, 405–14.

WYNNE-EDWARDS, V. C. 1939. Intermittent breeding of the fulmar (*Fulmarus glacialis* (L.)), with some general observations on non-breeding in sea-birds. *Proc. Zool. Soc., Lond., Ser.* A 109, 127–32.

YOUNG, E. 1994. *Skua and Penguin: Predator and Prey*. Cambridge University Press, Cambridge.

YUDIN, K. A. 1957. [Certain adaptive peculiarities of the wing in birds of the order Tubinares]. *Zool. J.* 36, 1859–73. [In Russian.]

Scientific names of birds mentioned in the text

Abbott's Booby *Papasula abbotti*
African Dwarf Kingfisher *Ceyx lecontei*
Adélie Penguin *Pygoscelis adeliae*
African Penguin *Spheniscus demersus*
Ancient Murrelet *Synthliboramphus antiquus*
Antarctic Fulmar *Fulmarus glacialoides*
Antarctic Petrel *Thalassoica antarctica*
Antarctic Prion *Pachyptila desolata*
Arabian Babbler *Turdoides squamiceps*
Arctic Tern *Sterna paradisaea*
Atlantic Puffin *Fratercula arctica*
Audubon's Shearwater *Puffinus lherminieri*
Audouin's Gull *Larus audouinii*
Auckland Island Shag *Phalacrocorax colensoi*
Bald Eagle *Haliaeetus leucocephalus*
Band-rumped (Madeiran) Storm-petrel *Oceanodroma castro*
Band-tailed Gull *Larus belcheri*
Bank Cormorant *Phalacrocorax neglectus*
Bank Myna *Acridotheres ginginianus*
Beck's Petrel *Pseudobulweria becki*
Black Guillemot *Cepphus grylle*
Black Skimmer *Rynchops niger*
Black-browed Albatross *Thalassarche melanophris*
Black-capped Petrel *Pterodroma hasitata*
Black-footed Albatross *Phoebastria nigripes*
Black-headed Gull *Larus ridibundus*
Black-legged Kittiwake *Rissa tridactyla*
Black-throated Loon *Gavia arctica*
Black-winged Petrel *Pterodroma nigripennis*
Blue Petrel *Halobaena caerulea*
Blue Tit *Parus caeruleus*
Blue-eyed (South Georgia) Shag *Phalacrocorax (atriceps) georgianus*
Blue-footed Booby *Sula nebouxii*
Bonaparte's Gull *Larus philadelphia*
Brandt's Cormorant *Phalacrocorax penicillatus*
Brent Goose *Branta bernicla*
Bridled Tern *Sterna anaethetus*
British Storm-petrel *Hydrobates pelagicus*
Broad-billed Prion *Pachyptila vittata*
Brown Booby *Sula leucogaster*

Brown Noddy *Anous stolidus*
Brown Pelican *Pelecanus occidentalis*
Buller's Shearwater *Puffinus bulleri*
Cahow *Pterodroma cahow*
California Gull *Larus californicus*
Campbell Island Shag *Phalacrocorax campbelli*
Canada Goose *Branta canadensis*
Cape Cormorant *Phalacrocorax capensis*
Cape Gannet *Morus capensis*
Cape Petrel *Daption capense*
Caspian Tern *Sterna caspia*
Cassin's Auklet *Ptychoramphus aleuticus*
Chatham Island Taiko *Pterodroma magentae*
Chinstrap Penguin *Pygoscelis antarctica*
Christmas Island Frigatebird *Fregata andrewsi*
Common Eider *Somateria mollissima*
Common Diving-petrel *Pelecanoides urinatrix*
Common Loon *Gavia immer*
Common Murre *Uria aalge*
Common Tern *Sterna hirundo*
Cory's Shearwater *Calonectris diomedea*
Cotton Teal *Nettapus coromandelianus*
Crab Plover *Dromas ardeola*
Craveri's Murrelet *Synthliboramphus craveri*
Crested Auklet *Aethia cristatella*
Demoiselle Crane *Grus virgo*
Dolphin Gull *Larus scoresbii*
Double-crested Cormorant *Phalacrocorax auritus*
Emperor Penguin *Aptenodytes forsteri*
European Shag *Phalacrocorax aristotelis*
Fairy Prion *Pachyptila turtur*
Fiordland Penguin *Eudyptes pachyrhynchus*
Fluttering Shearwater *Puffinus gavia*
Fork-tailed Storm-petrel *Oceanodroma furcata*
Forster's Tern *Sterna forsteri*
Franklin's Gull *Larus pipixcan*
Galápagos Cormorant *Phalacrocorax harrisi*
Galápagos Penguin *Spheniscus mediculus*
Gentoo Penguin *Pygoscelis papua*
Glaucous Gull *Larus hyperboreus*
Glaucous-winged Gull *Larus glaucescens*
Great Auk *Pinguinus impennis*
Great Black-backed Gull *Larus marinus*
Great Cormorant *Phalacrocorax carbo*
Great Frigatebird *Fregata minor*
Great Shearwater *Puffinus gravis*
Great Skua *Catharacta skua*
Great White Pelican *Pelecanus onocrotalus*

Grey-headed Albatross *Thalassarche chrysostoma*
Guadalupe Storm-petrel *Oceanodroma macrodactyla*
Guanay Cormorant *Phalacrocorax bougainvillii*
Gyrfalcon *Falco rusticolus*
Hartlaub's Gull *Larus hartlaubii*
Herring Gull *Larus argentatus*
Hornby's Storm-petrel *Oceanodroma hornbyi*
Horned Puffin *Fratercula corniculata*
House Martin *Delichon urbica*
House Sparrow *Passer domesticus*
Humboldt Penguin *Spheniscus humboldti*
Hutton's Shearwater *Puffinus huttoni*
Ibisbill *Ibidorhyncha struthersii*
Iceland Gull *Larus glaucoides*
Imperial Shag *Phalacrocorax atriceps*
Inca Tern *Larosterna inca*
Ivory Gull *Pagophila eburnea*
Japanese Cormorant *Phalacrocorax capillatus*
Japanese Murrelet *Synthliboramphus wumizusume*
Juan Fernández Petrel *Pterodroma externa*
Kelp Gull *Larus dominicanus*
Kerguelen Petrel *Lugensa brevirostris*
King Penguin *Aptenodytes patagonicus*
Kittlitz's Murrelet *Brachyramphus brevirostris*
Kumlien's Gull *Larus glaucoides kumlieni*
Labrador Duck *Camptorhynchus labradorius*
Lammergeier *Gypaetus barbatus*
Laughing Gull *Larus atricilla*
Laysan Albatross *Phoebastria immutabilis*
Leach's Storm-petrel *Oceanodroma leucorhoa*
Least Auklet *Aethia pusilla*
Least Storm-petrel *Oceanodroma microsoma*
Light-mantled Sooty Albatross *Phoebetria palpebrata*
Little Auk *Alle alle*
Little Penguin *Eudyptula minor*
Little Tern *Sterna albifrons*
Long-billed Murrelet *Brachyramphus longirostris*
Long-tailed Cormorant *Phalacrocorax africanus*
Long-tailed Duck *Clangula hyemalis*
Long-tailed Jaeger *Stercorarius longicaudus*
Macaroni Penguin *Eudyptes chrysolophus*
MacGillivray's Petrel *Pseudobulweria macgillivrayi*
Magellanic Penguin *Spheniscus magellanicus*
Magnificent Frigatebird *Fregata magnificens*
Manx Shearwater *Puffinus puffinus*
Marbled Murrelet *Brachyramphus marmoratus*
Masked Booby *Sula dactylatra*
Mew Gull *Larus canus*

Northern Fulmar *Fulmarus glacialis*
Northern Gannet *Morus bassanus*
Northern Giant Petrel *Macronectes halli*
Northwestern Crow *Corvus caurinus*
Oilbird *Steatornis caripensis*
Oriental Darter *Anhinga melanogaster*
Pacific Loon *Gavia pacifica*
Parakeet Auklet *Cyclorrhynchus psittacula*
Parasitic Jaeger *Stercorarius parasiticus*
Pelagic Cormorant *Phalacrocorax pelagicus*
Peregrine Falcon *Falco peregrinus*
Peruvian Booby *Sula variegata*
Peruvian Diving-petrel *Pelecanoides garnotii*
Pigeon Guillemot *Cepphus columba*
Pink-footed Shearwater *Puffinus creatopus*
Pomarine Jaeger *Stercorarius pomarinus*
Pycroft's Petrel *Pterodroma pycrofti*
Razorbill *Alca torda*
Red Phalarope *Phalaropus fulicaria*
Red-billed Gull *Larus scopulinus*
Red-footed Booby *Sula sula*
Red-legged Cormorant *Phalacrocorax gaimardi*
Red-legged Kittiwake *Rissa brevirostris*
Red-necked Phalarope *Phalaropus lobatus*
Red-tailed Tropicbird *Phaethon rubricauda*
Red-throated Loon *Gavia stellata*
Rhinoceros Auklet *Cerorhinca monocerata*
Ring-billed Gull *Larus delawarensis*
Rock Pipit *Anthus petrosus*
Rockhopper Penguin *Eudyptes chrysocome*
Rough-faced Shag *Phalacrocorax carunculatus*
Rough-legged Buzzard *Buteo lagopus*
Royal Albatross *Diomedea epomophora*
Royal Penguin *Eudyptes schlegeli*
Roseate Tern *Sterna dougallii*
Ross's Gull *Rhodostethia rosea*
Sabine's Gull *Xema sabini*
Salvin's Albatross *Thalassarche (cauta) salvini*
Salvin's (Medium-billed) Prion *Pachyptila salvini*
Sand Martin *Riparia riparia*
Sandwich Tern *Sterna sandvicensis*
Saunders's Gull *Larus saundersi*
Savi's Warbler *Locustella luscinioides*
Short-tailed Shearwater *Puffinus tenuirostris*
Shy Albatross *Thalassarche cauta*
Snow Goose *Anser caerulescens*
Snow Petrel *Pagodroma nivea*
Snowy Owl *Nyctea scandiaca*

Soft-plumaged Petrel *Pterodroma mollis*
Sooty Shearwater *Puffinus griseus*
Sooty Tern *Sterna fuscata*
South Georgia Diving-petrel *Pelecanoides georgicus*
South Polar Skua *Catharacta maccormicki*
Southern Giant Petrel *Macronectes giganteus*
Spectacled Cormorant *Phalacrocorax perspicillatus*
Steller's Sea Eagle *Haliaeetus pelagicus*
Stewart (Bronze) Shag *Phalacrocorax chalconotus*
Streaked Shearwater *Calonectris leucomelas*
Swallow-tailed Gull *Creagrus furcatus*
Thayer's Gull *Larus glaucoides thayeri*
Thick-billed Murre *Uria lomvia*
Trindade/Herald Petrel *Pterodroma arminjoniana/heraldica*
Tuamotu Sandpiper *Prosobonia cancellata*
Tufted Puffin *Fratercula cirrhata*
Turkey Vulture *Cathartes aura*
Blackish Cinclodes (Tussacbird) *Cinclodes antarcticus*
Wandering Albatross *Diomedea exulans*
Waved Albatross *Phoebastria irrorata*
Wedge-tailed Shearwater *Puffinus pacificus*
Western Gull *Larus occidentalis*
Westland Black Petrel *Procellaria westlandica*
Whiskered Auklet *Aethia pygmaea*
White Tern *Gygis alba*
White-chinned Petrel *Procellaria aequinoctialis*
White-faced Storm-petrel *Pelagodroma marina*
White-rumped Vulture *Gyps bengalensis*
White-tailed Eagle *Haliaeetus albicilla*
White-tailed Tropicbird *Phaethon lepturus*
Wilson's Storm-petrel *Oceanites oceanicus*
Yellow-eyed Penguin *Eudyptes antipodes*
Yellow-nosed Albatross *Thalassarche chlororhynchos*

Index

Indexer's Note: Pl. denotes a reference to the captions of numbered Plates.